STORIES UNITED

Harvesting Elders' Wisdom

'Old age is the time when the meaning of the play becomes clear to us.'

This vivid insight of Rabbi Schacter-Shalomi is only one of the many gifts I have received from these pages. As an elder myself, everything about Stories United affirms and respects the stage of life I myself now live daily.

The pastoral insight that first imagined this enterprise, the immense commitment and seriousness that brought it to fruition, its rich intergenerational quality, not to speak of the rigorous training and sensitivity that drew out this flood of elder memory and wisdom — for all of these things we owe a great debt to the leadership and the community of First Metropolitan. The cover speaks of this work as 'harvesting elders' wisdom.' In this harvest there is much golden grain.

— **The Rev. Dr. Herbert O'Driscoll**,
Anglican priest, author, international
speaker and hymn composer

STORIES UNITED

Harvesting Elders' Wisdom

From the Spiritual Companions Program
First†Metropolitan United Church
Victoria, B.C.

Terry Dance-Bennink,
editor and contributor

Published by First†Metropolitan United Church
Victoria, B.C.
2008

Disclaimer: *Stories United* consists of elders' personal memories only; it is not an official history of First Metropolitan United Church.

Library and Archives Canada Cataloguing in Publication

Stories United: Harvesting Elders' Wisdom/Terry Dance-Bennink, editor and contributor.

Includes bibliographical references.
ISBN 978-1-897518-36-6

1. First Metropolitan United Church (Victoria, B.C.) – Biography.
2. Older people – British Columbia – Victoria – Biography.

I. Dance-Bennink, Terry, 1948.
II. First Metropolitan United Church (Victoria, B.C.)

BX9882.8.V48S76 2008 287.9'20971128 C2008-902088-X

Published by First Metropolitan United Church, 932 Balmoral Rd., Victoria, BC V8T 1A8, (250) 388-5188, www.firstmetvictoria.com

Printed and bound in Canada by First Choice Books, www.firstchoicebooks.ca

Graphic design by Bronwen Duncan, Quite Write Designs, Victoria, B.C.

Cover art by Ken Faulks, www.kenfaulksillustration.com

Stories United is dedicated to the elders who
harvested their memories
and to the companions who prepared this feast.

CONTENTS

Foreword

As I look back on my life... I think of roads taken and roads not taken, of decisions I have made and of decisions that have been made for me.... But I do not dwell on these things; I have long ago learned to accept them....

The one great challenge left me, I suppose, is the challenge of death. But I have been prepared for that for some time. Years ago my Christian convictions led me to accept life as a gift of God's grace. It was not something I had earned or deserved, but something given. If I were to die today or tomorrow my attitude would be the same: I have had a good life, and I would thank God for it — for the gift that was given. Dying, after all, is no great thing. The least of us will achieve that. It is the living that matters.

These candid reflections are found in memoirs my father wrote for his children and grandchildren. As his memoirs have been a lasting gift to our family, so this book *Stories United* will be a lasting gift and inspiration for many. In the book, you will meet 15 elders with 15 different life journeys. None of them lived without hardship, yet all of them possess a deep and resonating hope.

They speak on a range of key facets of life, from early memories to thoughts on aging, loss and death. They reflect upon the significance of relationships and a sense of calling. They share personal thoughts about God and faith and what they wish to pass on to the next generations.

Individual readers will find much to ponder about what gives significance to our life journeys and how we choose to engage life. The book also provides valuable resources for congregations to develop dynamic intergenerational programs involving elders.

Rob Dalgleish of the United Church of Canada General Council offices has this to say about *Stories United*:

Every congregational leader concerned about congregational transformation would benefit from such a book. I see congregations across the United Church yearning for ways to refocus and clarify their sense of identity and mission in a changing context. Of course, such discernment, when it is effective, draws deeply on the wells of the spiritual experience of their congregation and especially those 'earthy saints' we name 'elders.' Stories United *offers a model that can help root congregations in the treasures of their past, yet in a narrative and personal way that leaves the path open for deep transformation and a renewed future.*

Even more impressive and hopeful is that this is an inherently intergenerational model, the wisdom is 'harvested' for following generations. The Emerging Spirit research (not to mention my children) tells me that post boomer populations don't want instruction so much as engagement, conversation AND the potent stories that invite such engagement and conversation. This book shows us an important way forward for recovering the practice of passing our faith on to our children, and our children's children.

The enthusiasm with which the Spiritual Companions team has taken on this project underlines that, for them, it has been a labour of love. As they review their lives, the elders often express special thanks for those who have been beacons of light for them over the years...and I rejoice in the beacons of light they themselves have become.

— The Rev. Dr. Allan Saunders
Lead Minister
First†Metropolitan United Church

May 2008

Acknowledgments

Our deepest thanks go to all the elders and companions who have participated in the Spiritual Companions Program. Their names are listed in the Elders' Gallery section of this book. It's been a labour of love on both sides. Countless hours of sharing, listening and writing are core ingredients of this feast that celebrates our elders' wisdom.

The Pastoral Care Committee at First Metropolitan United Church sponsors the program and we thank the members, past and present, for shepherding this unique program through unknown territory. Past chairs, Helen Simpson and Shirley Chatfield, and the current chair, Patti Buchanan, have offered enthusiastic support from start to finish.

The Rev. Margaret Harper, First Met's former Minister of Pastoral Care and Outreach, was there at the moment of conception. As we sipped our tea in my living room in December 2006, I shared my dream of writing a book about elders' wisdom based on my spiritual director training, and Margaret shared First Met's urgent need for a lay visiting program. We put two and two together, and with help from the Holy Spirit who loves all things novel and creative, the seed was planted.

In moments of doubt later on, we needed only a hallway encounter with the Rev. Dr. Allan Saunders who looks for the light rather than the dark. As lead minister, his "can do" attitude gave us the courage to dream big. Parish Nurse, Ann Maffey, steered us through administrative hoops during our first year and continues to cheer our efforts. The new Minister of Pastoral Visitation, the Rev. Gordon Cann, now provides backup pastoral support. He has a heart with ears, like the rest of our companions, and a Down East sense of humour — an unbeatable combination.

The program would have faced a longer and harder road were it not for a seed grant from the Watkins Fund of the national office of the United Church of Canada. Special thanks goes to the

Rev. Dr. Jacqueline Harper, who encouraged us to submit a funding application, guided us through the process, and recommended we document the outcome in book form.

The Stewardship Fund at First Metropolitan United Church also seeded the program with a grant in 2007 and continues to support the program as part of the church's commitment to broadening pastoral care through lay visitors.

A program is only as good as its training component. We acknowledge all those who helped train our companions, including Lindsay Barber, a Victoria counsellor/trainer, who assisted me in designing and leading the first training program; Tim Scorer who helped us reflect on biblical models of spiritual friendship; Dan Curtis, a documentary filmmaker and personal historian, who taught us how to evoke and record life stories; and the Rev. Wilda Cottam who shared some of the joys and sorrows of aging based on her many years of ministering to the elderly.

Adeline O'Gorman from Hospice Victoria reminded us of what *not* to say and do when faced with grief, and Jane Sheaff from Seniors Serving Seniors assured us we were not alone as she highlighted local community resources to support elders. The Rev. Gordon Cann and Ann Maffey also assisted with our training and continue to attend our monthly support meetings.

A hard-working Editorial Committee made sure the right stories were selected for *Stories United* and presented in a readable format. We had to cull 200 pages worth of stories from the original 700 pages submitted. "How do you choose between a ruby, an emerald and a diamond?" we often asked ourselves.

As editor, I knew I could count on the collective wisdom offered by my colleagues: Caroline Mufford (copy editor), the Rev. Gordon Cann, David Bray, Edeana Malcolm and Penny Bond. We gelled as a team from our first meeting and felt comfortable disagreeing with each other when necessary — and all with incredible good humour.

Stories United owes its attractive appearance to Victoria artist, Ken Faulks, who designed our beautiful front cover; Bronwen

Duncan of Quite Write Designs who laid out the text and photos with such great care; and Johanna Socha at First Choice Books who ensured the book was printed within a month of delivery and always offered a word of encouragement during my frequent visits.

The *Stories United* marketing team deserves a round of applause for ensuring wide distribution of the book locally and across Canada. We are particularly grateful to Patricia Gilmore, Coordinator, United Church Resource Distribution in Toronto, for promoting and distributing our book across Canada. We also want to thank the Epiphany Explorations Conference team at First Met and conference chair, Joan Mason, who also is a companion, for allowing us to share the lessons of our experience with others at a plenary session in January 2009.

And finally, we wish to thank those hidden and not so hidden individuals at First Met who offered our team unfailing hospitality and support. Phone inquiries, room bookings, room setup and cleanup, processing of book orders, printing of promotional material, proofreading, power point presentations, payment of bills — it's a long and sometimes thankless list of tasks that can make or break a program.

We are grateful to Sharon MacDonald, Candace Bourchier, Sheila Anderson, Sue Clough, Jayne Kirby, Carol Goy, Brian Shields, Cullen Morton and Bruce Davies.

One man remains to be thanked — my husband — who has put up with the clattering of computer keys outside our bedroom door day and night. For his patience and loving support of anything my heart desires, I thank Theo Bennink.

The last word of thanks goes to God who has sustained us throughout our journey and blessed this harvest of soul friends.

— T. Dance-Bennink

Introduction

What is most personal is most universal.

— Henri Nouwen

Welcome to this feast of wisdom! We hope you enjoy this harvest of memories gathered from elders in Victoria, B.C., by their new soul friends at First Metropolitan United Church.

We had no idea what to expect last year when we began to interview 15 elders about their life and faith experiences. To our delight, we discovered that deeply personal stories have universal meaning. Anyone who has been born, loved, worked, grown older, lost a loved one, held hands in community or sensed the Sacred in their lives can relate to the stories in this book.

Everyone has a story to tell. "There was never yet an uninteresting life," Mark Twain insists, and Rudyard Kipling claims that "if history were taught in the form of stories, it would never be forgotten." Even the most ordinary of lives has pathos and meaning if you take the time to thresh — to remove the husks of your life and celebrate the life-giving seeds. "The doors of wisdom are never shut," Benjamin Franklin reminds us, and memory is the foundation of wisdom.

Our elders are not, for the most part, famous people but have lived ordinary lives with amazing courage and hope despite life's challenges. They are not formally designated Elders in our church, but simply much admired members of our congregation. Sit back and listen to stories from women and men who've lived in nearly every Canadian province at some point in their lives — pioneers who have:

- weathered drought, dust storms and plagues of insects during the Depression
- served as RCAF officers, a pilot, and a secret service agent during World War II
- organized hundreds of youth camps for the YMCA and the United Church of Canada

- comforted and fed countless visitors in manses across Canada
- pioneered sex education in Victoria
- taught gifted children
- established a citizens counselling centre
- cared for family caregivers
- healed those in pain
- helped families get out of debt
- raised millions of dollars for the B.C. Cancer Society
- found a true love
- challenged a workaholic husband to slow down
- rejoiced in the birth of children
- lost a mate but loved again
- discovered the art of letting go in retirement
- mourned the death of beloved parents and mentors
- witnessed miracles in the face of life-threatening illnesses
- trusted that life goes on beyond the grave
- celebrated a new amalgamated faith community
- encountered God in many disguises

The elders' voices vary in tone, pitch and depth. Some elders love to philosophize; some enjoy telling a funny story; some expect you to read between the lines; and some hope to spark a debate. Personality and background shape the stories. We've presented the stories in the first person and kept editing to a minimum to reflect each elder's authentic voice.

The female voice dominates, not because we chose to exclude men, but due to illness among the male elders and companions who initially volunteered and the fact that the majority of First Met elders are women.

Four elders chose to write their own stories (noted as "written by"), and the rest were interviewed by their spiritual companions with the stories transcribed and edited (noted as "as told to"). Some of our spiritual companions had no experience with writing but embraced the pen with enthusiasm. The ongoing mutual spiritual friendship between elder and companion led to trust and deep personal sharing.

More than 700 pages of stories were submitted originally — way beyond what the Editorial Committee had hoped for. We chose stories for publication which reflected the diversity of our elders and had a compelling message. Each elder has at least one story published in the book.

The **Elders' Gallery** follows the stories and presents each elder's biography and photo, together with the companion's photo and the **Wisdom Learned** from the elder. The **Story Behind the Stories**, including a bibliography, ends the book for those who wish to learn from our experience.

The stories are not meant to glorify our elders but rather to stimulate you, the reader, to follow in their footsteps. The **reflection questions** at the end of each chapter should prompt you to pick up your pen or turn on your computer, chat with a friend or a spiritual companion, join a life-review group or record your memories in whatever way you wish — but do it *now* — before the unique story named YOU is forgotten.

Every creature is a book about God, says Meister Eckhart, so let *your* book be read.

— T. Dance-Bennink

Early Memories

You can't possibly know where you're going if you don't know where you've been. — Ken Burns

Getting educated — A school memory

Written by May Deller as shared with Irene Baddeley

I was six years old, several months into Grade 1 and had quite mixed feelings about school, some of them less than positive. I couldn't figure out why anyone should be forced into this routine day after day, when there were so many interesting things to learn in my world outside school.

One day, however, the opportunity presented itself inside school to learn one of those interesting things.

"Do you know the difference between boys and girls?" whispered Henry who sat straight across from me.

"No," I whispered back. "Do you?"

"Yes," he said. "Do you want me to show you?"

"Of course," I replied as my admiration grew for this classmate who possessed such important knowledge.

"Come down to the boys' washroom in five minutes." With that directive, he raised his hand and asked for permission to "leave the room" as it was delicately called in my day.

As the classroom clock ticked off that long five minutes, my logical six-year-old mind put together some information that did seem pertinent to the activity at hand. Henry had brothers only, so he must surely know all about boys. I had several sisters. My only brother at 13 and "grown up mostly," certainly hadn't bothered to enlighten me about this interesting lack in my education. Just maybe, my being an expert on girls could help in Henry's education too. I knew it all had to do with some physical difference but what? I hadn't a clue.

May (Turnbull) Deller, 3, in 1936

Five minutes ended. Up went my hand as I squirmed in my desk. I really needed to "go" badly. I received permission in spite of the rule that said only one student at a time could leave the room.

How fortunate I felt. Down the stairs I skipped to the landing where two flights of stairs presented themselves. The stairs to the right led to the girls' washroom, those to the left, the boys' washroom.

"Well, this is easy," I thought. "I just make the wrong turn." That was when the great god Conscience struck full force. The rules said that girls only went to the right and boys only went to the left.

The inner voice of authority could not be defied especially when a "big" boy came down the stairs behind me and turned to the left. It took but an instant to make up my mind. I went to the right. "So much for that intriguing addition to my education," I thought sadly as I perched in one of the girls' cubicles.

Of course, my curiosity never ceased. But I discovered that missing tidbit of knowledge after my older sister and her husband had a baby boy some years later.

I must say I wasn't all that impressed. Sometimes this education stuff isn't always what it's cracked up to be, is it?

On discipline

By Ruth Howell as told to Edeana Malcolm

The principal at Girls Central School in Victoria was Miss Williams. None of us liked her. We called her Meanie Williams because she was really very strict. We were lined up in the basement, and she used to stand on a platform, turn on her gramophone, and march us up the stairs to the sound of her gramophone.

When I passed from Miss Keith's room into Miss Williams' in

Grade 8, I didn't want to join her class. So my dad wrote a note to Miss Williams and said that I would like to go into Miss Barron's room. But Miss Williams said, "I take all the people who pass the highest from Grade 7 to 8 and I want you." So I couldn't go with my friends.

She would leave us to do some assignment and go off into her office and tend to her plants. Some of the girls would cheat and compare notes while she sat in her office. When she came back in again, I was a tattletale and told her what had been happening, but she didn't do anything about it. I passed out of her room eventually and entered Victoria High School.

The Grade 4 teacher, Miss Sherwood, was lovely. I always walked home with Miss Sherwood as she walked down Fernwood Road, and one day her brother came along on his bicycle and stopped to walk with us.

"Sorry, I can't walk with you," Miss Sherwood told him. "Miss Williams says we're not to walk with the boys."

"Not even your own brother?" he asked her.

"No," she replied.

That was the kind of person the principal was. Men were taboo. Maybe she had a bad experience with a man. I don't know. I thought it was sort of silly. But those were the rules and, boy oh boy, if you were caught! There was a fence between Girls Central and Boys Central. If you were caught down there, maybe throwing snowballs or something like that, you had it.

The principal usually took you into the office or made you stand outside her room in the hall. She didn't strap, but you had to stand in the hall outside her door for a certain length of time or she would send you to a lower grade where you had to spend some time in this classroom. That was her method of punishment. I heard years later that she had elderly parents to care for, but I didn't know this then. We weren't very sympathetic at our age.

I never strapped my own children.

When my son, Donny, was not very old, he went into our next door neighbour's garden. She had a long row of tulips planted at the side of her house. Don promptly went over to her place and picked the heads off all her tulips, and I was furious with him.

"Do you know what you've done?" I said to him. "You've picked all the flowers off! You know what you've got to do. You're going to go next door and tell Mrs. McKay what you did and that you're very sorry."

So he had to go and tell her what he'd done, but this backfired on me because she said, "All right, Donny. Never mind. Will you have some ice cream?"

In disciplining him, it didn't take any force, as long as you took him by the hand to his bedroom and sat down with him and explained to him what he'd done. That was the way to handle him. Not by spanking or anything like that. It worked every time. So I guess mothers have to learn that too, as well as teachers, and I should have done more of that as a teacher.

When I look back on my teaching career now, I regret several times using the strap. I shouldn't have done it. I'll defend myself by saying that there was this boy in Grade 4 who was a regular upstart. I was told that his parents couldn't discipline him, so he lived with his grandmother, and she used to threaten to send him to Vancouver to some boys' school where he would be disciplined.

I should have taken that child by the hand and spoken to him and tried to reason with him, even though his own parents couldn't handle him. But I was young and green and just starting out. However, I regret it. Sometimes the teacher gets all steamed up too, especially when she has a full classroom.

I had four grades — Grades 1 to 4 — all in one room. And one of the hardest things about it was keeping Grade 1 busy. I was forever trying to keep the younger ones occupied while I was teaching the other three grades. It was quite a problem.

Not an easy life

By Sheila MacDougall
as told to Terry Dance-Bennink

Wash day was a big day on our Saskatchewan farm in the 1920s. It was no easy life. We had to do our washing by hand, boiling up the water and soap on the wood stove. As the eldest child, I'd haul in the wood and maybe a bit of coal. We'd bring in chunks of snow to put in the box beside the cook stove, so we always had lovely hot water.

Bathing wasn't an everyday affair, although we washed ourselves each day. We eventually got a bathtub, but without running water, we had to ladle the water in and re-use the water. More than one person had a bath in that water, which we'd frown on today, but it was a necessity then.

Our first washing machine was very heavy, and you had to swing it from side to side, so Dad operated it because Mom didn't have the strength. Eventually, we got a different kind of machine which went flip-flop, and I could handle that one.

For a toilet, we had an indoor bucket in the cupboard close to Mom and Dad's bedroom. We didn't have a vacuum, so dusting was all we could do — we'd bang the rugs on a line in the spring. I knew Mom wasn't as strong as me, so I scrubbed and waxed the floors and did all the washing. I didn't do much ironing — she must have done that. Mom was a very good cook and often canned meat and fruit. I learned to cook just by watching her.

Sheila MacDougall, 2, on a farm horse

I'll never forget the day my mother scalded herself with boiling water while she was canning. My father eventually arrived from the fields and she told him, "I couldn't get Sheila to go down to the

Sheila MacDougall's family farm in Saskatchewan

fields to find you." I was probably two or three years old then, and she wanted me to go out into the fields. I clearly remember her telling my Dad this, and I felt guilty for not going. But I'd probably never gone out into the fields before to find my father. It's funny what you remember.

If I had to describe myself as a young girl, I'd say I was precocious! I always knew everything. Nothing ever surprised me. I handled a team of horses when I was eight years old and went off to school. I was the eldest and my parents trusted me, so I just did it. When my brother grew older, he accompanied me.

It's a standing joke that when he was six he was allowed to drive the team for the first time. We got to an intersection and another family arrived with a cart, and the race was on to the school. My brother turned a little sharply at the gate, and I flew out into the gravel. He looked back to see what had happened to me, and then he hit the school itself! To this day, I've never let him forget this! But we never told Mom or Dad. "Don't tell" was our motto.

Mom used to say I was just like my dad. "She's just like you," she'd say when I was being stubborn. Dad could be stubborn sometimes — he wouldn't give in all the time. "How do you expect her to be any different when you do… " she'd say to him. He'd laugh and so would she. I was very lucky to be born into such a loving family.

The way it was

By Ross MacKinnon as told to David Bray

How it started

Mom and Dad met in our church. It was originally First Presbyterian Church on the corner of Blanshard and Pandora. It moved to our present site in 1912, the year Dad came out here. Mom came out in 1913 with her folks and they met in that church.

Dad worked for the BC Coast Steamship Service before going off to World War I where he became a stretcher bearer — his eyes weren't good enough to be in the infantry. They had to pack out people who'd been gassed.

During this time Mom and her family had moved to New Zealand. Dad's family was still in Glasgow so he stayed behind after his war service and worked in London for about a year. When he came back here, of course, Mom was in New Zealand. He went down to book a trip on a ship and the guy said, "OK, there's a bit of a waiting list. I can put you down for a year from now." There was a shortage of ships after the war. That wasn't good enough for Dad so he signed on as a steward in the kitchen and worked his way down there.

He had to sign on through to Sydney, Australia, so he saw Mom briefly in New Zealand while the ship was there; then he had to leave and finish his trip in Australia. Mom said when he got out to New Zealand he worked on a couple of dairy farms which she thinks did an awful lot of good to get him back in shape again.

One of his army buddies wrote to him from Hawaii saying they were making all kinds of money on sugarcane — there was a shortage of sugar after the war. So Dad and Mom and her folks — they weren't married — all moved up to the Big Island, Hawaii, and Dad and Grandpa got jobs as overseers in the sugarcane fields. They got married there.

It was sort of multiracial there and they wanted to be where there were more white people — although they got along fine. A friend of Dad's said, "Come on over to Seattle, I can get you work here." So they came to Seattle. I was nearly born there because Mom was pregnant with me.

There happened to be a downturn and Dad couldn't get work. A fellow who worked for the BC Coast Steamship Services where Dad had worked before the war got in touch and said he could fill in for this guy who was sick. Well, the guy never got better and Dad stayed on and eventually Mom had to pack up in Seattle and come here to Victoria. I was born a few months later.

Fun, fun

We lived on Chapman Street, about two blocks east of Cook Street Village. It was a one-and-a-half storey house built in the boom before the First World War in 1912.

Nobody had very much money. We didn't eat out that much but there weren't that many restaurants in Victoria anyway.

We never had a car — the first one in our family to have a car was my young brother. He got an old Model A Ford with a rumble seat and I remember my dad and I climbing into that.

Victoria didn't seem to grow up with a great number of tract houses side by side. They were individual ones and there were a lot of empty lots where we could play soccer or baseball.

We played roller hockey on the roads in the wintertime. The arena had burned down in 1929 so there wasn't any ice hockey. It was quieter then, not the same traffic. We could play and not get interrupted too often. We'd just haul a couple of rocks out for goal posts and away we went.

We had proper rubber pucks. We didn't need masks or anything like that because there wasn't any raising of the puck. That went fine until a puck went down one of the sewers and then we had to lift the storm drain and fish it out. We did that periodically.

I never learned how to ice skate until I was about 18 or so. Once in a while Goodacre Lake in Beacon Hill Park froze over, but then you had to have enough money to have a pair of skates and we didn't have that much. They finally put an ice arena in about the beginning of the war and I learned to skate there.

In the nicer weather, we used to play down at the beach. We'd take a pile of nails and make rafts — we spent all of our time getting the thing made; we never spent any time on it because the water is so darn cold there.

We played on the banks a lot and they used to get quite eroded. My mom used to wonder how we got our pants so dirty — it was just from sliding down the bank.

Riding the rails

Dad was a clerk for the CPR–BC Coast Steamship Service — and being part of the CPR he could get a pass. Even though he wasn't making any big money — because CPR isn't Santa Claus — when my grandparents moved from here back to Saint John, N.B., we were able to visit them.

We'd get on the train and in those days they had a fridge or an ice box and a kitchen at the end of each car and you could prepare your own meals. We'd take enough food aside from milk and what we could get along the way and we had our meals on the train.

I had a paper route and worked as a golf caddy for extra cash. As a special treat when I was getting older, we'd come back from Saint John on the train and I'd be able to afford to take the folks and my brothers into the dining room car for one meal.

The dining rooms were first class, and there were roomettes or some sort of bedrooms there, and then there were the tourist ones where we went. They had bunks or berths — and the kitchen at one end and the bathroom at the other end. There were the day coaches, too, because even though the train was going across Canada there were lots of people just sitting up.

They didn't have the dome cars then. Air conditioning was just coming in. I remember the first trip or two that we made in tourist class without air conditioning and it would get pretty hot on the Prairies.

We made five trips during the Depression, becoming well-travelled across Canada: Montreal, Toronto, Niagara Falls, across the Bay of Fundy by CPR ship, and day trips by paddle steamer up the Saint John River to Fredericton and back by train.

We were very fortunate. We did it on the cheap because we didn't have any money. But we used to manage.

When we were in Toronto, we'd take in the Canadian National Exhibition which was a good show. The last time I was there I was a bit self-conscious. I was 18 by then and a civilian and saw this show at the grandstand where they had the precision squad from the Air Force and lots of the kids in it were just my age. With war on, you could see you were going to have to join something or you were going to be called up.

'Extra, extra, read all about it. Carrier saves shoe shop'

I got a *Colonist* paper route at just about the start of the war which meant I had to be downtown at quarter to five in the morning. It meant early to bed. I had a route that was right in town.

One time I came along Douglas Street from Fort and I was passing a shoe store — Art Chapman's — and I looked in the window and saw a fire starting. It was a little electric sign that he'd had on the floor inside and it had caught fire. That whole block, from View Street through to Fort, was all living quarters, and there were apartments up above.

It was the only time I ever pulled a fire alarm. I went to the corner, broke the glass, rang it and then I stood there. The fire station used to be just behind City Hall, so I stood there until I could hear them crank up and then they came out onto Douglas and I stood there with my flashlight and signalled them. I didn't hang around because I was going to be late in getting to my papers and you got points knocked off for that.

The fireman didn't waste time at the door; he just walked right through it, glass and all — he put his shoulders to it. They put out the fire without any damage, and nobody was hurt. They got the fire out so quickly they didn't even have to evacuate the people up above. But it probably could have been a serious fire — it was an old, old building. I remember going up the stairs to the living part up above and just the smell of those old buildings!

It was a little while later that Andy, the guy who gave out the papers, said, "Were you the one who turned that alarm in?" Somebody had been phoning.

I think I got a shirt from one store and a new pair of shoes from Art Chapman's, the shoe store. And I delivered papers upstairs and they must have taken up a collection — I don't remember what it was — maybe $20 or $25, which was a heck of a lot of money then. I would have been about 16 or 17 then.

War!

By Ross MacKinnon as told to David Bray

The gathering storm

We used to hear the broadcasts of Hitler at home, and he was an orator par excellence. He got the people really worked up. And growing up when we did — I was 16 when the war started — you knew if it went for any length of time you were going to be involved in it. It was just a matter of where you were going to be involved. I guess I was pretty young for my age at that time and when I got through high school I didn't have any great yearning to join up as soon as I was 18. So I went to college for a year and during that year Pearl Harbor happened.

I stayed at college until the end of the year and Mom and Dad never said anything but I told them, "You know, I'd like to join the Air Force." So I wrote over to Vancouver and they said, "Here's what you do." And then one day soon after, I happened to meet a buddy from high school downtown who said he'd joined the Air Force and said I should ask to get in his draft. I did and we went all through our training together.

RCAF pilot, Ross MacKinnon, back from overseas with his wife-to-be, Patricia, 1945

Pearl Harbor and the Japanese internment

We got pretty nervous there, you know, in December 1941 — man!

I know the Japanese who lived here and were natives got pretty rough treatment. They were shipped off to camps in the B.C. Interior and it was the same in the States.

We were watching "The War" recently, the PBS television series on the Second World War. It was done from the American viewpoint but it was the same in Canada — the program failed to look at the feelings of the general population at the time. It didn't really emphasize how nervous everybody was here. It's kind of hard to get across the feeling that existed. I can remember as a young person going up to Beacon Hill Park to a meeting on a Sunday afternoon — this would have been probably in January 1942 — about how to treat the Japanese here in Victoria. People just didn't trust the Japanese people at all.

There were all sorts of rumours going around spread by fishermen who knew the coast well. But the Japanese people got a raw deal. It was just a very bad time.

A bit of adventure or fighting for the cause?

I joined up in June 1942. I knew what had happened overseas and knew it wasn't right, and I believed that our side, the Allies, were fighting for the right cause.

If you were healthy, you felt a little conspicuous if you were of conscription age and hadn't joined up. The last summer before I joined up, when I got out of high school, I had just turned 18. Nobody ever said anything but you just sort of felt "gee."

'But it's a dry cold!'

When we were going to college, it was the start of the air cadets and another fellow and I were interested in them. We'd been going to some of the first classes and learning Morse code and a little bit about navigation, and I knew people in the Air Force. It seemed like a more interesting thing.

We were sent to the manning depot in Edmonton, out in the old fairgrounds.

We drove in from the train station in the back of a truck and when we got through the gates, the guys who had been there for two weeks were saying, "You'll be sorry, you'll be sorry!"

We were in basic training in Edmonton for about six weeks. Then we got shipped off to guard duty in Yorkton, Sask., for about a month. Then we started what they called initial training school which was ground school. The Air Force had taken over the old normal school in downtown Regina. They put up huts on the grounds and they used the classrooms for our training.

We were there for about 10 weeks and studied mathematics, navigation, Morse code, Aldis lamp, different armaments and meteorology. By the time we finished it was December and getting cold. That was my introduction to a Prairie winter. Coming from Victoria, that was a shock — I didn't know it got that cold but it certainly does in Regina.

The wild blue yonder

People who were going in for aircrew got posted to all the different pilot/navigation/air gunner bases. Some of us who were going in for pilot training got posted to the airfield right in Regina. We started our pilot training in Tiger Moths. They sort of looked as though they were left over from the First World War. They were very sound but cold. There was just a thin covering and your hand was on the throttle right next to where it was -40 degrees outside.

We didn't use the runways. They just rolled out a section of the field because it was all snow-covered then and we landed on the snow. After they figured you were fit to go solo, the instructor would get out and pass his parachute in and you got a red streamer on your tail which indicated you were on solo flight and away you'd go.

It looked pretty empty up front. It was kind of neat, you know. I thought, "Hey, I'm in charge here, there's nobody else to take over," and I quite enjoyed it.

We did aerobatics, mostly to make you feel at home with your aircraft. They'd take you up and say, "OK, now we're going to stall the aircraft to show you how to recover." You had to do it on your own and they'd say, "Be in control at least 3,000 feet up." I remember the first time, I got up to 4,000 feet and thought, "Well, I won't come down more than a thousand feet in a stall," because the ground looked pretty close to me. So I climbed up a bit higher because when you put it in a stall or a spin, there's no control for a while.

It was nearly a year after I joined up that I got my wings. My folks were there for the graduation and my dad pinned on my wings. I was thrilled about that.

Over there

By the time we were ready to go overseas the British Commonwealth Air Training Plan had been so successful that there were an awful lot of aircrew. So they sent us on a get fit course in Exeter, England and we saw what had happened. The place had been levelled because it was right on the south coast where the Germans could come across, flatten it and get away.

They would take us out in a truck, dump us off and say, "OK, find your own way back from here." You'd get in pretty good shape.

And then we went on a flying course over Britain because it

was completely different from flying in Canada. If you got lost in Canada you could just follow the railway tracks to the nearest granary but not in Britain. There are so many tracks going all over.

We did some instrument flying as well. You'd take off, go up through the clouds and you'd be up there all alone, depending on your instruments, keeping on a radio beam, and you had to come down through the clouds back to earth.

It was the luck of the draw where you got assigned. You just went overseas and where you got shuffled to is where they needed pilots at the time. I got sent to a Coastal Command operational training unit which is where they crewed you up. I was the only Canadian in the crew — there was one Aussie who became my good pal — the skipper was a Brit and the rest of the crew were Brits.

Good-bye skipper

Our Catalinas would take off fully loaded and by the time you had burned off a bit of fuel you were up to 105 knots — about 150 miles per hour — not very fast. But with overload tanks they'd stay up 24 hours.

We had some night flying toward the end of our training in Northern Ireland. It's not like a runway — there are just flares on a lake — and they don't always stay in a straight line and there'd only be about four flares. The skipper couldn't seem to land at night because his depth perception was off.

They gave him another try. He dropped one in from about 50 feet, sprang the rivets in the hull and it started to fill up — the pump couldn't keep up and they ran it up on an island and that was it. He was scrubbed.

One day the chief flying instructor called me into the office with another guy and he said, "OK, there's a fellow here looking for a second pilot — you call it," and he flipped a coin. I called it and won, so I went with the fellow and it was a Canadian crew.

The fellow was from Alberta. He was 29 and we all called him "Pappy" because he was so old. I was 21. He'd come to pick up a new second pilot which was me. I was kind of lucky.

We got posted out to East Africa. It was interesting flying up the Nile and across Lake Victoria. I see these places now and think, "Oh, I've been there." I've seen the pyramids but under different circumstances.

Out to Africa

I'm not a good sailor and going across the Bay of Biscay in a convoy, you'd look out and see the escort ships disappear behind a huge wave. Then we got to Gibraltar — it was safer in the Mediterranean by then, near the end of 1944 — and the convoy broke up. We spent Christmas Day in the Mediterranean and got to the port for Cairo. They had a great big camp in the desert outside Cairo at a place called Heliopolis and we just lived in tents there.

We got used to sleeping under mosquito nets in Mombasa. We did patrols out of there. One time we were going to the Seychelles but didn't make it because our plane developed engine trouble, but we did get down to the Comoro Islands — it took about six hours — and out to Madagascar. It was seven hours, 25 minutes from Mombasa to Diego Suarez on the north end of Madagascar. It took all day to go one way.

Coming back from there we saw all these waterspouts which we avoided. It gave the navigator a bad time because the skipper kept saying, "Oh, we've got to change course again!" They were all over the place. It was just about the start of the monsoon season so I guess that was a normal sort of thing.

The longest flight I made was a convoy escort — almost 12 hours daytime and two hours at night. You'd go around the ships one way, then back the other way. You could feel the kite under you for quite a while after you came off.

Give us the tools

In the last stage of the war, we changed over to Sunderlands. They were beautiful aircraft. They had two decks on them. You came in on the lower deck where the wardroom was and the flight deck was up above where the pilots sat. In the Catalina you always had the feeling your pants were just about in the water because you were down low and when you opened up the throttle all you could see was water in front of you. In the Sunderland you were on top of everything — sort of like the difference between a car and an SUV — you're sitting way up.

On the last flight I had in a Catalina we flew from Mombasa to Dar es Salaam and then to Kisumu on Lake Victoria. We flew right between Mount Kenya and Kilimanjaro — quite something!

It's over, over there

Our squadron was an old Royal Air Force (RAF) squadron and all Canadians had to go home because our squadron was going East. They knew then that victory in Europe, VE Day, was coming very soon.

A Canadian fellow came down from Cairo and said Mackenzie King, the Prime Minister, says that before any Canadians go out to the Pacific theatre — and the Far East was considered the same thing — you have to get leave in Canada. So they yanked us off the squadron.

Some of us got put in a troop ship and sent back up the Indian Ocean, around the Horn of Africa and up the Red Sea. We stopped before the Suez Canal. I've been to both ends of the canal but never through. When we got back to Heliopolis again, the war had ended in Europe.

Coming home

Some of us had volunteered for the Pacific and we spent a couple of weeks in Cairo and then flew back on a Canadian DC-3 that was on a mail route from Cairo to Athens, Naples, Marseilles and then back to England. It took two days.

I had nine weeks' leave up in Scotland and back to Bournemouth and then we shipped home. We pulled in to Quebec City one afternoon and there were a few French Canadians on board who got marched off first. They had quite the ceremony that night because it was a big deal for them in Quebec, and we got regaled in French for the better part of an hour and none of us knew what they were saying. Finally, somebody said something in English and a big cheer went up because we knew what they were talking about. The next morning we got on trains and were sent from Quebec to Montreal and then home.

It's over, over there: part two

I was on leave before I was to report back to Nova Scotia where we were going to train for bombers for the Pacific theatre and, of course, they dropped the two A-bombs.

We were on a trip to Vancouver and had just pulled out of Ganges on Saltspring Island when we got word the war had ended in Japan.

I know they bemoan the use of the A-bomb, but it saved an awful lot of lives. The Japanese were working on their own. The Japanese wouldn't surrender: you had to kill them. There would have been hundreds of thousands killed in an invasion of Japan.

Motivated to succeed

Written by Helen Mau and shared with Cyndi Frame

My earliest memory is of having hot grease poured on my head as a baby while I was lying in a carriage! I may have been told this, but I can still feel that grease. My mother had been cooking bacon in our rented home in Guelph, Ont.

We lived in five rented homes while I was in elementary school in Toronto during the Depression. All this moving about to get better housing made me a sociable person, able to relate well to new teachers and friends. The economic times were difficult though when I started high school in 1934, so I tried to do things cheaply whenever I could. I'd buy a dress I liked on credit, for

Helen (Dickin) Mau with her mother and grandfather

example, and copy the pattern onto newspaper or tissue paper, and then adjust it to my size and sew it for myself. I learned to sew on a treadle sewing machine and made my first cotton dress when I was 12 years old.

I was sent to the principal's office at St. Mary's Public school in 1926 to show them something I'd done and I remember feeling that I could achieve anything I wanted to mentally. I was always motivated to succeed. My earliest dream was to do my best at whatever challenged me. And as an only child for quite a while, I knew that I needed to make friends and be faithful to them.

I had little playtime with friends after school because my mother insisted I practise piano and pass progressive piano exams. I played at recitals until I reached the Grade 12 examination and begged to stop. I was not that talented as a pianist though I did well on the Conservatory exams. My mother had a familial hand tremor and so did I. But all this piano practising helped me appreciate classical music, and I've attended and enjoyed many symphonies and musicals in New York City, San Francisco and Victoria.

I was not athletic as a child like many of my friends and my sister, Louise, but I enjoyed bicycling, horse and sleigh rides in the winter, tobogganing, skating and badminton.

My mother's family was well educated and kept encouraging me to do well at school. I discovered in Grade 9 that I was good in botany, zoology, mathematics, French and Latin grammar but not in English or French literature or British history. I did not care to remember dates of history or where a line from Shakespeare came from, but I liked the rules of languages. To this day, I can recognize 72 birds in Ontario.

My interest in birds started in Guelph at age five when I

discovered a nest of baby robins without their parents in a tree beside our house. Dad took the birds and put them in a tub with soft lining under our back veranda. Mother baked custard for the birds and we fed them. Only one robin survived whom we called Lindy after Lindbergh who'd just flown over the Atlantic. Lindy was tame and came to my windowsill every morning and sat on my shoulder when I went down to breakfast. He gave me great joy.

The onslaught of nature

By Irene McDonald
as told to Terry Dance-Bennink

The Depression meant unemployment or low wages to many people, but I remember the onslaught of nature the most: the drought, dust storms and plagues of insects.

On the farm, we were lucky to have a well with good water so we could maintain a garden, but along with the drought and dust storms came cutworms and grasshoppers. Just when you thought your garden was off to a good start, you'd either have a plague of cutworms nipping it in the bud or grasshoppers coming later to finish it off. Potato bugs also reduced our crop. You can imagine what these same pests did to the crops in the field. The drought and the dust storms, though, were frightening.

I remember my sister, Marjorie, coming home from school just a little behind me, when a dust storm caught her and she couldn't see. She had the good sense to sit down on the ground and pull her coat over her head so she could breathe, and she just stayed put until somebody came out to find her. She was only a short distance from our home. A family member went back through the field and found her and led her to the house.

When the dust storms hit, we always kept lamps burning in the house so anyone on the road could see. I don't know how

The King family on the steps of the family farm, 1926

people with asthma managed because the air was full of dust. Our home was better than many, but friends told me that when they set the dining room table, they'd invert the plates to prevent the dust from gathering on them.

Farmers faced many crises during the Depression, and not just from the drought and pests. The grain prices were very low and yields were almost nil, so you were lucky to get your seed back for the next year. When the rains did come, we had hail storms, and crops would be wiped out. It was subsistence farming; we had just enough to get by on for a number of years.

My parents and neighbours reacted to this onslaught of nature with surprising equanimity, even though it must have been devastating. They always expected that the bad weather wouldn't last, that next year would be a better year. They had a quiet philosophy of trust. Some people may have prayed for better years, but I don't recall anyone blaming the bad times on a God who'd turned against us. My father never lost his temper during these crises, but the merriment in our house was gone. I'm sure the stress contributed to my mother's nervous breakdown.

A person who's lived through the Depression never totally changes their frugal ways of life. I don't think anyone growing up during the Depression would ever think of wasting something or not shopping carefully or not having extra provisions on hand in case of emergencies. Growing up in that period also made each of us much more family-centered, so we expected the same closeness when we had our own families. The Depression brought families together and made us value community a great deal. I felt this sense of community around our church, our athletic facilities and even politics.

My parents were both quite active in politics, as this was the era of the Social Credit in Alberta. No one growing up in Alberta at that time can forget the "Back to the Bible" with William Aberhart on Sundays, because it was probably about one-third Bible and two-thirds Social Credit. He stirred the community. Social Credit became the government of Alberta for over 35 years.

My father served as a municipal councillor for a long time, but he's the only one in the family who actually ran for office. I continue, however, to have a tremendous interest in the political affairs of my community and country, both provincially and federally.

Political leaders often stayed overnight at our home if they were out in the country, as our home was bigger than most. This changed after the 1940s, because the politicians by then all had cars and travelled more. My mother was very involved in helping to gain the vote for women. She was also active in the United Farm Women of Alberta. Our home certainly broadened our education in all aspects.

Highly secret work

By Irene McDonald
as told to Terry Dance-Bennink

Canada declared war against Germany in September 1939. Rumours of the impending conflict had been circulating for years. I had hoped peace would prevail, as surely great men knew the folly of fighting. I'd also known many people of German origin when I'd taught at Beiseker, Alta., so it was difficult for me to think of us being at war with their nation. The RCMP kept a very close watch on Canadian citizens whose families had come from Germany and Europe. But the practical and moral grounds for this war seemed indisputable.

Irene (King) McDonald, RCAF W310388, in 1943

The early months of wartime saw many changes in my family circle. My mother had passed away, and my sister, Eva, her husband and daughter had come to live on the farm to run a chicken and egg business. They were wonderful to my father and to each of us when we descended upon them for our holidays. The winds had abated, the fields and crops were flourishing and unemployment was no longer such a problem. Some of the early military recruits were from the ranks of the unemployed, but very soon, we all became aware that civilization was at stake. The voice of Hitler and the newsreels transformed our peaceful way of life.

The Ghost Pine community in Alberta soon began to say goodbye to those who'd joined the Army, the Navy and the RCAF. A commemoration of the valour of all those who served in the war is displayed on a large plaque erected today at the Sarcee Corner, with a star beside the names of those who gave their lives. When those whom I knew and loved had fallen, I became introspective, and finally decided that I, too, should enlist. On Mar. 1, 1943, I was sworn into the RCAF Women's Division at age 26 and served until Aug. 15, 1945, when the war ended.

I was sent to the Rockcliffe Manning Depot in Ottawa where we were drilled and marched and immunized for everything possible. Standing in line for needles made me aware that more men than women are prone to fainting. We also had to stand in line for our pay. I earned 90 cents a day and male recruits earned $1.20 a day. Our days were characterized by discipline, punctuality, bed-making and line-ups for everything, including ablutions and food in the mess hall.

Women as well as men lived in barracks. When the Sergeant inspected the barracks, the extra blanket at the end of each bed had to be in absolutely formal line with one another — even the garbage tin was polished. You had to be ready to reply when your name was called, so you learned to come smartly to attention and never to miss a beat. I learned the alphabetical order of the names preceding mine which I remember to this day: Kemp, Kent, Kiddle, and then King, along with my regimental number which was always on the tip of my tongue: W310388.

I started my term in the Manning Depot as an AW2 and worked in administration while awaiting a course. I was transferred to Guelph, Ont., where I began intensive study of codes and ciphers and learned how to operate the Enigma machine, a very early form of a computer used for coding. The greatest foe of the Enigma machine was dust, and throughout my career in the RCAF, we cleaned our machines with carbon tetrachloride every eight hours. I realize now what a hazard that chemical is to your health.

Upon completion of the course, I was posted to the Western Air Command Headquarters in Vancouver. We were stationed at Jericho Beach in a camouflaged building. Years later, when we held a reunion of air women in Vancouver, a group of us went to Jericho Beach hoping to see the building where we had worked, but we couldn't find it. It had probably been disassembled.

Irene McDonald on Remembrance Day wearing her war service medals and the Commemorative Medal for Volunteerism

I was transferred eventually to the Northwest Air Command in Edmonton. The Japanese war became part of the messaging I was doing. It became an interesting chapter of my life as I flew into the north with codes.

I flew into Beaton River once and when I stepped out of the aircraft, the fellows shouted, "It's a girl!" I met the commanding officer and gave him book codes because they had no machine at that base. Then we'd fly on to other places such as Watson Lake, Whitehorse, and Atlin. We flew in small RCAF planes which generally held five passengers.

The pilots were very accustomed to flying into these mountainous landing strips, but I was scared. While I was in Watson Lake, the fellows said, "You can't be here and not go out on the Alaska Highway!" So I went out in a truck in the deep mud of the Alaska Highway. Years later, when I returned to the north and travelled on the Alaska Highway, I thought, my, what a change!

Most of the work I was personally involved in came by way of Air Ministry Whitehall in England. Needless to say, our work as code and cipher clerks was highly secret. We were a very small group of people who never talked about our work when we were off duty. We held our work in such secret trust that I'm still reticent to talk about what was in our correspondence. But I do remember receiving long lists of the names of all those missing, presumed dead or killed in action which were to be forwarded to appropriate persons. War was brought to our very souls.

Early days in Victoria

By Helen Simpson as told to Joan Mason

My father had a general store and post office in Victoria, B.C., during the 1920s. From the age of eight, I had to help when needed, starting in the school lunch hour at the candy case. Our

The Seven Oaks Store, Victoria, 1927

Seven Oaks store included staples, bread, canned goods, flour, rice, barley, fresh fruit and vegetables, fresh farm eggs, dairy products, basic medications and some stationery. In addition, we stocked some hardware items, kegs of nails, chicken feed and coal oil. Our post office served people within a two mile radius of the store.

By the time I was 15, I had passed tests for assistant postmaster and completed the weekly audit sheet that had to be submitted by each post office. I had to balance the accounts to the penny. Incidentally, I'd been a stamp collector from the time I was nine years old.

A friend of ours ran the Colquitz Post Office at the corner of Wilkinson and Interurban Roads. When he was away for an entire summer, he asked Dad whether I would undertake their audit sheet as well. They arranged that I would bike over from our corner at Glanford Avenue and Carey Road and help his wife, who was not a bookkeeper, to do the weekly audit. One of my special memories from our post office is of handing mail over to Mr. McKenzie of the Craigflower Farm family, who had a house of his own at the bottom of Christmas Hill.

Summer in Victoria in the '20s was hot and dry and all the

young folk liked to go to the Gorge for a swim. Tillicum Road was a dirt track and our canvas sandals oozed with dirt by the time we got to the Gorge. There would be a long trail of us walking past the large Wong farms rented from J.W. Rowland, with at least one of the group over 12 years in age. It was two miles each way. We went to the "Free" where the change room cost five cents and you put your clothes on a bench. At the "Pay" it was 25 cents, but you got a locker for your clothing. We had our swims — boys and girls were not separated except in the change rooms.

Mother and Dad wanted to buy a radio in 1928. They explained it would be a family present and we would each be given one small present. What a joy it was to hear Dad chuckle over the comic groups of the day and to hear the news! We often had visitors because many of Mother's family lived "up-coast" in Kingcome Inlet, Alert Bay, Campbell River and Comox and other family members lived in the B.C. Interior in Kamloops, Quesnel, Grand Forks and Nelson.

We had a wonderful childhood with family picnics and outings to pick blackberries as a family (including the occasional encounter with a hornets' nest). On quiet Sunday evenings, after dinner visitors had left, Dad softly played the piano and Mother read passages of the Bible or *Pilgrim's Progress.* I remember being scared by the line, "Yea though I walk through the valley of the shadow of death… ." It gave me fearful thoughts.

The practice of medicine was very different then. In 1921, our family doctor came to the house to see my one-year-old brother, Jim, who had a fever. After assuring Mother it was not serious, he looked over at me and said, "What's the matter with Helen?" Mom said it was just a tummy ache, but he examined me and realizing it was more serious, took me to the Jubilee Hospital. He admitted me and took me to a bed in the Children's Ward. At 11 p.m., he came with a stretcher, gave me chloroform, wheeled me into the operating room, took out my appendix and then wheeled me back to my ward. He was a true Scot with big bushy eyebrows.

I still didn't know about the facts of life when I was 15 years old. A friend of one of our neighbours asked me if I would like to go for a ride one day and told me, "Helen, I think you are getting in beyond your depth. I've been watching you go out with some of the fellows and I think some of them are tough characters." Then he told me what I needed to know. From then on, whenever I went out and anyone started anything funny, I just told them I wanted to go home.

My Prairie origins

Excerpt from *Finding Gold In My Memories* by Madge Struthers as shared with Barbara Robertson

I was born in a bedroom at Dr. Cumberland's farm house on Jan. 8, 1913, in Elfros, Sask., where the ice in the jug on the commode was two inches higher than the top of the jug. My birthplace was registered six months later as being in the Northwest Territories, even though Saskatchewan was made a province in 1905. Perhaps the officials were short of staff and an official provincial registry had yet to be established.

My mother and father both immigrated to Canada from Scotland, along with my father's brother, Jim. When my mother first arrived on the farm my dad had bought, she was bothered by the frogs in the springtime and the owls at night. Sometimes she missed her old life in Scotland, but when she sat on the top step of the cellar, which Dad had cribbed and shelved, and looked at all the home-cured hams, the rows and rows of fruit and jellies and bins of vegetables, all her anxiety faded away.

How my father, who had pernicious anaemia and was considered "delicate," ever thought he could come to virgin soil and break the land I'll never know, but he had guts and pulled out roots from land covered with bush and then he sowed wheat. In Scotland, he'd owned Muirs Bakery and was a master baker.

Haying in Saskatchewan, 1917

The threshing machine arrived in 1910 like a big dinosaur. The threshing crew moved from farm to farm as it ate the sheaves of wheat which had been stooked for some time (dried out). The straw went one way and the wheat went into the wagon boxes to be hauled by the horses to the elevator. Every town had three, four or five elevators which were situated on the other side of the railway tracks from the town. A few years later, the railway put on a harvest excursion and the lads who came to work on the harvest, mostly from Ontario, often stayed on to homestead. Such was the romance of the west!

A narrow escape in Elfros, Sask., 1913

We relied on our horse and buggy, with a sleigh in the winter, to get around. While crossing a little bridge one day, the cutter tipped and I rolled into the stream, which thankfully had some ice and snow still on it. I was wrapped in a lovely down quilt, so I probably would not have gone down the stream anyway.

My dad was superintendent of the Presbyterian Sunday School and for some time the superintendent of the Anglican Sunday School. Elfros was treated to what was known then as the "saddle-back ministry." My parents were very strict but we always knew they loved us. The Bible and the Sunday school paper were the only two things we could read on Sundays and no playing was allowed outside. We attended church twice a day on Sunday and Sunday school at 2 p.m.

I can remember the trimming of the coal oil lamp wicks; the little enamelled basin where you washed your hands as you came in the door; the cast-iron pump for water; and the telephone on the wall with a party line shared by four or more families. A few yards from our back door was a small patch of bushes where chokecherries, pin-cherries, raspberries, thorn-apples and hazelnuts grew down by the creek.

Nothing was wasted in our family. Bags which had contained flour and sugar became dish towels and embroidered table cloths. My dad and mom, like most people of that era, had to use their ingenuity to keep the wolf from the door so our house became a boarding house even though there was very little room.

I'm thankful that I grew up in an era when a "grief counsellor" happened to be your own mother whose simple but effective remedy was support, patience and love. I'll always remember how patient my dad was in trying to allay the pain I suffered from rheumatic fever as a child.

My parents stretched their budget to give me music and dance lessons which I really enjoyed. (I have certificates from the Toronto Conservatory of Music on file.) But I was forced to stop at age 13 when Dad was out of work, although I took occasional lessons with a local teacher. Music has always been part of my life, a very dominant part, but I feel sorry I did not make more of my excellent training. I often joke about being on the stage, but it was true. Freddie Heath and I danced the sword dance, the Highland fling and the cake walk each year at the Empire Theatre and we were sometimes asked to perform in smaller towns in the Saskatoon area.

The year 1929 was a memorable one for me. I was 16 and had my first job at the YMCA, earning $35 a month. Many girls and boys turned up to audition for the job at the Y. I was the last girl to audition and on the spur of the moment I played "In an English Country Garden," which I'd played on the radio not long before and I got the job. One night after a dance at the Y, eight of us did the equivalent of the snake dance down Second Avenue, the main street in Saskatoon, singing our hearts out.

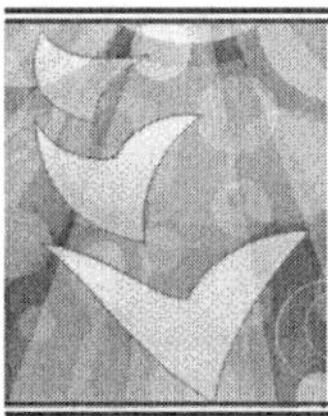

A "lucky" life

By Mary Thomas as told to Edeana Malcolm

Rural Saskatchewan in the '30s

I think I was very lucky to be born into the family that I was and to have lived the life that I have. Both my sister, Anne, and I really appreciated life on the farm. My dad gave each of us a calf to fatten and exhibit in a show that was held every April — we belonged to the "Baby Beef Club."

We had whist drives and those sorts of things at the United church, and the United church minister had to come from Esterhazy, Sask., a distance of over six miles, which wasn't always easy in the wintertime. We had services every other Sunday and the children attended Sunday school too.

My mother taught Sunday school for a while and we had many different teachers. Often it was the school teachers who took part in teaching Sunday school. Our school teacher and her mother had a girls' camp one year at Crooked Lake. It was the most wonderful two weeks in my life because we learned how to row a boat, and I enjoyed doing all sorts of things with other young people. It was a most outstanding two weeks, though I know it was hard on my mom and dad. They had to do all the milking and chores we normally did when we were at home.

Electricity

Not even townspeople had electricity in the years when I was growing up. Electricity was brought into Saskatchewan by the Cooperative Commonwealth Federation (CCF) in 1940, although I'm not certain of that date.

Those people who had electric light also had a stack of batteries that had to be charged regularly. My uncle's farm had that kind of power because my cousin and his older brother bought the batteries and set them up properly and wired the house. The wires were obvious because they hadn't been built into the house like they are nowadays. So they had electric light but they didn't have an electric stove or anything like that.

We had coal oil lamps. We had one lantern with a little bulb, just a cloth wick. It lasted a long time but you had to be very careful. That's how most public buildings were lit at that time. We had one lamp that was used in the kitchen or in the living room, wherever most of us were gathered. But it was the coal oil lamp that we took upstairs when we went to bed. I lived a good deal of my life under that kind of light.

Plumbing and heating

Our home had been properly built, so we had a furnace in the basement and there were pipes put up to all the rooms including the living room, the kitchen, the service room off the kitchen, the bedrooms, of course, and the bathroom upstairs. But we used wood for fuel because nobody I knew had a coal furnace. We had to cut down our own trees. At the beginning that was good because the property could then be used for other purposes, but a lot of the trees were around sloughs and the sloughs were a source of water for the animals.

We had no indoor plumbing. The water had to be carted in and out. I remember the drought while growing up that took its toll on the Prairies for about 10 years. My sister and I hauled water at least twice every week in a great big water tank on a horse-drawn wagon.

One time we brought two little pigs from the neighbour. My sister, Anne, and I did most of the milking, and we had lots of milk throughout the summer. So Dad bought two little pigs to fatten them, and we placed them in a gunnysack. I don't remember which of us was driving; maybe we took turns while the other one hung on to the sack with the two little pigs inside. We had some funny experiences like that.

Transportation

We used horses in the wintertime — only a few people had cars to get around. I was on my way home one day on my bike from Esterhazy, Sask., and it had snowed. I was trying to steer my bike in the tracks of cars that had been along but I was having some difficulty. A car stopped behind me and a man got out and I knew instantly who it was because he was our family doctor. My mother worked with him a lot because she was a nurse — he always asked for her when he was called out. Anyway, he said, "I think we'll put that bike in the trunk of my car and I'll take you home," which he did. I really appreciated that drive home.

When I became a teacher, I used to ride the bike back and forth between my home and the school every weekend. I didn't take it to school during the week because I boarded about a mile away from the school. I just walked because it wasn't too far. But I went home on my bike a good part of the winter.

It was kind of an isolated life on the farm. You didn't see too much of other people except for the men working on the crops and the neighbours going by. They used to drop by frequently to see Mom if they had a bad cut or something like that because she was a trained nurse. She was always kept busy. Many times, my dad used to call to me, "Mary, you'll have to get up this morning. Your mother's at so-and-so's." Then I knew a new baby had arrived.

NOW IT'S YOUR TURN

Some questions to ponder

- **What is one of your favourite childhood memories?** Use your five senses to describe it *(sight, smell, sound, taste and touch)*.
- **What is your *earliest* memory?**
- **Where and when were you born? What did your home look like?**
- **What was your relationship like with your parents and siblings?**
- **What was it like to grow up during the Depression and war time?**
- **What were some of your early dreams and goals?**

LOVE AND FRIENDSHIP

Kindness
Warm cloak of love
Enfolding hurting heart
Encouraging return to life
Hope sings! — May Deller

Neighbourhood saints

Written by May Deller
as shared with Irene Baddeley

Mr. Simpson

I grew up in the little village of Hamiota in western Manitoba. My parents owned a very small home in a spacious lot at the east end of town. The railway bound us on the south side with very few scattered houses on the north. Farmland and bush bound us on the east and some distance to the west, the "downtown." We were isolated from that downtown area with its neatly manicured streets, real cement sidewalks and large important houses. This untamed, less sophisticated and more remote corner of the village became my beloved neighbourhood.

Very few homes in our corner had children in them. Most of our few neighbours in the randomly scattered houses were, to my young mind, "old" people.

A couple of these old people, Mr. and Mrs. Simpson, lived down our lane and across the gravel road in a huge, draughty old ramshackle house that had seen better days in a previous century, I'm sure. She was a quiet, shy woman, not to be seen outdoors much at all. He was the partner who fascinated me. His lanky, thinly clad body supported a gruff, grizzled countenance, camouflaging rather well a kind and caring heart. He proved to be a somewhat inept conversationalist, so unlike the members of my talkative family, but he and I managed to communicate reasonably well.

My childhood ears had picked up gossip from older children that he must be avoided at all costs. The tales suggested that he had come from "away" Down East somewhere, so he was an outsider and that he had a wild temper, especially when drunk. He had supposedly killed a man when in a rage and had fled to our little community under an assumed name. Be that factual or not, I quite enjoyed the brusque old chap.

Mr. Simpson chewed tobacco. His few remaining teeth were brown, very brown. The few times I was in their home, my eyes were drawn to a terrible looking spittoon situated beside his chair. Spittle fastened itself to both inside and outside of this queer dish and on the floor surrounding it. I tried not to look in that direction but found my repugnance overcome by the fascination of this awesome sight, never more so when suddenly the wad in his mouth would move, he would take aim and spit in the general direction of this odorous container.

Since our home was almost a mile from the school, we children took all the shortcuts we could as we made our way there and back four times a day. His spacious yard provided a welcome shortcut. Each morning as we ran past his kitchen window, we could see him sitting there waiting for us, or in the summer at work in his garden. He always waved and we waved back. If a school day passed with one of the Turnbull children missing that cut off, by 10 a.m. he would be on our doorstep asking Mom if we were all right.

If we did not see him at the window, his absence would be duly reported to my mother and she would go over to their home to see if they were okay.

Some days, especially cold, cold winter days when we children hurried through the Simpson yard, we would meet Mr. Simpson running to the "little house" that rested lopsidedly on one corner of his property and was partially screened by shrubs. (This type of plumbing was common to us all, at least in our neighbourhood.)

As he ran he would call out to us, "I've been took! I've been took!" Respect and decorum could control us for just so long. We would hurry faster, placing as much distance as possible from our distressed neighbour before we burst out laughing.

My children probably have no idea where one of our oft-repeated family phrases comes from. And a useful one it is indeed. The path to the bathroom clears instantly when someone hollers, "I've been took! I've been took!"

Mr. Simpson's candour and sense of humour delighted me. I remember one other winter day when I came upon him in his back yard with his arms full of stove wood from the woodpile. His arms, amply overloaded, could not carry the ash pail he no doubt had taken to empty on the ash pile near the privy. To save himself a trip in his shirtsleeves on a cold day, he kicked the pail in front of him along the frozen path. As I came into view he called out cheerfully, "Here I am, kicking the bucket!" I noticed a big twinkle in his gray eyes and heard his hearty chuckle.

I can't remember exactly when Mr. Simpson actually "kicked the bucket." I believe Mrs. Simpson returned Down East after he was gone. I do remember, though, how much I missed them.

Geordie

Some time after the Simpsons were no longer a part of our lives and I was a teenager, another neighbour moved into one of the many vacant lots down the road. I had known Geordie previously when, as small children on very cold winter days, he would stop his school van to pick up my younger sister and me and give us a lift to school.

Our school was one of the first consolidated schools in Manitoba. The municipality paid drivers to pick children up from the farms and bring them to school. The "van" was on wheels in the summer and sleighs in the winter. It had a little wood stove in it to keep the interior warm. Benches lined the sidewalls of the van. About eight or nine children could be picked up in each van. The exit door was at the rear. At the front, a small-hinged window provided space for the driver to see out and to use the harness reins to urge the horses to move along at a good speed.

Geordie had a shrivelled leg and used crutches to get around. He was not known for cleanliness, and we much preferred the smell of the horses. His language would curl your hair. He chewed tobacco and spit wherever he pleased. We little girls were afraid of him. When we rode with him, he would not let us leave the van until we had given him a kiss. That did not suit me at all and after a few attempts to make me comply, I told my father. It was not long before we were able to leave the van without this undesirable hassle.

Geordie eventually retired from farming and driving school vans. Then a small shack moved into our neighbourhood and Geordie with it. His wife had taken off for other parts and he lived on his own. One of his sons lived in town a few blocks away. There didn't seem to be much love lost between father and family. The old chap truly was on his own. Not everyone had telephones at that time. When I look back it must have been a lonely existence for the poor old sod.

We no longer used the Simpson property as a shortcut to school as it had changed hands. So my route took me past Geordie's place. I kept my distance but whenever I saw him outside, I would stop and have a bit of a chat with him. I felt sorry for him. He had not been a neighbour for very long before my life and his were to connect in an unexpected way.

I was returning from school on a cold January day. The cold snap of near –40 degrees had continued for some days. As I walked past his house something moving back and forth across the window caught my eye. I recalled that I had not seen the old chap in several days. I had noticed the fresh snow had no tracks in it save for a cat or dog or bush rabbit track, and I'd seen no smoke from his chimney. I had assumed he was away for a few days, something that occurred occasionally.

Being both curious and concerned, I went to his door. I knocked and then opened the door when I thought I heard a faint call for help. (None of us locked our doors in those days.) When I went in through the late afternoon gloom, I saw Geordie on the floor near the window. The room was ice cold. The fire in the stove had long since gone out. The water pail on the table was frozen over, as was the chamber pot near the bed in this one-roomed house.

He looked so frail and weak and half frozen. I asked him how long he'd been lying on the floor. "Two days," he said. He dragged himself as close to the window as he could and grabbed his cane which he waved in the window for a few seconds as his strength allowed. The clock on the wall told him the approximate time one of us might be passing his place on our way home from school. He saved his energy until then.

I pulled blankets from the bed to cover him and lit a fire in the woodstove. Then I ran as fast as my legs would carry me to get my mother. She phoned the doctor and hurried over to Geordie's house with water and soup while I ran to where his son and daughter-in-law lived to see if they were home. They were not.

By the time I returned to Geordie's house, the room had warmed and the doctor was there preparing to take Geordie to our little village hospital.

Years later, whenever I met Geordie, he would say, "You are the girl who saved my life, aren't you?" I think his own survival instinct and his ingenuity, as well as the clock on the wall, were what saved Geordie's life.

The Liefs

The lane that took me to Miss Cochrane's home led me past the home of a couple I loved dearly. She was a tiny scrap of a woman, Mr. Lief's second wife, his first having died many years before I knew him. They had no children. In his first career he had been a school teacher. His second career as an elevator agent (a grain buyer for a major grain company) in a nearby village ended at the time of his retirement. It was then the couple moved to Hamiota, our village.

He knew all the neighbouring communities well. He loved a good story and could tell many a good one himself. And he loved to sing!

As this couple grew older, I became their chore girl. Every morning before school in the spring, summer and fall, I would bicycle to the post office to pick up and deliver their mail. There were ashes to remove from the cook stove and furnace, firewood to carry in as well as drinking water from the well. The slop buckets had to be emptied and the indoor toilet pails as well.

Snow to shovel in the winter and grass to trim in the spring and groceries to fetch once a week from downtown kept me busy. I also had duties in my own home. I never knew what boredom was. I loved doing what I could for them. They were such a neat couple.

Accepting money for doing these chores was unheard of. Such a thing never entered our heads when we were young. It was just what you did for neighbours, but I was amply paid nonetheless. After the chores were done, Mrs. Lief would have milk and cookies ready for me while he and she enjoyed a cup of tea, and then Mr. Lief would launch into one of his happy, humorous stories. I was enthralled. These stories never lasted long enough. Eventually his beautiful tenor voice would fill the air with song. Mrs. Lief and I would join in and far too soon the time had come for me to leave.

One winter he was not at all well. He died in his home on the morning of Christmas Eve. That was my first encounter with the death of someone I loved. That Christmas Eve, the little Canadian Girls in Training (CGIT) group to which I belonged went out to sing carols to shut-ins as was our Christmas Eve custom.

The girls and our leader debated about going to sing at Mrs. Lief's home thinking it might not be appropriate because of his death that day. They asked me to decide since I was close to this couple. I suggested we do as we had always done. That seemed to me to be so very appropriate though I knew I would find it emotionally difficult.

Their little home was the farthest from downtown and the last on our list for that night. We gathered outside their door and began to sing. The door opened and little Mrs. Lief came out on to the doorstep. She told us she had been so afraid we would not come and that when she heard us, she burst into tears of both joy and sadness. She asked us if we would sing *Silent Night*. I have never heard a more beautiful rendition of that old beloved carol than we sang that night. Our beautiful young voices lifted in harmony rose and fell out over the quiet, frosty, starlit night. Tears streamed down all our faces as we finished singing.

It is All Saints Day as I write these memories of a few folk from the neighbourhood of my childhood, these wise, foolish, broken, wonderful ones — saints — who along with my passionate and compassionate parents taught me about life and loving, respecting and caring for each other. That little village, that little neighbourhood became for me the loom on which my heart wove its first sacred places of human connection.

On friendship and loneliness

By The Rev. Colleen Erb
as told to Terry Dance-Bennink

I've experienced many different forms of friendship during my life. When I left Victoria in my 20s to be trained as a minister, I cried all the way on the train to Toronto. When I arrived, I had no friends and was terribly lonely. It was the most devastating time of my life. I can remember going to church on a Sunday night and walking down Bloor Street bawling my eyes out. I felt so empty. But after Christmas I met a woman who was studying to become a doctor and she helped me with some of my homework, and it made all the difference in the world.

It's hard to feel God's presence when you feel really lonely. I wasn't probably as mature in my faith in those days, but since then, I've explored the Ignatian practice and developed a much deeper relationship with God. It's easier now for me to truly believe God is my companion.

Over the years, I've learned you can't form a friendship based on preconditions. Some people have attributes you may find hard to handle or accept. I have a friend, for example, who lives in the moment all the time and sometimes it drives me nuts, because I want to know what we're going to do on Friday!

"What are you doing next week?" I'll ask her, and she'll

respond, "Oh, I don't know, let's wait and see." We have to understand and accept our differences. A good friendship involves a sacred trust, especially if the two friends differ in some ways.

Friendship takes many forms

There are many kinds of friendship. You can have friends with whom you relate on a fairly superficial level, friends, for example, in the music or business world whom you see once in a while. You may have another level of friends whom you see more often, and then an even smaller circle of friends, and perhaps one person with whom you really feel close.

Whether you have friends or not depends on how much initiative you take to reach out. Sometimes you have to initiate a friendship and be the person to invite someone over for dinner or out to a concert. You have to make the first call. To be an initiator can be a gift. I don't sit around and wait for people to visit me.

Friendship also takes effort. I have a dear friend whose ministry involves phoning anyone she knows who needs help. She has a bond with all kinds of people over the phone. It's a true ministry for her, and others who are home-bound can do the same thing.

Friends influence and shape one another. I remember telling couples before they got married, "You will become part of each other and shape each other as you grow to understand one another." I once lived in a boarding house, for example, with a woman who saved money. At the time, I loved to spend what money I had, but after living with her, I learned to save my money. It's the same with any deep friendship or relationship. You rub off on each other.

A minister's life can be lonely

I found it hard to make friends at certain points in my life, especially when I was a full-time minister. I was always concerned that I'd become "ministerial," that I wouldn't be just an ordinary friend, so I leaned over backwards to adopt a more natural approach.

The Rev. Colleen Erb, Minister, Gordon United Church, Victoria, 1989

In my former ministry at Chilliwack, B.C., I made friends with the minister and his wife, and my landlady and her family, but I was studying and had little time for extracurricular activities. When I moved to Victoria as minister of Gordon United, it was totally different because I was on my own — I had no ministerial team. I used to see my mom and dad every Sunday, and sometimes a member of the congregation would invite me for dinner, but I felt I couldn't really let my hair down.

I found it hard to maintain a balance between being a professional and a friend. The church teaches ministers that you don't make friends with the people you're serving, which is hard to practise sometimes. For example, I had to let a long-time Sunday school superintendent resign at one point, and this was hard on both of us. The rest of the congregation wanted to see some changes in the Sunday school curriculum, but it sure upset the teacher when she realized she needed to step down from her role. Despite our friendship, I had to make a tough decision based on the congregation's wishes. Perhaps this is what managers in the business world experience. Being a leader can be lonely.

After retirement, I joined First United and often had lunch and dinner with the minister and his wife. It took a while to get to really know people. One day after church, a group of women sitting in the Doreene McLeod room said to me, "You look lost and lonely! Why don't you come to lunch with us?" So I joined the "lunch bunch" and really enjoyed their company. At the time, however, I was spending a lot of time caring for my mom and dad, so my friendships were more family-based. When Mom died, my dad had me over for dinner every Wednesday and Sunday. When he died, it was hard on me

More recently, I've made quite a few friends in my townhouse complex who are very caring and mean a lot to me. I've consciously cultivated this because I'm a social person. I need to be in connection, in contact with people of like minds. I've made sure I have people around me with whom I can relate.

Friendship is not a 'cure' for loneliness

To be lonely is to be human. We're all gripped by loneliness at some point in our lives. It could be due to the death of a family member, the loss of a friend or any change in our lives. Sometimes we don't even know what we long for, what we desire. And sometimes we can feel lonely in the midst of a crowd of people.

Connection, I think, is the "cure" for loneliness — being able to share and accept one another, regardless of our differences, which involves getting to know one another. We need to know we are loved and cared for. A good friend, for example, cares whether you stubbed your toe or not and what you did about it! It's a silly example, but it's true.

Holidays are the hardest time of the year for me. Most people have family obligations and aren't available to get together. "Where is everybody?" I sometimes ask myself. One friend is out of town, another has a family commitment, and my younger friends are busy with their kids. So friendship is not a panacea for loneliness. It's part of the answer to loneliness, but not always and not completely.

You can have as many friends as you want, but even a husband and wife don't always feel supported by one another. God works through our relationships, however, even through a person who doesn't reciprocate our friendship. That's how God walks with us.

A friend of mine once told me about a nun who was feeling lonely and said, "It's OK for my spiritual director to tell me to talk to God, but sometimes I'd like to have someone with skin on!" Isn't that the truth? God does work through people, but when it comes down to the crunch and no one is there, you can either sit around and mope and be worried and say you're lonely, or you can decide to go out by yourself and do your thing.

Focusing on God makes a difference for me. I often go out to my local Tim Horton's for a coffee on Saturday mornings and put a tent over myself and am with God. Sometimes I read a book or a meditation to quiet myself, even though people are bustling all around me. It doesn't matter. I have a sense of God being at home with me.

God is with me no matter where I am. If I go for lunch alone, I often take a book that will stimulate my thinking about where I'm at in my relationship with God. This is how God becomes my companion and friend. It's the only way I can go alone. But sometimes it would be nice to have someone with skin on!

I learned this the hard way. For a while I felt I had to go out all the time and be with people. It cost me a fortune to go out and eat with friends, but I didn't want to be alone. After my stroke last year, the whole thing shifted. I discovered I could stay at home and be at peace. I was forced to make this shift because I couldn't keep up the pace anymore. My back was sore and I was on medication. I still came to church but I quit the choir for a while. I was just too tired to sing.

My whole life had been about going, going, going and giving, giving, giving. As I sat at home, I realized I *can't* go anymore. I don't have the same energy. So then your close friends become much more important, like my neighbours.

A lot of that former busyness was due to my work and social life being so closely linked. I found it hard to discern where my work ended and my social life began.

"Why are you still doing all this stuff for the church when you're retired?" someone asked me a few years ago.

"It's my life, it's where I connect, where my heart is," I replied. "I'm interested and still want to be part of it all."

But now, I've backed off a bit and have given myself permission to be on my own. I'm content to spend more time alone conversing with the Friend who's always at home.

Love lost and found

By Barbara Henderson as shared with Gloria Stott

Before starting my teaching career, I worked as a secretary in the B.C. Government High School Correspondence Department at the Parliament Buildings in Victoria. At age 21, I was asked to move to Prince Rupert, B.C., and supervise the Commercial Department of King Edward High School. I looked very young in 1936 so I let my hair grow and put it up in a bun in order to command more respect from the students, many of whom towered above me!

My starting salary was $125 a month for 10 months of the year. A lot of my Normal School friends who were teaching in elementary schools thought I was really in the money as their minimum salary at the time was $78 a month!

After teaching in Prince Rupert for three years, I moved to a new junior high school in Port Coquitlam, B.C., just outside of New Westminster. Unfortunately, my recurring throat and voice problems ended my teaching career and I became an inside instructor in the High School Correspondence Department of the government, marking papers of students taking commercial subjects by correspondence.

I met Kenneth Whitworth in 1939 when I was a bridesmaid at my cousin's wedding. He was my first serious boyfriend and I fell in love. Two years later, we were married in Metropolitan's sanctuary by Dr. A.E. Whitehouse. Ken was an engineer on the CPR passenger ships travelling between Victoria, Vancouver and Seattle — the "triangle run" it was called. We lived in Vancouver so we could see more of each other.

As World War II escalated, Ken felt he had to do his part for his country and joined the Navy. He was posted immediately to Halifax and after several months, I travelled by train across Canada to become one of the many "navy wives" much disliked by Haligonians. I was alone a great deal of the time as Ken was out on the frigates doing convoy duty, so I got a secretarial job with the CNR Express.

We were in Halifax for the big explosion and slept out on the boulevard that night until the "all clear" signal told us the worst danger was over. When the war ended, Ken was discharged from the Navy and we settled down to civilian life in Vancouver, living with his parents until we found a small basement apartment to rent. Housing was hard to find right after the war.

Due to his war service, Ken had lost all his seniority as an engineer with the CPR and had to work his way back up, so he decided to try and make a living on shore. We also wanted to start a family. We sank all of Ken's war service gratuities into a small engineering firm, but after a year of struggle and precarious living, the firm went bankrupt and we lost all our money. We never did have a home of our own but always rented and moved frequently.

I was overjoyed to find out I was pregnant at age 32 with our first child — it was the happiest moment in my life. Wendy Muriel was born in Vancouver General Hospital and soon after we had another daughter, Patricia Ann, so we had two beautiful girls. Ken tried to make a living selling life insurance but he was an engineer not a salesman, so finally he was forced to return to marine engineering to support his family. He joined the Union Steamship Co. which ran a fleet of smaller passenger steamships from Vancouver up the coast as far as Prince Rupert.

To get his diesel ticket, Ken had to serve time on a diesel-powered ship — an ocean-going tug called the Chelan which went up to Alaska and brought back barge loads of iron ore. Ken asked for a transfer to this ship, but on his very first trip in April 1954, the tug and barge were caught in a very bad storm and sank and the entire crew was lost. I was left with two young children, aged 3 and 7, and only $50 in the bank. It was the saddest time in my life.

A very good neighbour and friend gave me a copy of Catherine Marshall's book, *A Man Called Peter,* at that time.

Catherine Marshall had lost her husband suddenly from a heart attack and was left with one small son. Her book gave me a wonderful sense of the Lord's guidance and presence. I've since read every one of her many books and gained much spiritual strength from them all.

Barbara Henderson, secretary, Lansdowne Junior High School, 1956

I knew I had to go back to work, so I moved back to Victoria to live with my father and sister at 94 Linden Ave. Eleven months later, my father died. My mother had died in 1949. I found a job as a secretary at the Lansdowne Junior High School in 1954. I didn't feel I could return to my teaching career after 15 years away from it, and I had two small children to raise on my own, but I was happy to find a secretarial job in an educational atmosphere.

Love returned to my life a short while later. I'd been a member of Metropolitan's church choir ever since my teens, so when I returned to Victoria, I joined the choir again. In the baritone section was a 47-year-old bachelor named Keith Henderson. It seems he thought I was married with two small girls coming into the choir room to meet me after church each Sunday. He assumed I had a husband who never attended church!

After some time and a bit of help from a friend, Keith learned I was a widow and we became good friends. We were both musical and our first date was to the symphony. We soon fell in love. Brave soul that he was, Keith married "us" on April 20, 1957. My girls and I always said that the Lord saved him especially for us. Dr. F. E. Howley James performed the ceremony in the Ladies' Parlour at Metropolitan with Wendy and Pat standing up with us as our attendants.

The two girls — only 10 and six years old — were delighted to have a Daddy again. He gave them a real sense of security. We all went to church together every Sunday and attended many church activities. Keith was the biggest blessing of my life, and we spent 36 very happy years together. He was a wonderful husband and father, and we eventually became proud grandparents of four girls and one boy. We bought a house at 193 Werra Rd. for the horrendous amount of $12,800, where we lived until Keith died in 1993. I lived alone in the house for six years until I bought a condo in View Royal where I still live happily.

I've made a lot of friends through the years, mainly through the church, although many of my friends have passed away. At age 92, I'm still active in the Unity unit of the UCW and regularly phone members to remind them of our meetings and I send out cards to members who are sick.

I use a cane and walker and, because I can't drive anymore, I do a lot of phoning and invite old friends and women without families over for tea in order to help them in any way I can. I think this is my ministry now and I feel fulfilled. I'm convinced God hears and answers our prayers. I start and end each day with a prayer and thank God for all I've received.

To keep myself healthy, I eat well, ride my exercise bicycle everyday and attend weekly exercise classes. I'm ready to go whenever the Lord wants me but I hope it won't be before September 2008, when my first great-grandchild is due!

A marriage of equals

By Ruth Howell as told to Edeana Malcolm

I was 33 when I married my husband, Jack Howell, who was the manager of a meat-packing company here in Victoria.

When I taught at Smithers, B.C., one of the teachers on the public school staff was a girl by the name of Yateve Arthurs. She was also from Victoria, and when we came home from our teaching year she invited me over to where her mother lived and

Jack was boarding. Yateve and I were attending summer school and every week there was a dance and Yateve invited Jack to the dance. So he was well set up; he had two partners right off the bat!

I went with him for quite a while. I remember he had me out one night for a drive and told me he wanted to visit his home and his brother and sister and all his relations in Napanee, Ont., where he was from. He wanted me to go along. We were married in Vancouver, and our honeymoon was in Ontario. I remember someone on the train called out "Mrs. Howell" but it didn't ring a bell. In my mind, I was still Ruth Wilson.

A real satisfaction in my life was that my marriage turned out well. Thank goodness. I remember an aunt who visited us from Napanee, Ont., who said, "I never saw a couple that got along quite as well as you do." Well, I can't remember arguing, that's for sure. Everything was all right.

Jack was up at 6 o'clock every morning and down at the plant really early where he had a long day, standing most of the time. Then he'd come home and help me with the children and bring them to bed. Then he'd turn around and stand some more, helping me with any preserving that had to be done, like peaches or apricots. I think I was expecting a lot. I just accepted it.

You don't know really how your marriage will turn out until you're married. Jack always took time at night to help me with whatever needed to be done and that was wonderful. He was a good man.

My proudest moment

By Mona Hundleby as told to Terry Dance-Bennink

Our 60th wedding anniversary was a very proud moment in my life. I think our marriage was happy and long-lasting for three reasons. We practised open and honest communication between the two of us; we were both devoted to our children; and we shared a common purpose in life — to help others develop their potential.

Mona just before her marriage to Roy Hundleby

We rarely had disagreements, and neither one of us ever thought of anyone else. Our counsellor training in Banff and California helped us recognize and express our feelings. The course in anger, in particular, was a big help. Roy would say to me, "Sometimes you don't tell me the full story, and I feel left out." It annoyed him when I held back. I didn't do it deliberately, but both of us knew we could mention things like this and make the small changes needed to help the other partner feel at ease.

Sometimes I'd tell Roy that I felt he was getting a bit too friendly with one of the women in our counselling centre. I used to counsel the men, and he'd counsel the women, so we had to trust each other. Our counsellor training gave us a wonderful foundation for our own marriage.

We also shared a common purpose in life — helping others. The Counselling Centre in Victoria was the focus of much of our marriage in our middle years, and we were both equally devoted to helping it grow. It kept us focused outwards, not inwards — on serving others, not just ourselves.

We shared the responsibility for our two children as well and took those duties seriously. As they were growing up, we instituted a family council on Sunday nights so family members could raise their concerns or needs. We didn't have a TV when the kids were young, and they used to go next door to a neighbour's house to watch their favourite programs, which Roy and I didn't like. So at one of our family councils, we talked about how we could save to buy a TV. We taught the kids to be economical with toothpaste and to turn off the lights when they left a room. They learned about economy as they grew up — a gift that helped them later in life.

The kids could also choose what food they'd like to eat on Sunday nights (provided it was in the fridge!) They learned to resolve conflicts by talking about whatever was bugging them. Family holidays were a shared decision, with the kids as responsible as Roy and I for choosing our destination. We'd get out the maps and discuss how to save for whatever trip was our top choice. Our first big adventure was a round-trip across North America!

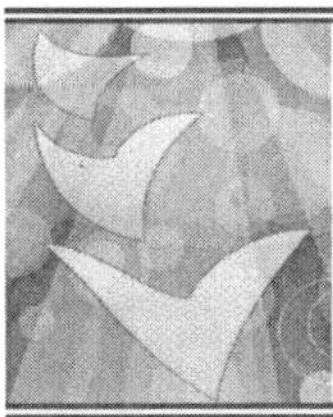

Meeting Jack

By Sheila MacDougall
as told to Terry Dance-Bennink

My nursing supervisor thought I was wonderful and she kept asking me over to her place for supper. I was reluctant — who wants to be a teacher's pet? But eventually I agreed.

On this particular day, I joined her on a trip downtown as she had to drop off some papers for a man at the Bank of Nova Scotia. He wasn't in the bank that day because he was on holidays, but there he was, on the sidewalk just as we came by. She introduced me to Jack and invited him to supper that night as well. As we walked away, she said to me, "He won't come, you know. He's afraid of women!" When I told Jack later about her comment, he said, "Yeah, I was afraid of *her*!"

Sheila and Jack Rice engaged

I met Jack about the first of July, and I had his ring before the summer was over. I was still working nights at the hospital and enjoyed showing all the girls my ring. My supervisor was absolutely delighted and took credit for our introduction.

Jack (John Rennie Rice) worked for the Bank of Nova Scotia, and I'm convinced he arrived in Edmonton, Alta., on the same train I did, because he started work on the very day I went into training. What a coincidence. He was the greatest! We had a very, very good marriage and endless fun. Everybody loved him. He was eight years older than I and in his 30s when I met him. He'd been around. He was a wonderful dancer — the best dancer I ever knew — and loved to play bridge and invite people over to the house.

His family came from Scotland — Rice was his father's name and Duncan was his mother's name. His ancestors all settled in Nova Scotia in the early days. His grandfather and father were in the army at Louisburg and then went to work in the mines. Jack started with the Bank of Nova Scotia when he was 16 and was transferred a number of times before he came west, initially to the town of Spirit Wood in Saskatchewan — a fair-sized agricultural farm community. He was the clerk, not the manager, when he arrived, and then he was promoted to be an accountant and sent to Edmonton where I met him.

We were married in 1947. He was transferred back to Spirit Wood in 1951 as the bank manager. He wasn't too enthused about this move, and didn't know anything about farming, but I did. We had a wonderful time there, tearing around doing all sorts of fun things. He was a very popular bank manager.

Jack was also very compassionate. An old fellow used to come into the office and sit around — a nosy-parker. A farmer came in one day and wanted to buy a truck. After he'd left, the old fellow asked Jack, "Did you loan him some money?"

"None of your business," Jack replied.

"Well, if you did, he lied to you, because he's got no money," the old fellow retorted.

When Jack closed the office at 3 p.m., he drove out to visit the man's farm. It was getting dark and when he arrived, he told the man he just wanted to count the cattle. To get a loan, you had to give a statement of all your assets and livestock. He could tell from the look on the man's face that he had, indeed, lied to him.

The man mumbled something about it getting dark, but his little boy piped up and said, "I'll get the lantern, Dad!" So they went into the corral and, of course, the number of cattle was not what he'd claimed. "You've got to come into the bank tomorrow," Jack told the man. He didn't want to say anything more in front of the man's youngster.

Everybody in the district knew that the man had taken home a new truck, so Jack felt badly for him and wanted to come up with a solution. The farmer would be mortified if the truck had to be returned. So Jack got on the phone to a good friend at the Chev Olds dealership and told the dealer he'd given a loan to a guy who'd lied about his assets and wondered what he could do for him.

When the farmer came into Jack's office the next day, he was literally crying. Jack calmed him down and said he'd see what he could do. He phoned up his friend at the car dealership and in front of the farmer, repeated the whole story and insisted the dealer would have to make sure the farmer made his payments on time.

"That's OK, that's OK, Jack," the dealer kept saying on the phone. They had the deal already cooked, but Jack was making the point to the farmer. Needless to say, the farmer was a happy man when he left that morning with his truck! After that, when people came in for a loan, they were more honest about their assets. Many people thought inflating their assets was just the way to do business. So it was a two-way lesson.

Jack was wonderful with our kids, and they have great memories of him. He always told crazy stories — he was a born story-teller. He was fun and we laughed a lot. Elsa, our daughter, went to work in the bank one summer during high school, and he used to come out of the office and make faces at her which cracked her up.

He was just full of fun. He taught Elsa to dance, and Eric, our son, learned to golf with his dad. Sometimes I felt a little resentful, because I had to be the one to lay down the law with the kids — Jack was the fun guy. But he could discipline the kids when it was needed.

We had a tremendous social life due to Jack's role as bank manager. You just step into this role when you arrive in each new town. I remember going to Moose Jaw and saying, "Man, I hope it's not Kiwanis again and selling apples. I'm sick of selling apples!" But apples it was.

The minister, Bob Morris, who later became a minister at First United in Victoria, was the minister of the United church in Moose Jaw, Sask., during our stay. He was there on the doorstep before I'd even got the furniture in! I was wearing my drudge clothes, directing the traffic, and here's Bob Morris wanting to make sure we came to his church and not the other United church in town.

Both my parents loved Jack. My mother said, "He's one of ours!" She was a bit of a snob, and Jack loved to tease her. There'd been some rows in the family about money, and mother wanted to be sure we all understood what was coming to us in their wills.

"Now, Arthur will have the farm because he's working on it," she said, "but there will be a little money for you girls."

Jack responded by saying, "If you think for one minute that I'll stand by if Sheila doesn't get her cut…!" Mother would erupt until she realized Jack was teasing her. She loved this kind of banter.

When I think about what I've loved most in my life — it's my marriage to Jack. They were very, very happy years. No marriage is made in heaven, but this one was pretty close.

A disappointment in love

Written by Helen Mau as shared with Cyndi Frame

I had a wonderful boyfriend from 1939 to 1942 — my first real love at age 18. He was a math and physics scholarship winner, a strong athlete and went on to become a prominent professor of nuclear physics. We came home from a lovely long walk together in North Toronto in 1942, but my father threw him out of the house because he'd discovered my boyfriend was a Roman Catholic. My father was prejudiced against Catholics and had a strong temper and I bowed to his wishes, something I've always regretted.

Today I say to myself, "Why did I not have the courage to leave home?" But this was before women's lib! My boyfriend was a Christian born into the Catholic faith, and I would have been a Roman Catholic, too, if Britain's King Henry had not protested. We are all Christian.

My dad's mother was a severe English woman. I decided early on that I didn't want to be like her. I think she was a large factor in defining Dad's temperament: his severity, his strong opinions and his tendency to control me. As a widow, his mother was forced to manage a family of five with no outside income. My dad went to work at age 13. These facts challenged me to rely on my own abilities and energy and to leave home when I could.

Sixty years later in 2002, I wrote to my high school boyfriend to apologize for the way my father treated him. In response to my letter, he hand-wrote an 11-page letter telling me all about his life. Five years after our separation, he married and subsequently had three children, all of whom became professional people.

Some years after the break-up of my first love, and perhaps on the rebound, I met and married Charles Mau who, unknown to me, had had tuberculosis. We lived in San Francisco for 37 years where I taught at San Francisco State University and then we eventually retired to Victoria, Canada. As time went on, I realized that my husband was looking for security, not love. I felt deceived. But I am responsible for my own choices, my attitude and my happiness.

This interracial marriage exposed me to many cultures and races through my life in San Francisco and extensive travel in the Far East; it helped me appreciate more fully the personal problems of others and to value tolerance and openness. I have had the opportunity to promote tolerance in my work, the church and my community. Perhaps this was part of God's plan.

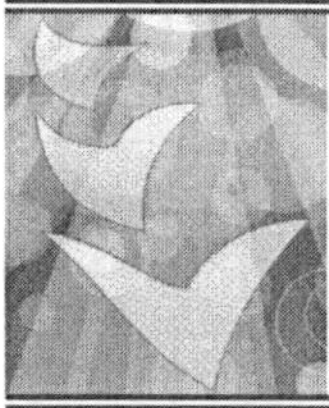

A war-time romance

By Irene McDonald
as told to Terry Dance-Bennink

While I was stationed at the Western Air Command of the RCAF, I met my future husband, Donald McDonald, on a blind date arranged by his very good friend, Peter Anderson. Donald's work was quite different from mine and I worked shifts, so our courting consisted of short quick walks to the mess hall for meals, and occasionally, we went to Stanley Park and enjoyed sightseeing in Vancouver.

Donald was a man of impeccable manners and dress. He came from an Irish family and had all of the wit of the Irish. He had dark, curly hair and was taller than me and somewhat heavy-set. He had many friends, but when he met me, who came from a large family, it was a different experience for him.

Donald's mother was bride, mother and widow in 13 months. His father died of complications from surgery when Donald was only five weeks old, so his mother brought him up by herself. When she went to work to support her family, Donald was raised by an aunt and uncle in Campbell's Bay, Que. His mother worked for A.J. Freiman's store in Ottawa for many years.

Donald's mother died of cancer, however, at the beginning of the war. It was before the era of Canada's medical health plan, and she suffered a long illness. During our courtship, Donald explained to me that anyone who became his partner had to know that he still had debts to pay off incurred by his mother's illness.

When the war broke out, Donald was in college at the time, but he enlisted as many young men did in 1939 and served for almost 30 years. Donald's wit and his manners certainly attracted me, and also the fact that he appreciated a woman's role in life, having grown up alone with his mother who supported them both. He was very much a man's man with his friends, however, and quite outgoing.

While we were in the courting stage, Donald was moved to the Northwest Air Command, because the Japanese theatre of war had become the focus. He helped set up field stations throughout Canada's north, which meant our romance had to be conducted through letters.

Our wedding

I was based in Edmonton until the end of the war. Donald was stationed in Whitehorse for a time and then he, too, came back to headquarters in Edmonton, and we planned our marriage. We were married on the 1st of March 1945 in McDougall United Church in Edmonton on a bitterly cold day. Donald was a devout Roman Catholic. He had a very sustaining faith throughout his life and certainly encouraged me to be more active within my church.

Irene and Donald McDonald's wedding day, Mar. 1, 1945, Edmonton

Our wedding in McDougall Church was a beautiful evening ceremony and our soloist, Sergeant Al, was the soloist for the

Theatre Under the Stars in Vancouver, and when he sang, all the wedding guests were enthralled with his voice. We held our reception in the Macdonald Hotel, and I still have our hotel room receipt for one night which cost $6.50. The CPR hotels had special rates for servicemen, and that was our room rate.

We travelled by train to Vancouver for our honeymoon and stayed at the Hotel Vancouver, also at a reasonable rate. During our stay we heard a tremendous explosion, and I feared we were being strafed or that something had happened in the war. It turned out that a ship of explosives had blown up in the harbour, and the windows in the buildings along the harbour, almost to the Hotel Vancouver, were blown out. It was a shambles of broken glass on Granville Street, but fortunately, our hotel wasn't damaged at all.

After our honeymoon, we returned to Edmonton where we'd rented a small apartment before the wedding. When we arrived, however, we discovered it had been rented to an American couple, despite the fact we'd paid for it. The landlord said he'd give us back our money, but that wasn't much help.

American servicemen were very much in evidence in Edmonton at the time and throughout the north, and their rates of pay were much higher than ours. Canadian servicemen really didn't stand a chance of getting housing. There was nothing we could do about it, so it was back to the barracks for us. We did find an apartment, eventually, in a private home within walking distance of the base.

Life-fulfilling moments

Donald and I entered our marriage with two quite different faiths and we recognized that there might be problems, but we faced these issues before we got married. We entered a marriage that was planned to be successful.

Some people felt that Donald would be kept from practising his faith by marrying in a church that was not Roman Catholic, but I discovered this was untrue. The only thing I was asked was whether or not I was a baptized Christian. From there on, the decisions we made about children were left up to us. I will never forget coming down that church aisle and seeing Donald turn and smile and greet me as I approached the altar. That moment brings me joy whenever I recall it.

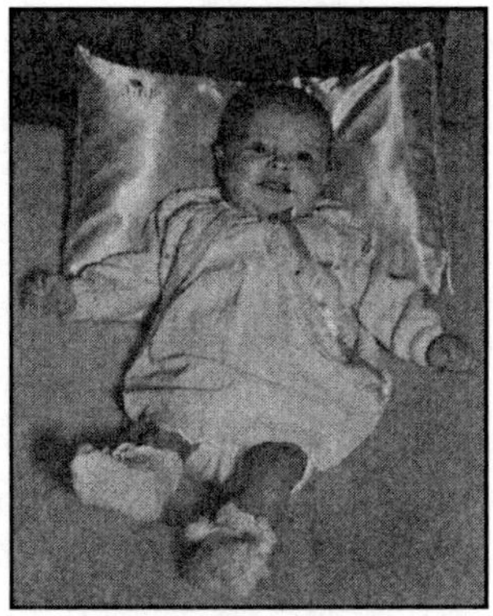

Catherine Ann McDonald, 3 months old, born June 15, 1946

Giving birth to my daughter, Catherine, however, has to be paramount in terms of fulfillment. To bring a new life into the world is not only a moment of tremendous joy, but it gives you a great sense of satisfaction, to be part of creating a new life. Giving birth brings you close to a sense of the tremendous mystery of life.

I sustained this life inside me for so many days and months and then all of a sudden, I had a bonny baby girl and a father who was *so* pleased to have, as he said, two girls to love. When he came to see me in the hospital, he brought me some red roses, along with a vase with a single red rose for his daughter. It was a moment of great joy for me. I was fortunate to have a routine pregnancy and gave birth on my birthday; it was also Father's Day weekend, so coupling all this together was a feat in itself.

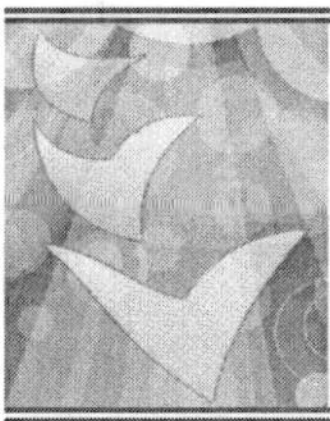

Finding my roots

By Helen Simpson as told to Joan Mason

When you start to talk to a stranger, you nearly always find a connection, even in New York City. Life is so short when you open up to others. I've never had any trouble in opening up and have made many friends on buses and ferries.

When my brother, Jim, came home in 1962 for Mother's funeral service, he said, "Helen, you've been here in Victoria looking after Mom for all this time." (It had been about two years since the beginning of her illness.) "When you feel like it, we would like you to come to New Jersey and meet the family."

Kenneth and Helen Simpson with daughters, Patricia and Elizabeth, 1951

I flew to New York a month later and started with a bus tour of the city. I had the whole of New York City to explore on my own. On the bus tour I spoke to my seatmate and it turned out he was from Vancouver and knew a lot of people I knew. It is such a small world when you start breaking down barriers and talking to people.

Genealogical research

I've made 18 trips to Salt Lake City to visit the Family History Library of the Church of Jesus Christ of the Latter Day Saints (LDS), mostly with the group from the Victoria Genealogical Society. I loved it there. I knew where the machines were and I could look things up. It was a lot better than chasing all over the United Kingdom or waiting months to order films. The LDS church has done a wonderful job of making microfilms of church and civil records available in so many countries. The information in their Ancestral Files, however, is not as useful as it often has not been thoroughly researched or documented.

I discovered that my mother's family was Quaker and had come to Pennsylvania in 1698 on the William and Mary. Some of her family members were early Quaker ministers and I was able to get their complete history. Using a reference in the notes I found there, I contacted someone in Toronto who had some of the Canadian Hughes history. It was absolutely fantastic.

My family background goes back to Wales, Pennsylvania, Ontario and Scotland and includes Quakers, Methodists and

Presbyterians. I've never been able to pin it all down, except the Airth family. I was able to find out whom they married right back to the year 1685. I remembered enough of my Latin to interpret the particular Airth entries which were written in Latin until the year 1700.

I found the greatest pleasure in learning where I came from and what the lives of my ancestors were like. I not only had the challenge of tracing my own family history, but explored the variable background of the Simpsons, Gemmills and Forgies who all came to Canada between 1821 and 1826.

Among these relatives, I met an active genealogist named Don who was a farmer in Manitoba and loved to come out to Victoria in March. He was a big man, six foot four in height and enjoyed talking about his research. He'd come for dinner and we'd trade information and talk for hours. When my husband, Ken, was alive, he would fall asleep and go to bed while Don and I talked and reminisced. That was my greatest pleasure — finding my roots.

I've read all of the newspapers for the first 50 years from Renfrew, Arnprior and Smiths Falls, Ont., where the early immigrants settled, and also from Victoria where Grandfather Halliday was vice-principal and then principal of Boys Central School. Family members were mentioned in the *British Colonist* from 1880 to 1890.

My uncle, Will, was in the headlines one morning in the 1880s when he graduated from high school at age 15. The next morning, he took the train and went to Comox to look after the farm. The paper wrote him up saying, "A great many parents should be like Mr. Halliday and have farmlands for their sons."

History has a human face through the research I've done. And that's how I interpret living on the coast. Mother's whole family came to British Columbia — they were all involved in the early history of the country with their farming, fishing and logging. Even Dad made a contribution and he didn't come until 1910.

A hard call

Excerpt from *Finding Gold In My Memories* by Madge Struthers as shared with Barbara Robertson

Margaret Muir and George Struthers, wedding day, July 8, 1936

One afternoon, I decided to do something about my husband, George, who was working too hard. George was a full-time minister at the time and worked seven days a week from early morning to late at night. We had no time for ourselves. Earlier that day, I'd visited another minister who worked a nine-to-five job, and the session of the church had spoken to me recently about George working so hard.

I prepared supper and phoned him, but he had a few things to do first, as usual, so I asked him point blank if I could make an appointment with him. I think he knew immediately there was something wrong. When we met, I talked about him being a workaholic and pointed out that it wasn't fair to him, nor his family and friends. At his suggestion, we often invited friends and relatives over for a meal, but George was never there to meet them when they arrived. Even after a phone call, we usually had to send one of the children over to bring him home.

He was very upset, and for some reason, he wondered if there was someone else in the picture.

"Of course not, George," I replied. "You're my man and I know you love me and I love you, but we owe it to ourselves to work on the potential we have, especially now that the children are away from home. I would be quite happy if you would take Monday off, like most ministers do. You work seven days a week! Maybe we could walk down to 16th Avenue to look at the city lights, even at 11 p.m. when you usually come home."

We also talked about the use of the car. "The car is yours, without a doubt," I told him, "but it would be nice if you would take Mom and me out on special occasions or to the symphony twice a year. You're usually quite reluctant to do this when we ask. Mom is 90 years old and even though it's raining cats and dogs, you leave us off by the Cambie Bridge."

I must admit I was not prepared for how upset George became, mostly over his fear that there was "somebody else" in my life. He reminded me of all he was doing — he'd become known as a counsellor, not just in our congregation, but city-wide.

On Thursday evenings, there was always a row of people waiting to see him. He insisted, however, that his whole life in the ministry was based on our relationship which he felt was wonderful. He wouldn't be able to go on without my love and backing, he told me.

After this talk, we did try to go out to a show on Monday evenings, but it seldom worked out. On the first Monday, he was called to the hospital, and the following Monday, he was detained in his office although we caught the 9 p.m. show and had a terrific night watching *Easy Rider*. It was one of several controversial films we talked about together, often at McDonald's with the young people of Dunbar Church who had also attended the Monday night shows.

Those were the days when ministers visited both hospitals and congregations. George hardly let a day go by without visiting and he was a regular hospital visitor. I had a call once from a lady who was in charge of the hospital visitors at Vancouver General Hospital and she said George was a perfect hospital visitor.

"That Scotch minister is asked for more than other ministers," she told me. She wanted me to know what a treasure my husband was. I knew he put his whole heart into his visiting. Nowadays, many fellows go into the ministry because it's an occupation they feel suited for, but I think George felt he had been "called."

Saturday was usually an exception, however, when George honed his Sunday sermon, and if possible, he loved to see a cricket or soccer game at Stanley Park. He'd always been a great athlete and loved a game with his son, Jim, until Jim could beat him all the time! George was still active at age 50, but by the time he reached his sixties, he had black rolls under his eyes and was diagnosed with diabetes. He also had angina and heart disease.

Much to my relief, George handed in his resignation in 1972 and a letter came back from the church officials saying, "Yes, we accept your resignation which will take place in three years' time when you retire in 1975." Initially, we thought we might go up the coast to a place that needed a minister, but in 1974, George was asked to move on his retirement to Victoria as a part-time visiting minister at First United which suited us just fine.

When we left Dunbar United Church, I told the congregation, "Today is the first day of the rest of our lives. George and I look forward to our second honeymoon in Victoria. Our life will be very much the same for the church will always be our way of life, but we do look forward to spending more time together and doing the many, many things Victoria is famous for, and of course, making frequent trips to see our family."

The happiest day of my life

By Mary Thomas as told to Edeana Malcolm

Sylvia, a chum with whom I'd become very close at normal school, suggested we move to Victoria to attend summer school. When I mentioned this to my cousin, she said, "Oh Mary, I think you should go. I understand it's such a lovely city and very different from most Canadian cities."

My aunt's brother and his wife and son lived in Victoria and that's how I met my husband, Len, who was a friend of their son, Ernie.

Mary and Len Thomas, 1942

Sylvia and I came out by train and had to catch the ferry. We got off the ferry that came into the inner harbour in those days. We were on Government Street, but we didn't know how on earth we'd find Blanshard Street. We didn't have a map or anything, and we didn't have any directions as to how to get to my relatives, and we were wondering if we could phone them because we had their address.

We were standing at the corner debating when a car pulled up at the corner and a young fellow jumped out and said:

"Are you Mary Pask?"

"Yes, I am," I replied.

"Okay," he said, "We've come to pick you up."

Those two, Ernie and Len, took us all over the place. Sylvia and I would be busy trying to finish our homework while Ernie and Len were sitting on the front steps playing a card game by the half-hour waiting for us.

Len would always have something planned for us to do. It was just unbelievable. Our time went so fast because we were in classes that were interesting and challenging, but we had to hurry through our homework.

Our wedding day

The happiest day of my life was my wedding day. Everything went so beautifully and the saddest point was after the reception. We had the reception at my home on the farm and we caught the Transcontinental at 5 p.m. so that we could come back to Victoria. There was no flying in those days.

My husband and I left the reception so quickly. That was probably the saddest part for me but we were booked on a three-day train trip. It was war-time so when we got on the train, very few seats were available. There were all sorts of single seats, here and there, but we couldn't find a spot where we could sit down together.

After wandering down several of the coaches, I decided to stay with our luggage between coaches while Len went to find the conductor. The saddest moment was when the train passed by my home farm — the railway goes through our property fairly close to the house. That was a bit of a bad moment, especially standing there alone with my luggage waiting for a seat to sit down with my husband.

Len asked the conductor if he could find a seat where we could sit side by side. The conductor went the length of the train and finally came back and said he'd found a place. The conductor had to ask somebody to move so that we could sit together.

We didn't have a sleeping compartment as they were very expensive and hard to get due to all the service people travelling across Canada. We used to think, "Why on earth do they ship them from one end of the country to the other?" Of course, the officers had the sleeping compartments.

The best decision I ever made, however, was to marry my husband. That was my happiest day.

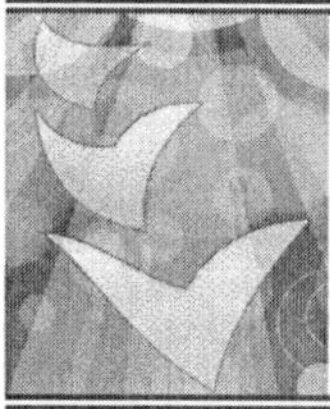

A miracle

By Esther Younie as told to Sheila MacDougall

I met my husband, Watson Younie, through my job as a home economist with the Ontario Agriculture Department in the 1940s. I was considered to be a good catch because I had my own car, a fur coat, and my wisdom teeth had been removed!

Esther Martin and Watson Younie on their wedding day

Watson was six years younger than I and we were married at my parents' home by a minister friend, and the reception was held at the local United church. We moved in with Watson's parents who owned a fruit farm near St. Catharines, Ont. We worked together to bring up our children on the farm and became active in the community.

Norman was our first born and a very busy little boy. Watson bought the makings for a crystal radio set and the two of them enjoyed putting it together even before Norman started school. Kindergarten disappointed Norman. "I don't want to play! I want to learn something!" he told me. Years later, we realized he was dyslexic, just as his father was. It seems this gene can be passed along.

Norman was only interested in electronics and held various part-time jobs during high school repairing radios and televisions. He also enjoyed his piano lessons. After graduating from high school, he worked on ships' radars on the Welland Canal and got his pilot's licence and bought his first plane. He acquired another plane later on and did a lot of flying for both work and pleasure — he even built his own plane.

He worked with pipeline and oil companies in Alberta for a few years but moved back to Victoria with his wife, Marilyn, to work in the electronics field for the City of Victoria. He also took a course in business administration and a paramedic course and then taught first aid to city employees.

Norman and I are very close. He looks after all my needs, takes me to appointments and visits frequently. He and Marilyn belong to a Baptist church and sometimes I go with them on special days. They have two adopted children.

My daughter, Lysbeth (Lys) is two years younger than her brother. She was an easy toddler, but when she reached the age of 12 she began having epileptic seizures. No medical relief seemed available and the seizures would occur at any time and place which magnified the usual teenage difficulties.

Lys went to the Montreal Neurological Clinic on a regular basis to have tests done. When she was 19, Lys made the decision to have brain surgery to relieve the cause of the epilepsy. Dr. Rasmussen, a colleague of Dr. Wilder Penfield, suggested the operation even though there was only a 10% chance of success.

The surgery took 11 1/2 hours but it was successful. It was truly a miracle! Our prayers were answered and all our lives were changed. Lys has never had another seizure. When she returned home, Norman had the Christmas tree up and beautifully decorated which was a lovely ending to some very difficult years.

Lys married when she was 23 and had a daughter, Margaret, who now has four children of her own. Watson and I have done what we can to help the grandchildren, one of whom may be dyslexic. I'm concerned that even today most teachers are not trained to identify these learning problems.

Lys left her marriage after 29 years but has since met a retired minister with whom she's made a life commitment. They had a special wedding in Victoria last fall. I have a lovely relationship with my daughter now. When I had my breast surgery in January, she gave me two weeks of loving care and support.

Watson and I have both had our share of health problems. Watson had a debilitating condition as a result of his days during the war on the North Atlantic in the damp freezing cold and rough seas. It continued to plague him for the rest of his life. His health problems intensified after we retired to Victoria in 1987 and he died in 2007. This is the first year of my bereavement and I miss him a great deal — the person he was and his companionship. We had a very good marriage.

I'm 89 years old now and no stranger to surgery. I'm plagued by weariness and various conditions that require medical attention. In spite of these handicaps, my attitude is, "That's just the way life is."

My family comes first in my life, and I know that we will always be there for one another.

NOW IT'S YOUR TURN

Some questions to ponder

- **Who was the most important person in your life?**
- **What was the happiest moment of your life? The saddest?**
- **Who or what has nourished you in your life?**
- **Who or what have you nurtured and cared for?**
- **Who or what has challenged you to grow in your life?**
- **Whom do you wish to thank in your life and for what?**
- **Whom do you wish to forgive and for what?**

A LIFE'S CALL

Work is love made visible. — Kahlil Gibran

A sense of call

By The Rev. Colleen Erb
as told to Terry Dance-Bennink

Early seeds

Colleen Erb, 4

The call to be a disciple of Christ came early in my life. I was fortunate to be part of a faith community as a child and absorbed the spiritual life by osmosis. I was baptized with my young brother when I was seven years old, by a Lutheran minister in my parents' apartment in Calgary.

I remember this vividly, because later on, when I was in ministry in Pincher Creek, Alta., I heard a man speaking at a church event and his name was Heideger, which rang a bell. I went up to him and asked him if he'd ever lived in Calgary and whether he'd baptized my brother and me. He was the one! I have a picture of him standing beside me that day in the presbytery beside the communion table.

In my early teens, I experienced another call to discipleship. When we moved to Victoria, I met a friend who belonged to the Baptist Church and she wanted me to join the Canadian Girls in Training (CGIT) at her church. I was reluctant at first, but when the CGIT leader spoke about what it meant to her to be a Christian and a member of the church, my whole attitude changed. I used to walk home with this CGIT leader and another friend, and we'd talk about God and church.

This faith-sharing was powerful — it was a conversion experience for me. I felt a strong desire to find out more about my faith, about God and Jesus, and to be with people who felt the same way. The turn around in my heart was dramatic, so much so

Colleen Erb, 15, practising piano

that I told my parents I wanted to be baptized in the Baptist church. Mom and Dad felt there was no need for a second baptism, because I'd already been baptized at age seven. My interest in the Baptist church, however, made my parents return to the United Church, and they invited me to join them.

Music also called me when I was in my early teens. I left school at age 15 and worked in the salad department at the Empress Hotel for seven years so I could pay for my music lessons. After years of study, I received two diplomas from the Royal Conservatory of Music in both teaching and performance. My piano teacher was a catalyst in my decision to embrace music as a career. "You're either going to teach music or you're not," she declared. "Make up your mind!" So I handed in my notice at the Empress Hotel and set up classes for students in Victoria, Colwood and Langford. I taught music full-time for the next seven years and loved it.

The call to ministry

The hardest thing I ever did was to leave home at age 30 and move to Toronto — a huge new city — in response to a call to enter the ministry. The call first surfaced during a wonderful experience at Pringle Camp (one of many) under the Rev. Laura Butler's leadership.

I went as a camp leader with a group of friends, and we were all touched by the spiritual fervour and love she demonstrated. We got a sense of God just being in her presence. She also knew how to have fun. She had a great sense of humour but she was also very wise and spiritual. She touched many people's lives, and mine in particular.

This call to ministry, however, caused a lot of grief. My mom thought I was throwing away my musical career and felt sad about this. My brother had left home at age 19 and kept urging me to do the same. In spite of how my mom felt, something compelled me to leave home. My dad supported my decision, and Laura Butler encouraged me along with many people in Metropolitan United Church. Some people felt I was too shy to become a minister, and it was true, I was shy at the time. But this didn't stop me from answering God's call.

God works most clearly in my life through people who stir me, move me and encourage me to choose a path that's life-giving.

The United Church training school was located in Toronto, and I was so homesick I cried every night for about six months, but I knew I had to answer this call. I couldn't turn back. I was on my own and found the courses at the University of Toronto really tough, because I had no background in subjects like psychology, philosophy, Near Eastern history and English. I'd leapt into deep water without knowing how to swim! But my faith sustained me, even though I was in a fog at the beginning.

God called again after my first year of training school. I was in Yorkton, Sask., completing my summer field work, and I remember driving around the Saskatchewan countryside and loving it, although bales of hay are not good landmarks for finding one's way on the prairies. I often got lost! During one of these drives, I sensed a call to ordained ministry, but it didn't come to fruition until several years later.

The actual call came during one of the United Church Conferences at Naramata, B.C. We always had communion and ordination at these conferences. Laura Butler was the speaker, and there was only one person being ordained this time — a woman. The dynamic itself gripped me, and when Laura and I passed each other during communion, I sensed something was in her heart about me, although I wasn't sure what it was. After communion, I went into the foyer, and she was standing at the door.

"When are you going to finish your studies and fulfill your call to the ministry?" Laura asked me.

"Oh never — I'm not going to do it — never, never!" I replied adamantly.

It was a shock to be confronted in this way, but I soon realized Laura was right.

Once again, I hit the books. I took courses at the Vancouver School of Theology one day a week while working full-time in Chilliwack, B.C., as Director of Christian Education. I spent every spare minute on my studies — for seven long years. I felt the urge to pack it in quite often, but something wouldn't let me. The call was so deep, I couldn't shove it aside.

The Rev. Colleen Erb, newly ordained, with her parents in Vancouver

Towards the end of my studies, I took a part-time job at a neighbouring church, which enabled me to complete the program. I graduated in 1980 and was ordained at St. Andrew's Wesley Church in Vancouver — a day I'll never forget. St. Andrew's is a wonderful church with glorious music, and busloads of people came from the congregations I'd served to witness my ordination. Laura Butler was part of the laying on of hands of the ordination service, which moved us both deeply.

After my ordination, I continued to work part-time at Carman United Church in Sardis, B.C., which allowed me to recover my strength, because I was exhausted after seven years of demanding theological study. I was discouraged at first as I looked for a suitable position. But then I received a letter from Gordon United in Victoria, inviting me to apply for the position of minister. It was an odd coincidence because I'd sent them a letter at the same time — our letters crossed in the mail.

A search committee of 30 people interviewed me! Oddly enough, I felt quite nonchalant during the interview and was out of character with my quips. The church had many needs, and I told the committee, "It seems as if you need a super-human being for this job!" The committee members thanked me for being honest with them when I left. Two weeks later, they called and asked me if I'd accept a call to Gordon United.

"I don't know," I said. "I might. I need to talk some things over with you before I say yes. I'm only one person and can't do all that you're asking of me."

After some back and forth discussion, I finally said "Yes." It turned out to be a wonderful match, and I remained their minister until I retired in 1993.

I never sensed a call to marriage. I had some boyfriends when I was growing up, and there was one fellow I was really drawn to at Metropolitan United, but somebody else got him. I found out later that she committed suicide after she'd had her children. The man was an upstanding Christian in the church and later remarried.

How do you know which path to take in life? If you're not sure and you don't feel divinely inspired, I think it's best to *wait* until you have a stronger sense of direction or calling. You can't just figure things out in your head. Your heart has to be touched. You have to look at your gifts and see whether they match a particular calling. I find it helpful to ask myself, "What do I feel passionately about? What is life-giving?"

A passion for counselling

By Mona Hundleby as told to Terry Dance-Bennink

I've always had good luck in my life. Meeting my husband, Roy, was certainly one of the luckiest things that ever happened to me, along with learning how to counsel people in Victoria's first citizens' counselling centre during the 1960s and '70s.

My daughter, Pat, was my first link with the counselling movement. After high school, Pat attended a Winter Session at the United Church's Naramata Centre near Penticton, B.C., where she met a minister who ran a counselling centre in Calgary. He offered training in Banff during the summer and brought in all the current psychology experts in North America to teach us.

Roy and I both attended this school and heard lectures in the morning from leading psychologists like Carl Rogers, and then we practised our skills in groups during the afternoon. I'd never heard of group work or sensitivity training before. I wasn't comfortable with opening up in a group because I didn't know how to express myself. After all, I'd been selling shoes in a retail store and teaching Sunday school, so I felt out of my depth at first.

Our time in Banff was a true awakening. When we got home, our daughter, Pat, and her boyfriend said, "Mom, you've changed!" I was so happy and chatty. I'd come out of my shell.

Roy and I studied with all kinds of wonderful teachers during the next few years. In addition to our Banff sessions, we visited California regularly and attended workshops presented by Carl Rogers and Virginia Satir. Virginia was famous for her approach to family counselling. When talking with children, for example, she suggested we get down to their level, in order to speak directly to them and not tower above them.

Victoria's first counselling centre

When we started our own counselling centre in Victoria, we took our counsellors to Banff for training and then met with them once a week so they could practise and hone their skills. We also offered groups for retirees who weren't sure what to do with themselves after a lifetime of working. They needed the support of a group to sort out their feelings. Some of them still wanted to work, and we helped them find part-time jobs. We offered marriage groups, as well, for couples who wanted to communicate better and resolve conflicts.

In the early days of our centre, many women joined our groups. A good number of them wanted to get back into the workforce, although some chose to be full-time mothers. The women's movement had just started up, and many women needed a job or career. For those who longed for some quiet time to take stock of their lives, we suggested they try being a "nun for a day!" I'd read an article in a Roman Catholic magazine about the benefits of silence. If women wanted to change themselves, a day or two in silence at a retreat centre often worked wonders.

Our home in East Sooke served a similar purpose. Many couples and single people came for a whole day, up to a dozen in fact, and we'd get them to pair off and discuss questions related to their strengths or the state of their marriage. East Sooke has some wonderful hiking trails, so we also encouraged them to spend time in the woods — to walk and talk together and get to know each other on a deeper level. Then we'd all meet up later in the day, sit on the beach and talk things over with a cup of coffee in hand. They loved these day-long mini-retreats.

Every Thursday night, our counsellors would gather to discuss whatever problems they'd encountered with their groups. If someone was really hurting, we'd urge them to lie down on the floor and each person would give them a gift like a back or foot massage and offer some kind words. The hurt would fade away.

Roy and I trained quite a few nuns and priests, as well, through live-in workshops at Queenswood Centre on Arbutus Road. The nuns came out of their habits the year we started our Centre, so it was a time of big change. Some priests and nuns fell in love; others decided the religious life was not for them. We tried to support them as best we could during all this turmoil. Bishop Remi J. De Roo backed us 100%, and we met often with him.

After Roy and I retired from the Centre, the government paid us to visit other communities in B.C. to encourage them to offer similar services. We spent a weekend in Fort St. John, B.C., for example, giving a number of workshops. As many as 80 people would show up.

On one occasion, Roy started his talk but then lost his voice, and I had to take his notes and carry on. This was my first big speech! After that, I felt quite comfortable giving talks. The next morning, we spoke to a large group of doctors, nurses and patients. We broke them up into groups of three to practise various roles as a counsellor, a patient and an observer. We kept changing the roles, and they loved it. It was a great way to learn.

The best part of teaching

By Sheila MacDougall
as told to Terry Dance-Bennink

My teaching career began in a funny way. I used to attend the Saskatchewan Registered Nurses Association meetings on a regular basis, and one day, I met the chairman of the nursing school at Regina's Wascana Institute. I inquired about teaching opportunities and told her I didn't think I was qualified to teach anything but social sciences. I'd been out of the nursing field for quite a while and hadn't taken the nursing instructor training program, although I had a degree in education.

When I put in my application, I made a mistake. I ran into this man in the personnel office whom I recognized and I said to him, "Oh, I know your mother!" He then proceeded to tell me that he didn't think I'd be a suitable teacher. "Why not?" I asked him. He didn't elaborate, but I'm sure it's because I mentioned that I once knew his mother. Perhaps there were some emotional or family issues going on for him. I was in a bind, though, because he was the personnel officer for the whole college.

Sheila MacDougall, nurse in training, 1944

The other students kept asking me, "Haven't you got a job yet? They're still advertising." So I phoned the personnel office and said, "I know you think I'm not a suitable teacher, but would you mind sending my application to the nursing school?" I got a phone call later that afternoon from the same man I'd originally talked to, and he arranged for me to meet the chairman of the nursing school. He never mentioned our earlier discussion!

The chairman of the nursing school was delighted to see me. "I know you think you'd like to teach social sciences," she said, "but wouldn't you prefer to teach nursing?" Would I!! I said I'd love to.

She offered me a nursing instructor's job on the spot and I took it, even though I'd already planned a holiday in Africa. "That's all right," she said. "Take your holiday and then come to work when you return." I was thrilled. I started in the fall when the students were finishing their first year and entering their full day clinical placements. It was a pretty tall order and I had to wing it. But it was great fun, and I loved the whole experience.

I had to supervise 10 students and during the first six weeks, we took them to a number of nursing homes to teach them how to interact with the residents. The students attended other classes at the Institute, but learned their applied nursing skills through these placements. It was a great curriculum.

We had to teach them the basics as well, like how to make beds without shaking the linen and bed mites on the floor, and we stressed the importance of washing your hands all the time. I had the same students for the whole term, but they were unhappy when it came time for the next rotation. They didn't want to move to another instructor but they had to learn to adjust. At the end of the year, I supervised students on a maternity ward in Moose Jaw for eight weeks. I was willing to commute and drive the 40 miles. It was great fun.

I loved my students — that was the best part of teaching. I loved getting to know each one of them as an individual. I ran into a woman just the other day and asked her how her niece was doing, a former student of mine. She's married now and has grown-up kids. I truly enjoyed my students and their tears and laughter.

I was very interested in the learning process too. I had a rather strange girl, for example, who had enrolled to get her nurse's assistant credential. She'd been working in the hospital for years as a nurse's aide, but she was very reclusive. I wondered about some of her written assignments, because she missed some things.

One morning, I had the students at a rehab hospital treating a patient with a shoulder problem. I told the students, "There's an article about his condition in this magazine. I'd like you to read it, and then we'll discuss it after your clinical session." At the end of the session, this one student didn't know what she'd read. I realized she had trouble reading.

When the students entered the school, they were all given reading tests. I soon discovered this girl was reading at a Grade 5-6 level. I took the reading test myself and found it really interesting. I enjoyed this part of my job. But this poor girl couldn't read, so I went to see the chairman.

"I have a student who can't read," I told her.

"Well, find a way to teach her," she said abruptly as she dismissed me.

"Yeah right!" I thought to myself. But I talked with the student and then explained to the rest of the students that Mary didn't read very well and needed a lot of help to get finished. They all understood and were more than willing to give her an extra hand.

In another one of my groups, I had a girl who'd had a very difficult life. While I was making my rounds one morning, I asked her how things were going. She was very depressed and told me she was having shock treatments on Mondays and then coming to clinical on Tuesdays.

"Oh," I said, "why didn't you tell me? That's what I'm here for!" Some other staff knew about the situation, but no one had told me. She graduated, however, and was thrilled.

I enjoyed the challenge of helping students like her. I think about some of my former students today and wonder how they've turned out.

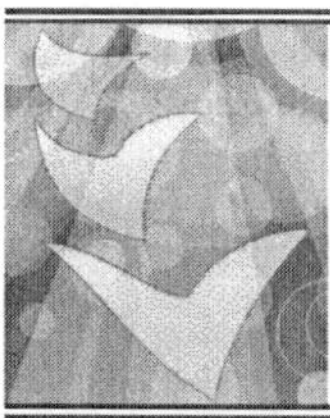

My healing ministry

By Sheila MacDougall
as told to Terry Dance-Bennink

I first encountered the healing touch ministry when a nurse who'd been trained in healing touch asked us one afternoon if anyone could feel the energy in the room. I had a cup of coffee, and it was really jiggling in my hands. "I guess I do," I said.

Then our Parish Nurse, Ann Maffey, invited Leslie Black to offer the first level of healing from the heart here at First Met, and I thought I should go. I ended up completing all three levels of the training. We began by offering our services on Tuesday evenings and now our healers are available on Monday afternoons.

People from the local area as well as the church come for healing and find it very helpful. A number of people with cancer say it relaxes them and eases their pain. It brings them peace. It's not about a cure but rather a healing. One woman had constant migraines for 20 years, and she participated with very good results. We have another woman who underwent serious surgery, and she comes every Tuesday for healing and brings her mom along too.

A woman who is profoundly deaf and relies on a hearing aid

panicked when she learned she had to have her cataracts removed. She was afraid she wouldn't be able to hear and follow the doctor's orders on the day of her surgery. So we invited her to a healing session the night before hoping she would experience peace the next day, and she did!

Many people have taken our training, including some Reiki masters. The healers have really bonded; we know each other well. I took on coordinating this ministry some time ago, and have been trying to find a replacement for myself recently. Fortunately, Suzanna Walma, who comes regularly for healing, volunteered in September to take the calls for the coming year.

I find the healing sessions energizing. The premise is that the outside Presence flows through you. I stand on my feet for four hours and I'm not tired at the end, and I'm not the only one who experiences this. I'm not bushed when I go home. After my husband, Jack, died, I was exposed to the power of positive thinking which is similar in nature. A sacred energy is available to you if you are receptive. I call it God, because that's what I've always called it.

You have to concentrate, however, as a healer. I'm fortunate, because I see a coloured aura and lots of light around the person, which not every healer sees. This makes it easier for me to concentrate. An old Reiki master once told us all you have to do is just be open. You don't have to look for all kinds of symbols. And this is how I feel about it.

I was horrified when some of the girls thought they had to physically manipulate the person. You just have to recognize that there are points of entry all over your body for the energy or power to penetrate.

Healing touch is a simple, simple thing. But it requires faith on the part of the healer and the person being healed. It doesn't matter if the persons being healed are Buddhist, Hindu or Muslim, as long as they believe in something beyond themselves. I don't have a problem accepting Hindu gods, and I don't think my God would object either. There are many paths to the sacred.

Helping families get out of debt

Written by Helen Mau as shared with Cyndi Frame

After graduating from high school in Ontario, I attended a two-year college program at Macdonald Institute, Ontario Agricultural College (OAC) at Guelph, Ont. I had a series of summer jobs as an assistant dietitian at Bigwin Inn, a popular high-class summer hotel in the Lake of Bays. This was the starting point for my later career working with home economists and dietitians.

During my studies in home economics at the University of Toronto in the 1940s, I worked for the General Engineering war plant in Scarborough — a bomb-making factory — to help pay for my tuition. The factory served 300 meals for each of three shifts. The dietitian, Mrs. Florence Ignatieff, gave me experience in managing every department, i.e. the dishwashing room, the bakery, the stores, the tasting of soups, main dishes and coffee and the work of three chefs.

One day, I was in charge of the bakery where we had two workers making pies for two huge ovens that took 15 or more pies at a time. I tried to help one of the workers who needed meringue for lemon pies. I made the meringue with the "sugar" and it looked beautiful. Fortunately, I'd been taught to always taste before putting it on the pie. I discovered the container was half salt and half sugar so I had to start all over!

I graduated from the University of Toronto in the spring of 1944 with a B.HSc. and attended the Ontario College of Education (OCE) the following year. That year I won the Laura Ockley Scholarship of $1,000. There was a shortage of teachers in 1944 because of World War II, so that spring I was asked to come to Ridgetown High School to teach home economics and English. I stayed on the following year.

My Grade 10 and 11 students and I were expected to come up with a Thanksgiving five-course turkey dinner for the school board and staff with a printed menu. This took lots of preparation and training and I hired a woman to help in the kitchen. The dinner was a big success. The next day, however, we used leftovers for the school lunch and I had four young students very sick to their stomachs. Someone had unclean hands, even though I had warned everyone repeatedly about cleanliness and how to taste food.

After teaching for one year in Ridgetown, I was invited to teach nutrition, safety and time/work management at OCE at the University of Toronto. My students were teachers in training for elementary and secondary schools in Ontario.

One day we were moving the refrigerator on wheels in our classroom across the room. The students were pulling it and I was pushing it. Suddenly the refrigerator hit a seam in the linoleum and went up one inch at the back and came down on my left big toe! Oh, how that hurt! My students rushed me to the Medical Arts building across the street. My toe was so painful — it took 30 years to fully recover.

I went to Columbia University in New York City during the summers of 1950-54 to get an MA with a major in family relationships and a minor in administration in higher education. By 1965, I had completed my Ed.D. at Columbia with a focus on cognitive objectives as they relate to creativity.

I spent the lion's share of my career during 1954-87 teaching family management at San Francisco State University (SFSU) and, at the graduate level, family and personal budget and credit counselling. I enjoyed teaching my students who came from all sorts of economic and cultural/racial backgrounds about value analysis, decision making, planning, organizing and evaluating.

One of my best friends, Frank Sperling, a Jewish man and retired director of credit for the Bank of America, took an interest in my work and urged me to become a member of the San Francisco and the State Board of Consumer Credit Counsellors. As a result, I was able to influence a change in focus in this organization from debt management and bankruptcy to budget counselling through the removal of interest on the debt until clients were able to live within a balanced budget.

Frank Sperling supported our development at SFSU of an interdisciplinary graduate certificate program in budget and family credit counselling. This was a huge task. Graduates of this program were placed as managers of Consumer Credit Counselors (CCC) offices throughout California in Napa County, Sacramento, Walnut Creek, San Francisco, San Jose, Los Angeles and San Diego.

Frank was a strong mentor and dear friend. I learned to respect the great qualities of several Jewish people through Frank.

Life-fulfilling moments

One of the most satisfying moments in my life was when I was made Honorary Business Person of the Year in 1975 in San Francisco by the business community at their annual dinner. This honour came because I'd been instrumental in changing the focus of the CCC organization in California from debt management which favoured the creditors to a budget/personal and family credit counselling orientation. The California Home Economics Association also named me that year's honoured Home Economist.

I have so many positive memories. I've enjoyed many leadership roles professionally and, to this day, I continue to have new insights that create a "Wow" or "Aha" feeling!

If I were to be honoured for something in my life, I'd hope it would be for the change I made for a generation in the teaching of family relations/family management. I encouraged my students to think critically and creatively and not just memorize facts.

Another life-fulfilling moment was my sabbatical leave in 1972 when I took 29 flights starting with a San Francisco to Tokyo flight and ending with the last flight from Tahiti to Los Angeles — all safe and on time! I had another sabbatical leave in 1980 and thoroughly enjoyed my BritRail Pass in England and

Scotland for one month. I love to travel.

I think I'm a fortunate lady. In fact, that could be the title of my life-story: *A Fortunate Lady*. I hope I'll be remembered as a compassionate person who inspired and challenged others to think and become better persons.

A young teacher on the Prairies

By Irene McDonald
as told to Terry Dance-Bennink

After high school, I went to normal school in Camrose, Alta. It's now a university, but at that time teachers were trained in a normal school. It was a good choice on my part, because I've spent nearly 30 years in classrooms since then and I've loved every moment of it.

After I finished normal school, I was fortunate enough to get a job right away, even though many teachers were unemployed. My first school was called Lakeview School, in Elnora, Alta., and was six miles from the town. On my first day as a teacher, at age 18, I faced 10 grades in one room! I had students in each grade, and the students in Grades 9 and 10 faced departmental examinations.

We only had standard training as teachers in those days, and yet we had to teach students from a wide range of backgrounds and with differing abilities. We not only had to teach but serve as janitors as well. I had to split the wood, build the fires and pump water for the school and the teacherage, which was a home for the teacher on the grounds, and all for the princely sum of $840 a year. The rent of $100 and $40 for fuel were deducted! But at least I had a job, and many people didn't. I was able to pay back some of the loans I owed my uncle who'd helped me attend normal school.

I lived alone in the teacherage. I didn't have a telephone but I had a battery-operated radio. I was too busy to be lonely. I had stacks of work to do every night to prepare for the next day. At Christmas time, every rural school teacher was expected to hold a Christmas concert. I'd grown up with this tradition so I knew what to expect.

My students performed very well indeed, and the concert was very successful. The woman who lived nearest the school, Hazel Hepburn, played the piano for us. She and her husband were my neighbours about a mile away and they were very good to me.

In my second year at Lakeview School, the school board couldn't pay me as it had run out of funds. I continued teaching and borrowed some money to carry me through, and the board paid me in full at a much later date. After spending two years at this rural school, I returned to Calgary and enrolled at the Garbutt Business College. This was a wise move on my part. I didn't enter the business world but I gained the ability to teach commercial subjects.

My next teaching assignment was in a rural school called Advent near the town of Beiseker, Alta. The school was situated in the Seventh Day Adventist community, a wonderful community. Every family was supportive of the teacher. Children in that school were expected to do well, and so they did.

The Campbell family invited me to their home on a regular basis for supper and an overnight stay, and I'd return to the school with their children in the morning. Other families also invited me over for meals — the rural families made you feel wanted and valued. Teachers were looked upon with a high regard, and you felt good about your profession.

Anecdotes of fright and fun

During my early teaching years, I experienced moments of fright and fun. At the Lakeview School, for example, I woke up one night to see something at my window and I was frightened. I was alone in my teacherage without a telephone and two miles away from anybody. Would I get up or not? I decided I should at least make an effort to see what it was. It was nothing more than a horse with its rear end up against my window!

On another occasion, I was quite alarmed although not particularly frightened for my own welfare, by a group of men whom I suspected had been duck-hunting at a nearby lake. They'd entered the school building and shaken up the fires to get warm. I assumed they wouldn't stay very long, but they remained inside longer than I thought. Eventually, they all got into their vehicles and drove away. There was no significant damage to the schoolhouse, but they had so much fire going, which I'd banked to last all night, that the children's crayons had melted. What a catastrophe it might have been!

I only knew of one woman teacher who was physically attacked while living at a teacherage, and she was raped. This frightened all of us who'd spent time alone in such a house. It's a sad time when a woman has to fear for her own person. Nowadays, women may have grounds to feel even more fearful. But the era of the teacherage is long gone.

I was often afraid for students in bad weather. One day, I was aware at dismissal time that a storm was brewing in the west. The windows of my school faced east and the door faced west, so you didn't have much chance to see what was happening on the westerly side. On this particular day, the wind had come up and the snow was beginning to blow, and I thought I mustn't let these youngsters go, because they won't get home before the storm hits.

We stayed inside the school for a while, but it soon grew dark, and I had no light in the school house. So I decided to take the children to my two-room teacherage. I took the smallest child by my hand and placed the biggest child at the end of the line and told them, "Whatever you do, don't lose your grasp on the child beside you. I'll take you to the teacherage where there is a light." So off we went.

I nearly missed the building, and we only just made it, because the storm was that fierce. We couldn't see our way at all. We got inside, and it grew quite dark. The hours passed, but no one came. I didn't expect anyone to come so I decided I should give the children some food. I made a large kettle of something hot and served it with bread, and then we told stories and sang while we waited. When it got quite late, I told the small children they could lie on my bed, while the rest of us lounged around. There was only one easy chair in the room.

Just before midnight, a farmer came on horseback, covered in frost up to his eyebrows — he looked like quite a character — but he'd brought us some bread, and I told him, "We're all here and just fine."

"Parents have been phoning," he said, "but they aren't worried because they knew you wouldn't send the children off alone." I thought what trust they have in me — I'm glad I'd earned their trust.

Teachers were obliged to do a lot of chores besides teaching. In my first school, the Province of Alberta had put a bounty on gophers, crows and magpies, and children were paid a penny or two for gopher tails. They'd come to school with an old tobacco tin with their gopher tails inside, and teachers were expected to count and record the number of tails and mail the tally off to Edmonton, so the children would be paid for their gopher tails, crows' feet and magpie eggs.

I soon learned to trust the numbers they told me! Then I faced the issue of what to do with the gopher tails, but the pot-bellied stove in the school proved to be a good incinerator.

Teachers, like their students, have things to learn, and sometimes we learn very hard lessons. I learned about discipline during my first year. I'd gone out at lunch time to my teacherage, and when I came back, I discovered the students had been having a merry time pitching this and that around the school house.

"Who did this?" I asked them. No one answered, of course, so I made the mistake of saying, "Well, if the person responsible will not admit to it, then everybody will have a detention and remain after school." So they all sat after school, and I wondered what else I could do.

I had to admit I rather admired them for not being tattletales on one another, so in due course, I said, "You have all remained a satisfactory amount of time, and I really compliment you on your spirit of caring for one another, but I'd like you to take more care of our school building the next time!"

They all went out with smiles on their faces. I thought to myself, never again will I make such a foolish mistake. I vowed in my early career never to belittle a person in front of others. If I had to scold a student, I'd remove them from the class. I didn't want to destroy the dignity of either of us.

Health and sanitation are big concerns today, and when I look back to my early teaching days, I wonder how we were all able to stay so healthy. There was a dipper outside near the well, and after playing ball, everyone just had a drink out of the dipper. We had one wash basin and we washed our hands with fresh water, but there was no bacterial soap nor paper towels.

Children were encouraged to bring their own cups for lunch and their own towels, but many times they shared. We had very little absenteeism, however, due to illness. For the most part, people were healthy and didn't seem to have dental problems. We were a healthy, strong lot of people.

Teaching gifted children

By Irene McDonald
as told to Terry Dance-Bennink

I was invited to teach an enrichment class for academically gifted children in Ottawa in 1955 and taught gifted children for the next 11 years. Much planning went into developing these classes and equipping the teacher to be able to enrich a program.

It was a daunting experience and tremendous challenge for me to teach a gifted child. Some students had great facility in reading and some in science. The purpose of the enrichment program was to bring them along in all subjects, but especially in the area for which they had a natural talent.

I organized some very interesting student field trips to such places as the National Research Council and the Parliament buildings. I arranged for the students to be more than just spectators in the Gallery — they learned how Parliamentary committee meetings were conducted.

Irene McDonald, teacher, early 1960s

On another occasion, I took my class to A.J. Freiman's store to learn something about merchandising. The students were so well-behaved and asked such intelligent questions that Mr. Freiman invited us all to have lunch in the dining room courtesy of A.J. Freiman's. We also visited a bank one day and the bank manager was most impressed with one of my students who could add three or four digit numbers in his head.

A school inspector came into my room one afternoon to find the students working away at their individual projects while I was sitting at my desk. I asked him if he'd like the students to do something, but he replied, "No — when it's running well, let her run." Afterwards, he told me that he'd asked one boy who was reading *Canterbury Tales* whether he had any difficulty in reading it. "No sir," the boy replied. "I don't spell that well either." What a novel explanation for the Old English in *Canterbury Tales*!

We always had a Christmas party each year and the parents would invite us to come to a home for the party. One year, a Jewish family invited us to hold the party in their home. The mother came over and talked to me about it and I explained that one person always read a part of the Christmas story during the party. She had no objection to this and asked if her son could read something about Hanukkah, which I thought would be wonderful. This inspired me later to take the children on visits to various churches, so they could learn about the architecture and core mission of each church.

When I listen to television or pick up the paper today, I see some of the names of my former students. One of them runs a men's clothing store; another is an economist; and another is a professor at Queen's University. One of my students even helped write the Free Trade Agreement. I have fond memories of them all and have been able to stay in touch with some of them.

Perhaps my favourite student tribute is a tiny chair made of gold metal wire an inch and a half high given to me by one of the boys at the end of his four years with me. It came with a little note which said, "For you — enjoy — you deserve a rest." I think it's lovely and I keep it on my kitchen window ledge.

In my kitchen cupboard, I also have a glass jar with a red lid on which is printed "pantry jar," and it came to me one Christmas filled with cookies which a girl and her mother had made for me, along with a little note: "You spent so much time with us, we're sure you haven't had much time for Christmas baking." I feel repaid just by knowing my students, but I cherish acts like these.

Sex education pioneers

By Irene McDonald
as told to Terry Dance-Bennink

Donald and I moved to Victoria in the summer of 1968, not without a few tears on my part. I'd hoped that Calgary would remain our permanent home when Donald left the military, and I'd actually unpacked everything. Now we had to sell our home once again and look for another.

When we arrived in Victoria, I thought I might like to work, so I went to the school board office and filled out an application form. But Victoria had a full complement of teachers and a waiting list of others who wanted to move here, because it's such a lovely place in which to live and work.

It wasn't long, though, before the superintendent called me and I started teaching Grades 8–10 at Central School in 1968. For the first time in my career, I had an opportunity to teach typing and other business courses which I hadn't taught since my initial training. I also taught English.

At Christmas time during my second year, the superintendent asked to see me in his office and I wondered what was up. He had a woman with him whom I recognized as Dr. Patriarche. I'd met her many years before when I was newly married in Edmonton.

Dr. Patriarche had become the medical health officer for the city of Victoria and was interested in teaching sex education in the schools. She'd offered a couple of lessons herself to Grade 8 students and now the parents wanted her to develop a full program in the schools. The superintendent asked me to become a teacher in the program called Family Life Education designed for every junior high school in the city.

I was now in totally new territory as I had no experience in this line of work, but Dr. Patriarche and the superintendent felt I could communicate well with both students and parents and had no difficulty with classroom discipline. I also had considerable experience writing curriculum that met the standards of the department of education.

It was Christmas time, and I was asked to assume this new role by Jan. 1. I had only a few weeks in January to prepare myself for this new undertaking, but Dr. Patriarche and I sat down and wrote up a course of study for Grade 8. The plan was for me to spend about a week in each junior high school in the city and talk to the Grade 8 classes about sex education. We agreed it was imperative that the parents should be informed and feel comfortable with the program.

Through medical sources, I acquired the necessary teaching equipment. I had the same pelvic model and charts as were used for medical training along with all kinds of audio-visual aids. A gynaecologist visited one of my classes one day and subsequently volunteered to join me at other schools. And then a doctor who advised medical interns in the hospital arranged for the interns to work with me and visit classes, so I was able to have a medically trained person in the classrooms.

The students reacted very positively, although sometimes it was a challenge for me to know whether the questions placed in the anonymous question box were designed to trip me up or were legitimate concerns. I answered each question, no matter its content, with the same seriousness.

Even though a question might seem flippant, I viewed each one as a means to teach. One questioner, for example, asked me, "What do *you* know about all this?" I replied simply, "I'm a wife and a mother." In very short order, the question box contained mostly genuine questions.

Education in family living is probably as important an aspect of formal teaching as any other subject because all students, regardless of their academic capabilities, are confronted with the development of their own sexuality. In my teaching, I tried to stress the development of not just the physical, but the mental, social and spiritual well-being of each person. Unless you're at one with your own conscience and actions, you can't really feel ennobled.

Someone once asked me how I got away with talking about spiritual well-being, and I said, "Everyone has some kind of inner soul; I'm not talking about faith or religion, but rather each person's inner well-being." From the very beginning, I tried to integrate sex education into the regular curriculum rather than separating it out as a distinct subject.

When Dr. Patriarche retired, my position expanded to include in-service training of teaching colleagues and yearly evaluation and revision of the curriculum for Grades 8, 9 and 10, as well as the preparation and presentation of the annual report to the Board of Trustees.

Another highlight of my career included an invitation to participate in a conference in Victoria of newly graduated medical doctors from across Canada. Their topic was human sexuality, and I felt honoured to be asked to contribute. The success of the program depended on an informed community, so I took every opportunity to speak to church and community groups when I was invited.

Victoria has been pegged as a city for retired oldies, so many people were amazed to see such a new and innovative program launched in the city. Representatives of teachers from various Canadian cities came to talk to me about our program and how it was designed. One person came all the way from London, England, and another from Washington, D.C. Victoria became a pioneer in sex education in the schools due to the vision and courage of Dr. Patriarche and the school board.

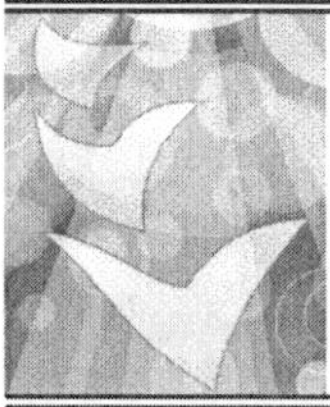

A challenge to the Cancer Society

By Irene McDonald
as told to Terry Dance-Bennink

Donald and I both felt that leisure time and travel in our retirement years had to be balanced with doing something worthwhile in our lives. I was soon asked if I'd like to become involved in the Canadian Cancer Society's education program and I agreed. I went along to the office on Cormorant Street to find out what this entailed. Upon entering the office, I was surprised to see an ashtray with cigarette butts in it.

Irene McDonald receives life-time achievement award from the Canadian Cancer Society

I carried on, however, because I was impressed with the educational materials developed for the Society by a team of volunteers and professionals who'd been involved in education in Ontario. My role was to talk to the students about lifestyles, the dangers of smoking and the various cancers and treatments available.

What concerned me the most, however, was the fact that Cancer Society board members and other volunteers smoked. I was now the chairman of the education program and a board member, so I made a motion at a meeting in 1976 that Cancer Society board members and other volunteers would not smoke when on Cancer Society business. The motion did not carry. I left the meeting and resigned from the Society.

"I'm urging school children not to smoke," I told them, "but here you are smoking! You don't even accept your own materials, so I can't be part of this organization." I always tell people I had a "sabbatical" from the Society at that point.

The Clean Air Society was championing clean air and no smoking in buildings, but the Cancer Society was sitting back. The press called me and wanted to know if I'd make a statement about the Cancer Society. I refused and told them, "I believe in the work of the Society and don't want to do anything that would jeopardize the fine work performed by the Canadian Cancer Society." But at the same time, I began a letter-writing campaign to get the organization to take a firm stand on not smoking.

After a year or so of my "sabbatical," the Cancer Society board decided it had been wrong to reject my motion and notified me that they'd support the motion if I'd rejoin the Society. At this time, I met Sheila MacDougall, who was also a volunteer with the Society, and she was instrumental in getting me to return. She was the president of the Victoria chapter of the Society, and I thought she wanted me to be involved in the education program, but to my surprise, I learned she wanted me to be the fundraiser.

Sheila can be very persuasive, so I agreed and became the fundraiser for the first door-to-door campaign in Greater Victoria. We had to get permission from five mayors and councils to have such a campaign, and then we had to get all the maps and divide up the city into areas and find enough volunteers to walk the neighbourhoods. But we did it.

Donald and Sheila's husband became our telephone answering service when the calls started coming in. Not only did we have to find all these volunteers, but we had to prepare the materials in order to leave packets at each door. We had a huge number of packets. Sheila was never one to think this was an impossible job, so she found people from sheltered workshops to help us.

It was slow going, but it almost brings tears to my eyes to recall that at the end of the week, a young man stood up and came over to shake our hands and said, "I've had a job all week!" He was so proud that he'd had this job. It made me think back to the days when I was working with exceptional children. Along with the academically gifted, there were many children who were unable to function well in their studies and yet were fine individuals like this young man.

Having served my apprenticeship as a fundraiser in Victoria, I was invited to become the chairman of fundraising for the B.C. and Yukon chapter of the Society which meant travelling to Vancouver every week. I had to encourage all the B.C. and Yukon units to take up door-to-door campaigning along with other fundraising methods.

During my first year as the fundraising chairman, the Society asked me to raise $7 million, which I thought was a lot of money at the time, but we made our target. During my last year in this role, we raised $13 million. It was a full-time job for both Sheila and me. We were at the office as volunteers all day, every day, because we were operating in new territory, although Sheila had a better handle on the work than me.

What I loved most about my role in the Society was our focus on encouraging people to take personal steps in order to try and avoid cancer. Some people are more prone to cancer than others, regardless of their lifestyle, but certainly the smoking issue is a huge factor for those who smoke. The other thing I enjoyed was meeting the hundreds of people who were helpers, who had the same desire as me to get rid of cancer, just as we'd been able to do with other diseases through immunization.

Fundraising is largely an educational activity. It's about reaching out to people to explain *why* you need their money. I often had to address meetings and explain the causes of cancer, and I always said you should never look into someone's pocket to decide how much they should give. Instead, you should look into their understanding of the *reason* to give.

I was the national fundraising chairman of the Cancer Society for a short time, but that role was far more administrative, and I was not so closely linked to volunteers. I didn't have to travel too widely, because the Cancer Society keeps its administrative costs low relative to funds raised. We volunteers refrained from any unnecessary travel, and when we did travel, we kept our costs as minimal as possible.

When Sheila and I went to Vancouver for meetings, I prevailed upon Sheila's son and family to put us up so we never had hotel bills, and we relied on buses to get around. Our costs were very, very low. We brought volunteers to Vancouver periodically to make sure we were all on the same page, but we limited the number of meetings. It kept our costs low and gave more independence to our unit chairmen.

By the time you've been a fundraiser for the Cancer Society, you've tried every conceivable method of raising funds, including floating rubber ducks down the street. The most effective method was door-to-door campaigns using local volunteers. I also learned how to organize large bridge parties as fundraising events. Some people offered Christmas wrapping as a fundraiser. We had long lists of ideas and tried anything that worked. We had 24-hour runs and 24-hour golf games, for example, in the Yukon. Unit chairmen joined us with lots of ideas. Everyone was encouraged to be creative.

A YMCA pioneer

By Helen Simpson as told to Joan Mason

By 1940, I was feeling bored. Most of the women I knew did not work outside the home and my husband, Ken, had joined the reserve army. I always discussed what I was planning to do with Ken. He had his own life and activities and enjoyed having time to go out with the boys. He always felt that we were a modern couple and could go our own separate ways when it came to work and volunteer activities.

The Young Men's Christian Association (YMCA) was putting on educational and social programs to attract both sexes in 1940 and I thought they sounded interesting. So I became involved in the Y programs and helped get youth groups going. Viv Shoemaker, who went to Metropolitan United Church, and I became good friends. He was the Boys' Work Secretary and when he took a job in the East in 1941, he threw me the keys and said, "Simpson, here's the key to Camp Thunderbird. It's your responsibility from now on."

I was the first woman program secretary in the YMCA in Canada and managed Camp Thunderbird from 1942 to 1944. Our camps for 100 youth ran for seven days, with only a cook, a handyman and me as the paid staff. Each year, there were two girls' camps, one CGIT camp and one Anglican Girls' Camp in July and boys' camps in August.

We didn't have any fancy facilities. Mr. W.T. Straith, who was a First United Church trustee, had been able to acquire a former forestry camp at Glinz Lake up in the Sooke hills for the Y. The camp had very basic facilities — seven cabins with wooden floors and canvas tops. The leaders and campers walked up to the camp from Sooke Road. To get there, you climbed the hill for two miles and then you came to a creek with a plank bridge which you had to cross before walking another half mile to the camp. I used a truck bringing out rail ties to get our supplies in the first year, and in the second year, a logging truck.

There was no emergency phone in those days. If there was a problem, you had to run down the hill to the 17 Mile House which was two and a half miles away. Jim McKellar and I kept ourselves fit doing that run and back up every night. There were cougars around, so we would sing or yell the whole time. It was fun!

Kids weren't homesick in those days like they are today. Actually more boys than girls were homesick then, but still very few. We had super people there as camp staff. Cliff Carl, who was the head of the B.C. Museum, came for boys' camps each year. I was there for all of the camps and had many experiences.

To prepare for our camp openings and closings, we were able to get help from some of the servicemen. We put on a coeducation weekend (well-chaperoned), charged a fee to cover food and all the labour was free including the cooking and cleaning. By then, I was also responsible for all the youth programs and had organized a background committee called the SoEd group. Jack Syme is one of the few people still around who was part of the SoEd Committee.

We had a concert party of 24 girls under the leadership of Mrs. Harwood who wrote a variety of programs. I found enough older people who were still young enough at heart to chaperone the dance groups at the various camps for which we had a pool of about 100 girls. The rule was that the girls were picked up by bus at their homes, had to stay with their group and were then returned home by bus. I still meet people who say, "Helen, I was in one of your hostess groups."

The SoEd series was offered twice a year. We put on programs that were a lot of fun as well as being educational every spring and fall at the old Y building at Yates and Blanshard, all planned by the SoEd committee. In addition, there were Saturday Night Dances, using Charlie Hunt's orchestra for two years and then Bernie Porter's orchestra. There was a strict rule of "No drinking allowed." It was my job to make it work.

War service and two great honours

I went into the YMCA War Services in May 1944 for a year and a half until Dec. 31, 1945. I spent that time in uniform as a recreation leader for Navy personnel. I was so thrilled when the Rev. Ed Horton, an assistant minister in Dr. Wilson's time, wrote me about five years after the war ended to tell me, "Helen, you will be very happy to know that a young man whom you had taken to First United with you joined our church this day." That was very rewarding.

At our house on Maywood we entertained many people and shared our home with four families, each with a year-old child. Archie Morrison, who came to Victoria to be the Boys' Program Secretary, and his wife lived with us during 1943-44. In early 1945, George Bagby came into the office at the Y when I happened to be on the desk.

"My wife and little boy are back in Regina and I can't find a place to bring them," he told me. I invited him home for dinner and we found we had a lot in common. The Bagbys stayed with us for five months. Bill Milligan, his wife Eleanor and their child were the next arrivals. Bill was also Navy and a friend of George Bagby.

After the end of the war in Japan, HMS Prince Rupert came back from the official signing of surrender treaties. I was part of the welcoming committee consisting of the Red Cross and the YMCA War Services that followed the dignitaries on board the ship.

In late 1945, a battalion of British prisoners of war (PoWs) from Hong Kong was released through Victoria. Part of my job was to welcome them and join a committee which had been formed to entertain the men. That was how Harold Skinner, one of the PoWs, became part of our lives. He was at the house for meals and had the loan of our camera. When he left to go home to Britain, he asked me my birthdate and from 1945 to 2005, he sent me a birthday card each Oct. 24.

In 1977, Ken and I prepared for our first trip to the United

Kingdom and wrote to tell Harold Skinner of our plans. He wanted to know what I most wanted to see. I replied Winchester Cathedral, Stonehenge and London. He wrote to the Winchester Cathedral staff who said they would be delighted to host the niece of their former organist and noted leader of the Pilgrim Choir, Dr. William Prendergast. We were welcomed to the Harvest Thanksgiving service.

We also received an invitation to attend the 25th Reunion of the PoWs and Service of Remembrance at the Royal Festival Hall at Waterloo Station which took place at the end of our three weeks' stay in England. When we presented our invitation, we were ushered to a box on the fifth level. After the ceremonies were completed, the master of ceremonies welcomed "Mr. and Mrs. Ken Simpson of Victoria, British Columbia who had entertained a number of the troops in their home when they passed through Victoria on their way home." What a surprise!

That trip to England was one of those dreams I could never have imagined happening to me.

The Citizens' Rehabilitation Council

One of Victoria's social workers phoned me in 1946 and said, "We've started a committee of business people and community leaders to establish a citizens' rehabilitation council for returning service people." She told me the person who had done a magnificent job of organizing the council needed a holiday and asked me if I'd take over for two weeks. This was my introduction to Scotty.

I ended up joining the staff and working with Scotty, who had been an Air Force officer, and two more women, one with a Navy background and the other with an Army background. They were good workers and we had a lot of fun. Our boss was Arnold Palmer, who was a First World War veteran with a peg leg. Mr. Palmer was absolutely fabulous.

During that period, we took over the army camps at Gordon Head, Macaulay Camp, Belmont Park and Moresby House and turned them all into housing units. I was the only one with a phone as the girls in the hotel didn't have one and as a result, I received any emergency calls. The only problem I had was with a man I knew from our own neighbourhood. I had to go out in a taxi at 11:30 p.m. one night and investigate when I got a complaint that he was trying to sleep with some of the women.

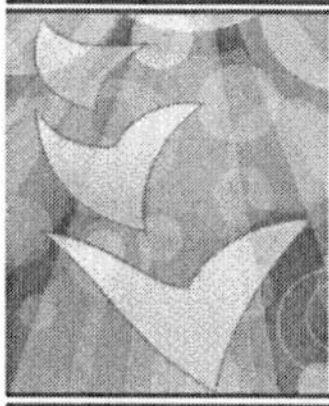

Caring for the caregivers

By Helen Simpson as told to Joan Mason

In order to help family caregivers in Victoria, a social worker at the Gorge Road Hospital, Faith Magwood, brought people together in August 1987 to form support groups. She started a few key groups throughout the community and called me, knowing that I'd asked for help earlier.

At that time I had to oversee the care of my husband Ken's two sisters, my foster sister and Ken himself. The Gordon Head Support Group was my first experience in a project to which I devoted time and energy from 1971 until 1997.

After about a year, everything started to fall apart in our support group and two of us were left to keep it going. Joan and I used to walk around the Cedar Hill golf course every morning, both of us crying. We had not known each other until we met at the support group. Joan had her father living in her home along with her husband, and my husband griped when he didn't have my full attention.

So I would get up early and walk with Joan before he was up for the day and wanted his breakfast. Those 45-minute walks gave me a life of my own and helped me get rid of my frustrations.

Later on, when Ken had passed away and the Caregiver Network was on stable footing, I volunteered to train facilitators for support groups. What I wanted to do more than anything was to create a support network for those who were family caregivers so they could discuss their problems and concerns with someone.

I knew enough about leadership to know that you don't sit there and talk about yourself when you are leading and assisting groups. You let them do the talking and find their own solutions within the group. The most important thing in leading a group is to let group members find their way and make sure that everyone has a turn to talk. As a leader, you have to sublimate your own feelings and needs so that others can share their needs. You can lose volunteers if you criticize them too much or seek to direct everything that happens.

Today, the Family Caregivers Association insists on sound training for board members and presents programs that truly answer the needs of caregivers, which I find gratifying.

I've been on practically every selection committee of the Family Caregivers Association in Victoria. Sometimes you think you have the perfect person but it just doesn't work out. I've learnt a lot about assessing people from Neena Chappell (UVic Centre on Aging), having been associated with her ever since she came to Victoria. She's now known worldwide for her work in bringing the responsibilities of caregivers to light. I was fortunate to have been sent to Ottawa three times to speak at caregiving conferences, one of which was a worldwide conference.

Madame Monique Vezina, who was federal Minister of State Responsible for Seniors in 1992, was someone with whom I had the pleasure of working. We really hit it off. She chose me out of all of B.C. to represent caregivers. Her Ottawa staff used to call me "that feisty little lady from British Columbia."

My greatest satisfaction in volunteering is helping someone else. My greatest frustration is people who hog the limelight — they frost me completely. It's that kind of person who takes all the time. I have worked on being able to compress my thoughts into a few minutes, even at a national meeting of over 400. I just rehearsed and trimmed until it fit into the allotted time.

Supporting caregivers is now recognized as necessary, but that wasn't always the case. When I wanted to talk to someone about the responsibility of caring for my family members, none of my close friends, not even the seven members of the Sewing Club, were there to talk to about this. No one had these issues or if they did, they hid them.

I've been involved in the Network since it was first formed. Joan Sefton and I went to bat and were promised money for an office downtown and signed for both federal and provincial grants. Now, I am the only one still left of the original board as an honorary member. If a support group needed assistance, I was always happy to help. This is why I went back on the Pastoral Care team at First Met United five years ago and I finished my term in February 2008.

I've been involved in volunteering from 1935 till 2008. I would like to be remembered as someone who made a contribution that is meaningful in the community.

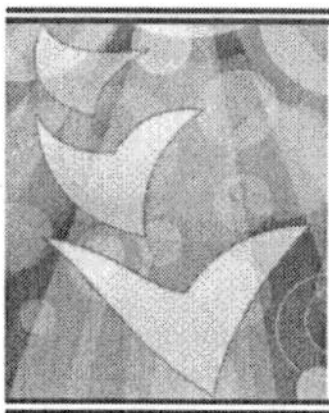

An officer and a gentlewoman

By Esther Younie as told to Sheila MacDougall

I grew up on a farm near St. Thomas, Ont. I finished Grade 13 in 1936 and went on to study home economics and dietetics at the Macdonald Institute in Guelph. In 1942, I joined the Air Force (RCAFWD) and went to Rockcliffe for basic training in Ottawa.

I was to be trained as a meteorologist, but they re-assigned me to the newly formed Aircraft Detection Corps (ACDC). We were trained by personnel sent over from England to plot aircraft on a large map based on phone calls from spotters who were located mostly in northern Ontario. I received my commission as a section officer and went to Toronto for officers' training.

The ACDC was disbanded in December 1943, and I was posted to Calgary. I had no experience in administration, however, so I was sent to Trenton, Ont., for the senior officers administration course for six weeks. I returned to Calgary as an

Esther (Martin) Younie inspects RCAF Women's Division in Winnipeg during World War II

assistant adjutant first in Paulson, Man., and then in Winnipeg where I was made responsible for the Women's Division.

I received my discharge in November 1945 and returned to my home near St. Thomas, Ont., but no work was available so I went to Toronto and found a job with Bell Telephone as a service representative. I didn't care for the job at all with its cut and dried routine!

In September, I found work related to my original calling as a home economist and was employed by the Women's Institute Branch of the Ontario Agriculture Department. I worked mainly with 4H clubs in four counties in southwestern Ontario. We trained local leaders to offer courses in cooking and sewing for girls. I enjoyed the work because I was finally in my own field.

It was through this job that I met my husband, Watson Younie, who was six years younger than I. We were married at my parents' home by a minister friend and the reception was held at the local United church catered by the women of the W.A. I still recall being escorted down the stairs on my father's arm and wondering, "What am I getting into?"

Watson's father, a doctor of veterinary medicine, had bought a fruit farm when Watson was discharged from the Navy and he ran a laboratory on the farm to develop treatments for poultry diseases. We moved into a suite above the lab and lived there until we could afford to buy our own house.

I continued to work for several months after my marriage but stayed at home once my children were born. When they started school, I held a number of jobs as the dietitian at the Hotel Dieu in St. Catharines, the Niagara-on-the-Lake Hospital and the T.B. Sanatorium in St. Catharines. I also taught sewing at high school for several years and was a substitute teacher in many local schools. My earnings went into the Younie Travel Fund. In hindsight, I regret that I didn't work longer in order to have a larger Canada Pension.

I've always enjoyed teaching and giving people tips on how to achieve better results. I love sewing and have made clothes for my children and myself as well as shirts for my husband — even underwear. My husband and son were very long in the torso, and I could never buy anything that fit them properly!

NOW IT'S YOUR TURN

Some questions to ponder

- **When you reflect on your life of service, what are you most proud of?**
- **What is your greatest accomplishment in life so far?**
- **What are three of the most life-fulfilling or satisfying moments in your life? Three of the most stressful moments?**
- **Can you describe a sacrifice you've made. How did it change you?**
- **Would you make the same sacrifice now, knowing what you know?**
- **If you were to be honoured for something in your life, what would it be?**
- **How do you want to be remembered?**
- **If your life were a movie or a book, what title would you give it?**

THE JOYS AND CHALLENGES OF GROWING OLDER

As we look back on our lives, we realize that
the harvest of youth is achievement,
the harvest of middle age is perspective,
and the harvest of old age is wisdom.
—Angeles Arrien

The call to retire

By The Rev. Colleen Erb
as told to Terry Dance-Bennink

There are moments in life when you sense you're standing on holy ground and you know it's time to move. After 31 years of ministry, a different sort of call came my way. When I turned 65, I decided to retire instead of pursuing other opportunities like being an interim minister. I was surprised to realize that I didn't want to continue in a paid, accountable form of ministry despite several calls from other churches after my retirement. I felt drawn, instead, to a more contemplative life style.

The Rev. Colleen Erb celebrates her 65th birthday

I grieved a lot before I left Gordon United which helped me let go of my earlier desire to stay active and involved. The psychology of my spiritual journey took precedence. I worked with Elly Bradley, my spiritual director, from January to June on the issue of letting go. Gradually, as I came to the end of the grieving process, I became aware that I had no desire to be an interim minister. I was tired and just wanted to be free. It wasn't such a traumatic transition after all, because I'd done my grieving ahead of time.

In retirement, the call still comes but in a different way. Retirees aren't meant to do everything! Initially, I experimented with my domestic skills. I took up cooking and renovated my house and enjoyed a wonderful trip to England in 1994. When I returned, I had to care for my aging father. Sensing a call entails reassessing your life and being open to change.

Retirement has distinct phases for me, each one marked by a call. I accepted the call to lead the women's spirituality group here at First Met, and it's been most rewarding. It's given me an opportunity to share my own contemplative experience and make friends with other like-minded souls. I've found a "little church" inside the big First Met community. I also find the choir life-giving, because I love the music and the people in the choir, even though my voice is not as good as it once was.

A matter of energy

At my age, it all comes down to energy. As a retiree, I could still be into everything and be exceptionally busy, but this no longer seems right for me. I feel called to let go of things that are no longer relevant. I feel called to go deeper into my spiritual life and relationship with God.

A special friendship five or six years ago was a catalyst to go deeper. I found myself searching, digging deeper and reading all I could about the mystics and authors like Gerald May. I learned about God's great love for me and my love for God. I also learned that darkness and light go together, and that friendship is not easy to maintain. Out of this experience, I sensed that God is with us in the muck; God does great things in the darkness. Now I look at whatever happens in my life and ask myself, "What is God trying to teach me? What is the deeper meaning behind each event in my life?"

In retirement, "ministry" can take many forms. Writing letters or phoning lonely friends can be important. These small acts of service are just as valuable as belonging to a busy church committee. Our church needs to acknowledge this more than it does. A lot of seniors may not feel useful any more, but they have a ministry in the "marketplace," in the places where they live, shop and bank. Somebody at my bank asked me the other day why I don't use the ATM.

"Why should I when I can come in here and talk to you?" I

replied. I'd rather talk to a person than a machine any day.

My concept of ministry may be foreign to some people, but I base it on the Jesus, Mary and Martha story. Jesus ministered to Mary, and she ministered to him. I think a congregation ministers to the minister as well as vice versa. It's a team relationship. I learned this out of my own experience at Gordon United. When my mother died, the congregation was there for me and supported me. I thought I should be able to handle it on my own, but they were concerned about my well-being. They ministered to me while I ministered to them.

Ministers are sometimes reluctant to let themselves be ministered to, but I've come to the place where I accept this. It's important for a congregation to know what's going on. It's no big deal for me to admit I get tired more easily, although I don't believe in going on all the time about my health. It's a question of balance. Yes, I had a stroke last winter, and I tell people this, if I think it's helpful for them to know. People sometimes forget that ministers are human beings too. We're not rocks, and ministers hurt just as other people do. We all have to minister to one another.

The art of letting go

As you get older, you don't have the same energy. Elders need to learn the art of letting go, and our church needs to hold the tension of the young working with the old. Sometimes it feels like young people are valued more highly in our church. Keeping an intergenerational balance is a challenge.

I'm no longer drawn to administrative roles. I've given up Presbytery and membership on the Spiritual Development committee. Even organizing a wedding can get to me these days! But I still enjoy being with people and talking one-to-one or in small groups. I try to live in the moment and respond to requests as my energy allows. My priority is to make sure I'm right with God and my neighbour!

A time to harvest

The theme of "call" is very important to me. I don't know whether I've been faithful to the call, but I've tried my best. "Being faithful to the call" could be the title of my life story even though I may not have been faithful all the time. I sense a whole new era starting in my life now, another call, which may be to feast on my life! I could enjoy looking at all my photo albums and diplomas and certificates, couldn't I?

I've wondered what people will say about me when I'm dead. Who am I, what have I done? Writing this story with you, Terry, is about lifting up and celebrating all the events, the story line, of my life. It's OK now to reflect on my life and where I've been. It's a time to harvest and enjoy the fruits of my labour, and to share that fruit, my life reflections, with others. This is part of my new ministry now — to share the wisdom I've gained over the years through this book *Stories United* and our Spiritual Companions program.

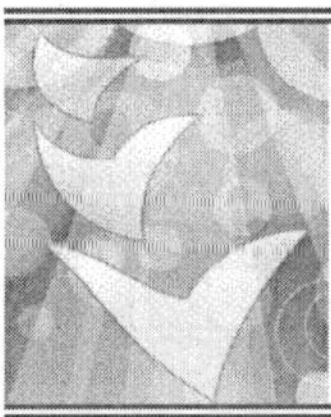

My attitude is gratitude

By Ruth Howell as told to Edeana Malcolm

I'm very grateful that I have lived this long and very grateful to see my two fine grandsons married, but I really find life a little more difficult now that I'm 100 years old.

I can't cope with having to be carried. That part of it I don't like. I can't walk and I can't use my own bathroom, which is humiliating to me. But I suppose that I have to admit that as you get older, you just have to learn to accept whatever comes your way.

The staff members here at Oak Bay Lodge are wonderful, both the men and the women, but you just have to reconcile yourself to the fact that your lifestyle has changed and, of course, one of the difficulties for me is that I can't walk. But I can talk, and I shouldn't say much more about that. If anyone lives to be 100, it's a blessing.

There are many things that I think and feel and hear so I don't miss much. For instance, at my table, there are two ladies, both of whom are very afflicted. Both women have burdens of pain which I have been spared. So to not be in pain — I am very grateful for that.

It makes you understand your blessings. It also makes you question the why and the wherefore of the suffering of others. There must be a reason for having to suffer so much pain. I don't know. Of course, it makes me grateful, but it's very hard on those who suffer. Maybe we shouldn't question and just accept. You have to accept your limitations and only do what you can do.

It's been a few years now since I've been in a wheelchair. But once again, I'm so grateful to have my mind. There are quite a number of people in here at various levels of life and some are affected mentally; they can't help it but they are.

I belonged for years to the UCW at my church and I was thinking the other day about how different ones have gone, including my sister. But a few of them still come to visit me. So, I can't ask for much more. My attitude has to be gratitude.

I think obviously that I have inherited my longevity, because my mother was about 105 when she died. She was very healthy up until the last year or so. She was in Mount St. Mary's, and in her last year, she wasn't quite with it, but she had it remarkably well up until then. There were three of us children and I am the oldest, followed by my brother. My brother and sister are both gone, so now I'm the oldest of the whole family.

I'm tired sometimes. Why, I don't know. You just learn to accept what happens to you.

I've kept active as long as I can. I lived alone in my house for five years after my husband died and then I moved to an apartment on Cadboro Bay where I lived for about 14 years. When I got to be 90, I had this habit of falling so I thought I should move to Oak Bay Lodge, and I'm glad I did. It's a very fine place and I have no complaints. They've got the church service on Sunday and I try to go regularly.

Make the most of each day

By Ross MacKinnon as told to David Bray

I am very happy to be alive each day. I'm thankful I can go for a daily walk and exercise regularly. And the other thing is the grey matter — when I do my volunteer work it makes me work up there. Maybe people who play bridge a lot get their exercise that way.

I make the most of each day.

On becoming a wise elder

Written by Kit MacMillan as shared with the New Vistas Forum, March 28, 2007

I'm somewhat surprised to be called a "wise elder" and feel it's presumptuous of me to instruct others on how they, too, can become wise elders. However, it is true that I am 80 years of age and I've been telling my sons for years that I'm much smarter than they are, so, perhaps, this proves something!

I confess I like being called an "elder" rather than a "senior" — or worse, a senior citizen — because to me, the term "elder" deserves much more respect. So when the census taker comes to your door and you're asked your occupation, don't forget to say that you are an elder in society.

My first 30 years in life were turbulent ones. The next 20 years gave me much food for thought, and the past 30 years have made me even more thoughtful and brought stability to my life. My children are grown and my time is essentially my own, so I'm able to consider more what I'm going to do and how I'm going to do it. I don't need to rush around in just any direction. Keeping a daily journal helps me to consider my choices. I can look back, compare situations, and then, hopefully, make better decisions.

My three criteria for living

1. Acknowledge my creator

I have three criteria for living. The most important one is to acknowledge my creator every morning — this guides me through the hours. I start the day with prayer or contemplation which is really a few quiet moments — solitude of a kind. I sit in my chair and at first, I'm not sure if I'm being heard but always, always, I feel support before my quiet time is over.

In the past, I used to pray only at night, but now I find that my morning prayer time is almost more valuable. It gives my day purpose and direction. This didn't come easily to me. I used to have a take it or leave it attitude about prayer, but now I feel differently. I give thanks to my creator and ask for guidance and assistance with the day ahead.

Sometimes I need peace of mind — anxiety-free hours. Sometimes I need more energy. Sometimes I feel overwhelmed and need guidance. And always, I feel supported at the end of my prayer time. It's an invaluable part of each day, and so is my evening prayer.

2. Nourish and care for my body

It's essential for me to look after my body and care for my health. My body is a gift of life from my creator, and it's my responsibility to care for and nourish it — to nurture it. It's foolish, perhaps even ridiculous, for me to ask my creator for good health if I don't eat properly and follow Canada's food rules. That's my responsibility.

I know from experience that my sense of well-being is greater when I exercise daily and maybe swim twice a week. I shouldn't have said "maybe." My body needs this swim, especially as I get older. I feel more energetic when I have a regular exercise routine. Daily exercise also lessens depression and promotes a zest for life.

I preached responsibility to my children, so I must practise what I preach in keeping my body in good working order. I owe this to my creator and to my family.

3. Help someone in need every day

I try to do something for someone in need every day. This can be simply baking for a friend, or taking someone out for lunch, or maybe going for a scenic car ride in beautiful Victoria with a companion who hasn't had a car ride in some time. You'd be surprised at how few chances people get for a car ride once they've given up driving. I've also found that people love a home-cooked meal if they're living alone in Victoria.

I don't feel smug or especially holy when I do any of this, but I can tell you the recipient's pleasure makes me feel good.

I try not to get caught up in the busyness of volunteering for a bazaar or a bake sale or a church supper without recognizing the theology behind the function. As a minister's wife for many years, I know that church people are great eaters. I've often thought that had there been four wise men, the *fourth* would have been carrying a casserole from the United church!

If I don't follow these three criteria — acknowledge my creator, nourish and care for my body, and help someone in need every day — I may get into trouble with my health or my spirit. It's essential for me to follow this daily routine, without which I'm incomplete.

On aging

Aging pleasantly and productively takes practice. It doesn't just happen. If you're a miserable man or woman at age 50, you'll be a miserable man or woman at age 80 — unless you change. People who say you can't change or teach an old dog new tricks don't understand Christianity or psychiatry, both of which demand change.

I had an Irish friend in Edmonton who always said, "People become more so as they get older." A typical Irish saying! Few of us enjoy being miserable, so why not think about a change?

No two people age the same way. No two people have the same energy level. We should just do the best we can and not fuss about it.

Many of us have memory problems and worry that this is some kind of a failing. I find increasingly that I don't remember what I've read, whether in the Bible or a novel. I've talked to many others with the same problem. I pray about this, but try to just let it go. Who really cares?

By the time you're old enough to be called a wise elder, there's more than one encyclopedia tucked away in your brain. And frequently the search machine is a little slower. Why worry about it?

There are many easy tricks for memory practice. Some people love to do the crossword puzzles in the daily newspaper. Others enjoy good old Scrabble. Anything that clears the dust out of your brain is a blessing.

Solitude or loneliness comes to almost every elder at one time or another. After my husband, Ian, died in 2000, and my family and friends all left, I was alone. Even though I didn't feel like it, I made myself go right back to church. Yes, I cried. I cried buckets. So many people said, "I couldn't do that. I'm afraid I would cry." But what better place than church in which to cry?

I cried on our minister's shoulder so many times that I really should have bought him a new suit. But Allan never ran away from me. The only thing that ran was my mascara!

There will always be crises in life. Don't be afraid of a crisis. It will probably not be as awful as you think. After all, what's the worst thing that could happen? If you seek, you will find strength. Prayer guides and comforts.

Friendship

Keep in touch with your grandchildren directly, not through their parents. Do this even if they live at the other end of the country. What youngster doesn't enjoy a letter or post card addressed directly to him or her, or a phone call about a game in which they're involved. Birthdays are very important to remember too.

My granddaughter, Kim, phones me when something special is happening in her soccer team. And the boys keep me up to date with their basketball team. I make sure I'm conversant with sports language. I even know how to say "Cool, man!"

When I talk to or write the kids, I ask about their friends, their school and what running shoes they think I should I buy for myself. They know all that stuff and like to be consulted. And don't forget the name of their dog!

Friendship is a two-way street. My grandkids and I are friends and I enjoy their friendship every day.

As the years go by, friendships change. I've made many new friends in the past 10 years since I moved to Victoria. I'm really amazed at that! I've also made friends with several bright people in their 50s and 60s. What joy! This is so rejuvenating and invigorating. They keep me up to date and I enjoy the breadth of subject in conversation.

Faith

The Christian faith is hard — hard to follow and difficult to understand. While I'm a Christian, I'm not so arrogant as to believe that my way is the only way for all mankind to worship.

Another strong principle in my life is that I won't leave the church because I disagree with the minister. The church is so much more than the minister. And so much more than me. The church belongs to the creator and is our community of faith. If we really care about the church, we'll pray for it and work for the good of mankind and the world.

I was raised an Anglican and attended church twice every Sunday. Sundays were no fun! My mother was a severe Baptist. I became a member of the United Church of Canada when I was about 22 years old, so today, I celebrate 58 years of membership.

If I were to share some words of wisdom with the next generation, I'd say "Don't hold grudges!" There's an old Arabic saying and it goes like this:

When you go to get even with your enemy,
Dig two graves: one for your enemy
And one for yourself.

So don't hold grudges! I also love T.S. Eliot's poem in which he says, *"We shall not cease from exploration, and the end of all our exploring will be to arrive where we started and know the place for the first time."* It's not farewell, but fare forward voyager.

Some practical tips

Written by Helen Mau as shared with Cyndi Frame

I have felt young until this year. Time fleets by faster as you grow older. These things help keep me young:

1. I continue to have younger friends.
2. I have acquired the habit of focusing on a task for 50 minutes and then relaxing for 10 minutes throughout the day.
3. I exercise on my feet for 20-30 minutes daily in the morning (treadmill and exercise bicycle). I also have a series of bed exercises. Both seem to help me get to sleep and control my weight.

4. I've put health first, i.e. balanced meals, not overeating and getting enough sleep.
5. I have maintained an altruistic, positive attitude and trust in God.
6. I watch out for and understand mental health problems that can cause people to be predators — they can be helped with medication.

What are my dreams now?

I'd like to continue with the above practices, be a good friend/ mentor and serve as many needs of others as my day allows. I hope to continue to live in my own home and have the resources to maintain it. I also hope to continue to keep in touch with a church.

What would I still like to do before I die?

I'd like to travel again, even if it's just to Sooke and Chemainus, B.C. I'd like to take a B.C. ferry over to the mainland and back again and just walk in the wind on the decks. I'd like to travel to California or Alaska again. I'd want to have two people with me on such trips for our own security.

And lastly, I hope to continue to be able to financially support important causes where there is need.

What do I wish to let go of? Nothing!

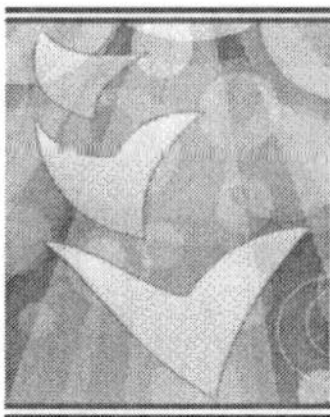

How am I?

By Gertrude Ethel (Trudie) Patmore, Jan. 10, 1909 – Mar. 24, 2007

Trudie was an elder who would have participated in our program had she lived a few months longer. She had a long history of service with the United Church of Canada, including as director of the Sunday school by mail and air program in the 1950s based in Toronto. Later on, she helped Dr. Alvin Cooper develop the New Curriculum for United Church Sunday schools and wrote much of the Junior Section in the Teachers' Manual.

After moving to Victoria, she worked with the Rev. Bob Morris at First United until her second heart attack in 1973. Trudie's sense of humour was always appreciated, so we've included one of her poems.

My feet are like two frozen TV dinners.
My step is unbalanced like I'm walking in a fog at night.

My hips, my back and one shoulder are stabbed by fierce
osteoarthritis
My fingers don't work and my hands don't hold.

My digestion's gone berserk and my plumbing is very old.
My scalp is encrusted with pesky psoriasis.
My eyes can't see my face in the mirror,
Nor your face when we meet.

My ears can't hear the organ in church,
Nor the fire alarm at Fisgard House.

My bones need a thicker inner lining
Beneath their very thin coat.

BUT

My mind's okay and
My heart's still beating.

So I am fine!
How are you?

Dealing with illness

By Helen Simpson as told to Joan Mason

I have to celebrate today. This is the first day in nine months that I don't have a bandage anywhere on my body. No more dressings, can you imagine that? I can have showers again.

Debbie at the Burn Centre said yesterday that she was not going to put a bandage on. I was terrified last night that something would happen because the wound is not completely healed. I still need to take care of the graft and donor sites. I was starting to feel that I would never get out of the doldrums after the injury, first the ankle and then the donor site and the skin graft. I guess I am not very resigned to taking care of myself so much and having to sit with my legs up three hours a day, day after day. I like being active and doing things.

I have to go for my walk a little later — about 20 minutes — along the block and back again. I am challenging my body to do this because I came back breathless when I first tried it. I knew then that I was losing my fitness and if I lose that, I'm in trouble. From the time I was knocked down by a car in March 2003, Dr. Huggett said, walk. So every day, I went out. People in my building thought there was nothing wrong with me because I was out walking. They didn't know that I would take about 10 steps and then come back again. One of my daughters, Pat or Elizabeth, was always with me.

Ever since the accident, I've relied on physiotherapy to help me keep going. Having the skin graft in March 2007 and spending two and a half weeks in hospital has set me back on overall healing.

I've lost almost all of my friends from the Sewing Club, as their lives started to peter out; some of them lost their minds and some of them couldn't walk at all. One was a "sundowner," phoning at two and three in the morning; I don't want to get into that state. I don't want to become a vegetable. There is a relationship between your body and your mind.

Right now, isolation is something I seem to need for healing. That is, perhaps, why I am reading all the time, mostly books with historical references but also novels or mysteries. I can forget the constant pain when I am reading.

I am lucky to have a grandchild who lived with us while she was growing up and is pretty feisty. She knows her own mind and now tells me what I should and shouldn't do. Sylvia is a groundwater protection officer with the B.C. Ministry of Environment, Water Stewardship Division, Vancouver Island Region and is based in Nanaimo.

Angels in disguise

Excerpt from *Finding Gold In My Memories* by Madge Struthers as shared with Barbara Robertson

The evening could have been a complete disaster if I hadn't been visited by three different "angels" all within about 20 minutes. At 6 p.m. on April 30, 2001, the sun came out after a stormy day and it was glorious, so I decided to attend a concert at Centennial United Church put on by the Penticton "Tune-agers."

Three weeks before, Bernice and Earl Harrison, my old time friends from Penticton, phoned to tell me Earl would be in Victoria and wanted to have a visit with me. He told me about the concert and said he'd be in the seniors' choir. Earl was well known in Vancouver as he had sung in over 40 operas with his deep rich bass voice.

I tried to find someone to accompany me to the concert that night but was unsuccessful. When the storm passed, I felt compelled to go. I knew it wouldn't be pleasant travelling on the bus having to change twice, and I had to wait a very long time for bus Number 10 to the Gorge. But I met four very nice young people in the bus shelter who were going home after work.

The conversation flowed and soon my bus was spotted in the distance. At the same time, the sky opened up and there was a deluge and a terrific wind. My umbrella was on the knob of my door at home, but one girl offered me hers and insisted I keep it as she had lots more at home. When I stepped the short distance to the bus, they all cheered me on. That was my first encounter with an "angel."

The bus driver was a lady and asked me with a smile where I was heading on such a night. The window wipers could hardly handle the wind and rain. She told me the regular stop was a block from Centennial Church but promised to let me off in front of the church. "You'll have to be very careful crossing the road," she cautioned me.

Getting off the bus was difficult. I had to hold the umbrella so that it didn't turn inside out in the wind and, with my other hand, I held my cane. I stepped down from the bus into water that ran over my shoes, rushing along the gutter. But lo and behold, my third angel stepped forward from a car wash establishment a short distance away and asked if he could help me.

"I'd like to get across the road safely," I said. He took my arm and we crossed the street, only to find the front doors locked. The stranger helped me around the corner to the David Street entrance and I told him what a treasure he was. I couldn't thank him enough. He told me it wasn't hard for him as he had a grandma who looked quite a lot like me. I was all wet but somehow floating because of my three angels.

I met two more angels at the end of the evening when I ran into a couple of women I'd met three days earlier in the laundry room at Robert's House. I was wondering how I was going to get home and they offered to drive me to my door!

Scooter encounters

Excerpt from *Finding Gold In My Memories* by Madge Struthers as shared with Barbara Robertson

One of the very special things a scooter affords me is to go out every Saturday with my good friend, Mary Mickleborough. I often go to Douglas House for afternoon tea with Mary and other people I know there. Although the church is one and a quarter miles away and on the other side of town, I go to church on my scooter, too, when it suits me.

I meet all kinds of people and very often they turn out to be somebody who knows somebody I know. I always say if you talk long enough to a stranger, chances are you will be related.

I slowed down on Toronto Street one day as is my habit when meeting an older person, especially someone with a walker. The lady thanked me for stopping and I remarked that she sounded like a Scot. She asked me how I knew for everyone thought she had no particular accent.

"I often go by the timbre of the voice," I replied. I asked her where she came from and she said, "Glasgow," but I knew by the hesitation in her voice that it was likely to be close to Glasgow.

"What place?" I asked her. "Eaglesham," she replied. After that it was old home week for she used to go back often and knew my cousin, Jean Greig, the owner of the Wishing Well Tearoom where she was a frequent visitor.

Fifty yards further on, I stopped for another lady with a cane who turned out to be 90 years old. "You sound like a Scot," I remarked and she told me she came from Galston in Ayrshire, so I told her my grandfather Anderson was born there along with his two sisters who ran a store in Galston. She couldn't believe her ears and said she remembered going to that store for needles and thread.

Before they left, both ladies told me, "You've made my day," and of course, they'd made my day as well.

Another really nice thing about this scooter is the fact that Alma, the previous owner, loves me to phone her and tell her some of my scooter stories.

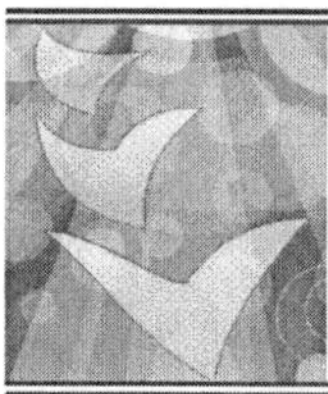

The comfort of faith

By Eileen Thorn as told to Gloria Stott

I've faced many losses in my life, including the loss of my eyesight, but my faith protects and comforts me in the midst of grief. I find sanctuary in my home and in my church.

I was only four years old when my mother got cancer and died in California in 1923. My dad took over and looked after me, even selecting and buying my clothes. We moved to Moose Jaw, Sask., to live with my Aunt Alice and Uncle Austin, and I grew up with their two children and felt part of their family. Their daughter, Glenys, was like a sister to me. We argued and fought just like sisters do.

My uncle worked for Burns & Co. Meats and we used to have a whole leg of beef or pork to roast for Sunday dinner. My aunt was happy-go-lucky and always asked the Sunday evening church crowd over to her place for tea and sandwiches after the service.

We all sang in the junior and senior choirs for years at St. Andrew's United Church. My father sang in the church choir, too, and I always sat in the front pew because I just had to see my dad. He worked for National Fruits at the time.

When I grew up, I became a stenographer and worked for Prairie Airways where airplanes were repaired. I was invited to a housewarming party one day and I went with a blind date, named Kenneth Thorn, an aircraft inspector from Ontario.

"That's the girl I'm going to marry," he told a friend afterwards. But it took me longer to get serious about him. When my dad found out that Ken's folks were Presbyterians and that his father published the Sunday school papers, he knew Ken came from a good family. That impressed me too!

After our marriage, we lived in Hamilton where my husband worked for Imperial Oil. Our daughter, Sheryl Anne, was born and then a son, John Edward (Ted). We moved a lot due to my husband's job and our last move was to Victoria in the early '70s.

My bridesmaid and her husband lived in Victoria, too, and were members of Metropolitan United Church, so we joined the church in 1971. One day they took us to an Actimets outing at Spooners and we happily joined this church group as well.

My husband died of Alzheimer's disease in 1995 and it was the Actimets group and their loving friendships which helped me through my loss. I felt as if all their arms were wrapped around me with love. I needed this because my bridesmaid died around the same time and we'd been so close over the years. Glenys had also died in Victoria in 1990, and she'd been like a sister to me.

I lost my daughter the year after my husband died. She had just visited us in 1996 and on her return to Edmonton, she died of a heart attack in the airport at the age of 55. This was a great loss to my family and me.

My own health began to deteriorate in 1994 when I was diagnosed with macular degeneration and glaucoma. I had to give up my car in 1998. I also have osteoporosis. After a day of lawn bowling and lifting bowls up some steps, I simply collapsed on the floor. I injured three vertebrae and needed pain patches of morphine to ease the pain.

I thought I'd never walk again. But I recovered and now I use a walker and a white cane.

Due to my vision problems, I have a telephone with large numbers, an Aladdin Reader screen to read written work, and a special screen in front of my TV so I can see the picture more easily. I go to the monthly CNIB meetings by Handidart and get taxi saver coupons so I can use taxis for half price.

When I go to the library for talking books, I use my walker with the basket on the front. Sometimes I go down to the Fairfield Activity Centre with my walker and drop by the pharmacy or grocery store; otherwise, I can get things delivered. I enjoy my walks in the fresh air and sunshine.

I play bridge occasionally too. I have a foldable halogen lamp that I take with me and the cards have large numbers. Two of the players have good eyesight and they help me. We take turns playing at each other's homes and eat dinner together before the card game. This is a challenge.

I had a fire at my suite on Oct. 9, 2007. I'd just returned from a visit with my son in Ontario only to face black smoke and a gutted bathroom in my lovely suite. The fire had come up through burned insulation from the suite below me due to careless use of a blowtorch.

The insurance company offered to put me up at a hotel but my close friend, Daphne, on the first floor kindly offered to let me stay with her and the insurance company has agreed to reimburse her. It's been a long wait getting my apartment fixed, but it should be done by the middle of March.

One of my grandchildren, Shawn, came and helped me pick out the tiles for the bathroom and some other things I needed. I'm very lucky because I have seven grandchildren and seven great-grandchildren.

I also have my spiritual companion, Gloria Stott, who takes me to church on Sundays and other church activities like the flea market and the New Vistas Program at Queenswood. I invited her to be my guest at a Valentine's tea at the CNIB centre.

I think I've responded to loss and death in my life by accepting it. I tend to keep grief to myself, however, because I don't want anyone to be upset or hurt by it. I believe in the resurrection, even though life after death is a mystery to me. I hope it means that I'll be reunited with my family again.

NOW IT'S YOUR TURN

Some questions to ponder

- **How have you faced the joys and challenges of growing older?**
- **What are your dreams now?**
- **What would you still like to do or be before you die?**
- **What do you wish to let go of? What is dying in your life now?**
- **What are some of your regrets, "if only's" or "I wish I had's"?**

ACCEPTING LOSS AND DEATH

Endings
Cause pain, sadness
God's strong arms enfold me
Carry me to new beginnings
Rebirth! — May Deller

For my mother: Maundy Thursday

Written by May Deller as shared with Irene Baddeley

Ellen Grace Turnbull, May Deller's mother

The shouting and acclamation of Palm Sunday recedes as the days move on toward the cross.

I sit by your chair, hold your thin hand, stroke your soft cheek.

I remember your strong arms and warm body holding me close. I am a hurting child, crying for help. "There, there darling, everything will be all right. I love you," you croon as you rock me quietly in the big old stuffed rocking chair. How safe and loved I felt. You could make my world OK again. And you did — year after year after year.

When I was a mother myself and heart-worn with nameless burdens, you were there with outstretched arms, gentle words and comforting food. No questions asked — accepting, knowing this daughter could find her own way and would, but also knowing a little loving along the bumpy road could help make her hostile world an inviting place once more.

Oh, gentle, wise woman — mother root, mother heart — how I have drawn from your great strength!

Now the cry comes from you. "Help, help! Please help! Oh help!" Minute by minute, day after day, the cry comes from your dry lips and pleading eyes. What depths birth that endless cry? Tragic, long buried memories of inexplicable pain and loss which no young girl should have had to face?

"Help me! Help me! Help! Help!"

"How can I help?" I ask. "Please tell me what you need dear

mother of mine."

You cannot tell me. You do not know. You seem surprised that it is you who are calling for help.

"Help. I want to get into bed. Won't someone help?" I cannot lift you alone, frail and weightless though your body is.

Caring folk come and help lift your thin, shrunken body into bed. The cries do not cease. You struggle, trying to find comfort for a body wracked by pain. And I? I stand by helplessly. Nothing that I do makes you more comfortable and the cries continue endlessly.

"Shall I read to you, Mom?" I read and gradually your cries and struggles cease and you momentarily sleep a restless sleep.

The long hours of sitting by your bedside, months of days and nights relive themselves in my memory. The pain of broken limbs and unhealed inner depths charged through your body and clouded your mind as minute by minute, hour by hour, day by day, month by month you cried out, and still cry out for help. How I longed, and still long to take you in my arms, rock you, comfort you as I whisper, "There, there, darling one, I love you. It will be all right. It will be all right!" knowing it will not.

Now here we are in this small room together, you lying there frail and helpless crying out, "Help, Help. Isn't anyone going to help?" And I, sitting here silently crying "help" for my helplessness.

"This is my body broken for you," the words of Holy Thursday. Here is your broken body lying before me.

Who do they say is hanging on the cross? I know who she is — my beloved mother — hanging, hanging, crying "Help," crying "Help."

"My God, my God! Why have you forsaken her? Where are you, God — the God of this woman of faith, this faithful woman? Where are you God?" I scream into the emptiness.

Only silence — then a still small voice — "I am here. I am here lying on this bed."

Nothing in life is lost

By The Rev. Colleen Erb
as told to Terry Dance-Bennink

There's truth in the saying that heaven and hell are on this earth. We do experience both during our life here on earth, and Jesus himself said that the kingdom of heaven is in our midst. But I believe there's also something beyond life on this planet.

We don't just die and that's it, although it's impossible to say for sure what happens next. It's a journey, and we don't know exactly where we're going and we seem to go alone, so it can be very scary. But nothing in life is lost — it's all gathered up into love.

I was reading the resurrection story this morning, about how Jesus encountered his disciples while walking towards Emmaus. They didn't recognize him at first. Who were they talking to? Was he in a different form? Were they simply remembering Jesus out of a longing to see him again? Was it a powerful experience they wrote down later in more graphic language? Or was there someone really walking beside them along the road? I don't know who can answer these questions.

But one thing that seems to be sure is when Jesus arrived at the upper room and they invited him to stay a while, he sat down and broke the bread, and that action, I think, indicates he was truly present. Whether he was actually in the room physically or the disciples just felt his presence strongly, I don't know, but I like to think he was there with them. He *did* walk along the road beside them — *how* doesn't matter.

Maybe the disciples didn't recognize him at first because he was different. Mary didn't recognize him when she first saw him — she thought he was the gardener. But when he said her name, something resonated in her heart and she turned around and called him by his name.

I recognize that "heaven" is within us, but I think we move into a deeper and nearer presence of God when we die. Teresa of Avila talked about the different stages of the soul's movement towards God, including the final stage of union with God, and I believe she's right. We experience some kind of resurrection when we die.

The whole universe is constantly being created and re-created. Everything dies in the winter and sits dormant until the seed or root starts to sprout again and give life. In the spring, there's a marvellous explosion of colour everywhere as trees and flowers bud — it's part of the rhythm of the universe. And it has to be the same for human beings, even though I can't tell you how it happens. Why would God deny us the fruit of the seed when we die, when we see birth, death, and re-birth all around us every day?

When I die, I think my relationship with God — and Jesus — will continue. I really do. I don't know how, but the relationship lives on. Wherever we go, it's not very far. A good friend of mine once described life on earth as a school. When we die, we keep on learning and growing.

A communion of loved ones

After my dad died, I had an experience which convinced me of this. Right after his death, I felt terrible. I felt I hadn't dealt adequately with his last moments of life, that I hadn't said what I should have, even though every time I saw him, I told him how much I loved him. But I still felt I hadn't done enough. He wanted me to be his daughter, not his minister. I knew that. But when it came to ministering to him at the end, I felt I'd let him down.

Louis Charles Erb, the Rev. Colleen Erb's father

Shortly before Dad died in the hospital, I sensed something was wrong, because his heartbeat changed and he was crying in agony with his tummy all extended. I sat in the hallway while the nurses gave him an enema. An orderly came along and I said to him, "It's a good thing I'm prepared for this."

"You're never prepared for it," he replied. I felt like saying, "What do you know about it?" But when I went back in to see my dad, I was not prepared. He was on the way out. I was expecting it, but not then. That's when I sat down and told him I loved him and that God was with him, but I still felt inadequate.

After his death, I went on a retreat and told my spiritual director that every time I thought about my dad's death, I cried. I couldn't seem to stop crying. I felt like a stunned daughter rather than a minister who should know what to do. "I'm stuck, I'm stuck," I told my director. He suggested I try an imaging prayer.

"Imagine yourself again at the bedside with your dad and recall all that you did. Then repeat the experience, only this time, invite Jesus to sit beside you," he suggested. So I tried this. When I did it the first time, I just wept buckets. But when I prayed the second time with Jesus by my side, I didn't cry at all, not one tear.

During this second meditation, I suddenly saw all my family — both my grandmothers and grandfathers, my mom, my niece Patty, and then I saw my dad and he had his arm around Patty. When I told a former minister at First Met about this, he told me one of his relatives had had a similar experience of seeing all their deceased relatives. It was like somebody had blown up a big picture of them. I saw them all vividly. It was amazing and I was elated.

We believe in the communion of saints, and I think loved ones who have died and gone on are still with us, and every so often, they come to visit us, as my dad did last year when I was lying in the emergency ward after my stroke. I felt his presence another time, as well, when he called my name. Sometimes when I'm feeling down, I feel my dad's presence strongly — the essence of my dad is very real. Perhaps these loved ones are angels who come to help us.

My dad had a similar experience just before he died. He told Bev Tracey, a former minister at Metropolitan, that he'd seen Mom in the room with him. He was not afraid to die, he told her, because he'd seen his wife alive and well. So it's truly the pascal mystery, even though we can't explain how we move from death to life, from this world to the next.

I believe wholeheartedly that there's something more than this life; otherwise, what's the point? Death should be the climax of our journey and offer us the opportunity to carry on our relationships, although not in the same way as on earth. Paul talked about the resurrection of the body. I'm not sure I'd go that far. Where's everybody going to live?! But it's not up to me to answer that.

When Mary recognized Jesus in the garden, perhaps she felt like I did with my dad — she had a powerful conviction of presence. Our souls — the part of us in which God and Jesus dwell — are indestructible. And I experience resurrection every time I go through hell and high water in my life. I don't have to wait until I die to find this out. Resurrection is about becoming whole again. Some people feel that you can never overcome a tragic loss, but I think you can.

Maybe it all comes down to my image of God. God is Love and love means relationship. I agree with Paul when he says that nothing can separate us from the love of God — neither death, nor life, nor angels, nor principalities, nor things present or things to come, nor any other creature can separate us from the love of God in Christ Jesus, our Lord.

On heaven and dying

By Mona Hundleby as told to Terry Dance-Bennink

Perhaps heaven is like a small community village with angels who meet you as you come up the passageway. I think my husband, Roy, will be one of the first people to greet me, and possibly others I care about like my mother and father. I'm sure I'll find them eventually.

Roy Hundleby just before his marriage to Mona

God is in charge of this heavenly village, and Jesus is there helping him. There's a lady God too. I've seen pictures of male angels, but who knows what God looks like? A record is kept of each life, and when I die, I'll have no regrets. I don't fear dying. I have nothing to be ashamed of because I've tried to fill my life with positive deeds and thoughts.

I'm ready to go because I miss my husband and my friends. I've talked to God all my life, and I think he has things for me to do in heaven, just as I've had a role to play on earth. I talk to Jesus too — maybe we can work together in heaven.

I can't really imagine where or how I'll live once I've died, but those dreams I had after Roy died probably come close to what it will be like. In my dreams, Roy always takes me to this lovely house, and I feel at home, at peace. A few nights after he died, the most beautiful angel visited me, dressed in white. It was real — not a dream. She had gorgeous hair. Maybe she's my guardian angel?

I'm losing the use of my arms and legs now and have very little strength. I need regular blood transfusions because my blood is getting thinner. My lymphoma has returned. I've signed the forms refusing all heroic means to keep me alive like tube-feeding and artificial resuscitation. When I'm finished, I'm finished. One thing that keeps me going, however, is working on this book and sharing my life story with others. It gives me a reason to live.

I was with Roy as he died, so I know what it's like. He was in bed all the time and I often fed him. He had difficulty swallowing after his stroke and coughed a lot at night. I'd call this wonderful male nurse, and he'd take the time to talk with us and reassure us.

I found it hard when they stopped giving Roy liquid, but we kept his mouth and lips moist. At this stage, he couldn't talk to me any more, but on his last night, he called out for me. He must have known he was dying. I used to talk to him about heaven and angels, and a member of the family always held his hand — we took turns. We were all there when he died. He went very peacefully, without a struggle, and his funeral was wonderful.

Close encounters

I've been having encounters with Roy recently. Some people might think they're just dreams, but I think they are real. A few weeks ago, when my daughter-in-law, Marilyn, had just left, I went off into a deep sleep. I was so tired. Then all of a sudden, I seemed to be in heaven, because there were about 15 to 20 people sitting on stairs in a fair-sized room. They were all dressed in material of a rosy-wine shade, and each one had slippers with a piece that came up to cover the bottom of their pants. Some had black hair; others had blond or red hair.

I didn't really know where I was, but just before I left this place, my husband, Roy, joined me. Then I looked down and saw my room here at the Lodge at Broadmead, and I said to Roy:

"Can't I please stay? I hate to leave you."

"I'm afraid you have to go back," he replied.

The next thing I heard was the phone ringing, and it was Marilyn. Since then, I've talked to Roy quite a bit and have told him about the story I'm writing with you, Terry.

"If I go to heaven," I told him, "I'll never see my book!"

"I'll get it for you, don't worry," he said confidently.

"How?" I asked him.

"The same way I brought you up here," he said. "This is my job — to travel back and forth."

This reminded me of the beautiful angel who visited me a couple of days after Roy died. It felt the same. I guess all kinds of things are possible in this world. It was a shaky experience for me, even though I was cool and calm, but I couldn't understand why I wasn't truly there with Roy and the others. Maybe I was still in a deep sleep, but I know I didn't want to come back to my room.

In my dreams since then, I spend most of my time with Roy. We go downtown and look into the stores or get a meal, just like old times. And you arrived today, Terry, like another angel, coming just when I needed someone. It's good to be able to talk about heaven and dying.

I think I had a little stroke the other day, I felt so weak. Last night, I wondered if Roy would still be there when I arrive — perhaps he'll have moved on. But now I'm sure he'll be there for me. I have a strong sense he's building a house for me.

I tell God he can put me to work as soon as I get there. I'm sure there are people in heaven who need help.

NOTE: Mona Hundleby died on Roy's birthday two months later, November 2, 2007.

Losing Jack

By Sheila MacDougall
as told to Terry Dance-Bennink

Sheila and Jack Rice and their three children, late 1950s

Jack died in 1970 in Regina when he was 55 and I was 47. He'd had more than one heart attack, and it was before the days of heart bypass. Another few years and he could have had an operation. But it wasn't to be. He'd had rheumatic fever as a child and wasn't eligible for the draft during the war, even though he tried everything he could to sneak into the army. He was also colour-blind along with his brothers.

What I miss the most since Jack died is all the fun and I miss listening to all his stories. Boy, was there a hole in my life when he died. Jack hadn't been feeling well for some time, and I told the bank that I didn't think Jack should continue working. The doctor agreed.

Jack found retirement hard at first, but then he started to really enjoy the lack of pressure. We were living in the bank house before he retired, so we had to move and buy a home for ourselves. We were getting the new house ready one day when he turned on the power saw to cut some wood.

I went into another room and when I came back, he was on the floor. I was a nurse but I couldn't do anything for him. It was February and our phone hadn't been hooked up, so I flew next door and asked a neighbour to call an ambulance. I sat in that ambulance with Jack and yelled, "Not now, not now, not now!!"

But of course, it was now. He was gone. It's a long time ago, but the tears still come when I think of him. It's his birthday today. I miss him. I still miss him. And the kids look like him and remind me of him whenever I see them. How thrilled he'd be with how they've turned out. Eric is the oldest, followed by Elsa, and then Ken who was killed in a car accident six months after Jack died.

Eric was enrolled in Dalhousie Law School when Jack died, and Elsa was studying in Edmonton. Elsa and I attended Eric's graduation in Halifax in 1971. I cried that day. I looked around at all the other fathers and couldn't see any that were even close to Jack. It didn't take me too long to realize that you can't program your life and it doesn't matter what happens to you — there's a reason.

Jack had suffered a heart attack before, and we talked at the time about what I might do without him. He thought I'd have an advantage by going to live in a small town. A few years earlier, he was hit by a car in Winnipeg in the winter time walking home with a Christmas tree. The impact broke his leg, and we talked for the first time about things like funeral plans. We had friends in the funeral home business and we used to joke and laugh with them. But we talked seriously about cremation and told our kids that this is what we wanted — no burial plots. After Jack died, we had a church service followed by the cremation.

We were married for 22 years — not very long when you think about it. I found it really hard one year when I looked around at all the couples celebrating their 50th wedding anniversaries. I felt another wave of sadness and hurt. I learned very quickly, however, to go and visit others who've lost a loved one, and to talk about my experience and let them talk. Don't leave these visits too long. One girl I knew waited two years and then told me, "Oh Sheila, I couldn't face you." You need to go quickly.

After Jack died, I had to move into this little house that we'd bought and one day, I was sitting in the bay window writing a slew of thank you letters, and I looked out and up the walk came a woman who once knew my mother. "I came because I have some things to say," she told me. She'd been married to a lawyer in Regina.

"We didn't have much money," she told me, "but we had one son and three daughters. Our son went overseas during the war and was captured as a PoW. That just killed my husband. He couldn't stand the thought of our son being imprisoned and he died shortly afterwards. My son came home, eventually… ." She went on to tell me that after her husband died, she got a job and was grateful she could manage for herself.

So I thought to myself, "OK, you think I should go to work, do you?" This was her message — from her own experience — even though she was much older than me.

It took me a while. My children had left home, so I was all alone that first winter as I stumbled around. A very nice woman at church asked me to sell UNICEF cards during the fall. I agreed and went out with Jack's briefcase to try to persuade local businesses to purchase these cards as their Christmas greetings. I can still remember how I felt trudging around with that briefcase.

People were very kind. I was invited to lots of teas and bridge games. And I had a wonderful, wonderful UCW group of women, all of them old enough to be my mother, and they were absolutely fantastic.

After a while I decided to go back to school and refresh my nursing skills. I ended up getting my degree from the University of Regina as well and went on to enrol in the Faculty of Education so I could teach. I spent a semester learning about teaching theory which was followed by a practicum and I quite enjoyed it all.

My kids were proud of me when I graduated at age 52. I would have gone to my graduation if they'd been able to join me, but they were living out of town, and I didn't want to go alone. I went to a wedding in Alberta instead. I loved studying and still do. I'd probably enjoy doing a master's degree, but at my age, I wouldn't waste the university's time. But I like to learn and be stimulated by new ideas.

The meaning of death

By Sheila MacDougall
as told to Terry Dance-Bennink

My son, Ken, was killed in a car accident when he was 17. He was three years younger than his sister, Elsa, and it was the same year that my husband, Jack, died — six months later in fact. Ken and his friends had been drinking. They may have been running a light when they hit a Saskatchewan Power truck. Afterwards, I never heard a single solitary syllable from that company, not a word.

Ken's brother, Eric, was terribly upset and cried. "We were just getting to be friends," he said. Eric was 21 at the time and about to finish law school. I had to attend his graduation in

Halifax and Elsa's graduation in Edmonton alone. I cried. It seemed so awful to have lost both my husband and a son.

I didn't cry much, however, because I knew my kids were suffering and I was determined not to be a burden. I don't cry easily, and when I do, I hate myself, because it's so explosive. I felt angry, though, and sad that Jack wasn't there to enjoy the proud moment along with all the other fathers.

When Ken died, I was still numb. What more can happen, I asked myself. So we had another church funeral. But my friends were wonderful, and the UCW women came out again to support me. They were always there for me, just like a bunch of mothers.

When you die, I think it's over. Heaven and hell are during your lifetime. Ken and my husband, Jack, were both taken from me, and after a while, I was able to think about why it happened and what I could possibly learn from the experience. When I eventually returned to teaching nursing, I was a kinder, more patient instructor, having suffered such losses.

What do you think they assigned me to teach during my first year as a nursing instructor? Death and dying! I used Jack's death and myself as a case study. I hadn't gone further than that one day when I heard a voice at the back of the class ask, "But isn't it worse when it's a child?" I was erasing the blackboard, and I stayed there with my back to the class for a while and gave that board a good cleaning. Then I turned around and explained that I'd experienced both type of losses.

"The answer is, I don't know," I said. They really got it, as some of them had suffered losses too. After that I thought to myself, I can do this. In a way, Jack's death was a big comeuppance for me. I slammed him on the floor the night he died, trying to bounce him back to life. I thought I knew so much about resuscitation that I would never be at a loss. But I was at a loss. It didn't work. My experience hasn't stopped me from teaching others, but resuscitation doesn't always work.

Life after death

I found it very interesting to read Mona Hundleby's account of her experience after she lost her husband. She clearly expected to meet her husband again as soon as she died. I don't have that feeling. I simply cherish in my heart all the memories — of my parents, of Jack, of Ken — the way they were. Memories are what last.

"It's funny, though," I said to my kids the other day, "Dad's always young — he never gets old." Here I am at age 85 and so aged, so different from the person he knew 37 years ago. I'm more than double the age I was when he died. I can't imagine how it would be if I met him again. I'm kind of glad he's not around to see this.

I think God orchestrates my life and always has — you don't have to like what happens in your life, but that's the way it is. Life is short but eventful and worthwhile. God allowed me those happy years with Jack, and I don't look for more years. I really don't. I believe I'm helped to do whatever God thinks I'm capable of doing every moment of my life.

The Resurrection story, I believe, is a metaphor. It's a *midrash* or form of biblical interpretation. A wonderful, wonderful story that presents us with Jesus — a man who lived and taught and was crucified — that's a fact. But he died. Yes, people felt his presence afterwards, but as a memory of Him and his teachings. I don't believe we go up to some pearly gates. If that is the way God wants it, however, that's fine. But I don't worry about it. I don't have any expectations of what will happen. I'll accept whatever comes.

I don't worry about the "hereafter." There may well be dimensions beyond this world which I can't imagine, but I don't worry about it. I don't feel anxious. I have no expectations. However, I wish I'd asked my father certain things before he died.

Maybe I'll give these reflections on my life to my kids, so they can ask me questions before I go. My mother was adopted when she was six years old, for example, but I don't remember her ever talking about being adopted. Did she not remember? I've not been able to trace my mother's ancestors because the birth records were burned in a North Dakota church some time ago, but I would have liked to have known more about this side of my family.

The right to live or die: an ethical challenge

By Sheila MacDougall
as told to Terry Dance-Bennink

Our church has invited discussion about euthanasia and physician-assisted suicide, but I think we have to do whatever we can to keep someone alive. I would qualify this by saying that if someone only has a short while to live and is in pain, morphine can and should be used to ease and speed their passing. It's a matter of careful balance, and that's as far as I'd go.

Personally, I could never give or assist with giving a drug that would kill a person. A while ago, I got to know a person who had ALS or Lou Gehrig's disease which is very unpleasant, but she was wonderful and her courage was a great example to others. It's a very fine line, and I admit, I wasn't with her in the last stages of her disease.

Sheila and her second husband, Mac Walter MacDougall

My second husband, Mac, wanted me to give him a needle before he died, but I told him I didn't have one and couldn't do it. His doctor suggested, however, that I give him an elixir of morphine every four hours which made it much easier on Mac. Morphine can speed up the transition but still allow time for last words with loved ones.

I don't have an answer for those who are experiencing dementia which is a much more protracted disease than cancer or a fatal heart attack. In the hospital, you can receive morphine when you're in pain, but those confined to a nursing home with severe dementia don't have this option. It's hard. I simply know I couldn't take a life. Just because someone has dementia, why should you take his or her life?

If a woman in her 60s takes her own life, the person left behind suffers. You don't want a loved one to go — you want to be able to touch them to the last second. I remember urging a woman whose husband had experienced a heart attack to go for a cup of coffee, because she'd been by his side all day. And of course, he died while she was gone, and she was wild at me for urging her to leave him. "You let him die," she screamed at me.

More often than not, loved ones are not there when a person dies. As soon as they step out of the room, the dying person often chooses to leave, perhaps to spare their loved ones.

The mentally ill pose a similar challenge. Are you going to pull the plug on those who grow up with a severe mental illness? My sister has a schizophrenic son who asked her recently, "Will I always be like this?" But to take that life? How does it differ from someone with dementia? Are we meant to suffer these things like Job?

I don't feel the same way about abortion as I do about euthanasia. Yes, there's life in the womb, but a fetus is not self-sufficient. I've seen victims of rape, and mothers with many children whose lives were in danger, and some beautiful babies born to women who couldn't care for them. I'm not inflexible. But I don't like abortion on demand or as a form of birth control. Each decision should be weighed carefully.

The issue of the right to die is not going to go away, especially as our society ages. We put animals down, I know, when they are in pain and near death. It's a huge issue. But I visit someone these days who's 101 and still sharp as a tack. Who is to decide?

My daughter invited her mother-in-law, who suffered from dementia, to live with them at home for a while, and they all managed, but not everybody can do this. And the mother eventually ended up in a nursing home. As I get older, I know my daughter would welcome me, but I'd think twice about moving into her home. Certainly not yet!

My daughter thinks I should be with her when I reach the stage of needing care, but I don't think it's such a great idea. However, given what we're talking about, maybe elderly people should be allowed to have the pills ahead of time and a will which stipulates when they are to be used, a bit like the way it's done in Holland. But I still have a hard time thinking that I'd administer the needle.

A sense of hope

Written by Helen Mau as shared with Cyndi Frame

My faith has certainly helped me accept loss and death. I believe there is a plan for everyone and it is beyond the powers of we mortal ones.

I've observed the death of my 73-year-old grandfather, my 93-year-old Aunt Lyle, my 83-year-old father who had a stroke when I was 53, and my mother's last evening in her 93rd year following a short stay in a nursing home. My husband, Charles Mau, caused his own death in a nursing home when, unknown to me, he hid and refused all fluids.

In every case, I felt the loss deeply. In my husband's case, I had pneumonia at the time and was 75 years old, so I'd placed him in a nursing home. To be put in a nursing home is against the wishes of all Mainland Chinese families because they have large families and someone can usually be designated to care for them at home. But I had no one to help take care of Charlie. He felt I had abandoned him.

In each case, however, I did everything I humanly could so I don't feel accountable. In most cases, age was a major factor in the death.

What protects me or gives me sanctuary at such moments? My faith, my own health and my realization that I did my best. I've been a responsible breadwinner for many years and have the financial means to cope. My sense of hope is also a great help in such circumstances.

As for life after death, no one really knows what happens at death. The experience of Jesus suggests that there could be life after death. There are many possibilities. Young babies, for example, may carry the soul of a human being who has passed on — perhaps a relative.

My main hope is that I've lived my life with compassion and altruism and that I've done my best with what I've been given in mind, body and spirit. I realize some of my limitations and hope for forgiveness where I've failed to do what I ought to have done.

The saddest time in my life

By Irene McDonald
as told to Terry Dance-Bennink

Irene and Donald McDonald, 1990

I lost my husband in 1991, which was the saddest time in my life. It came as a most unheralded death, because he'd only been ill for a day. There's no way to describe the shock and the loss. You eventually get over the shock in a way, but I'll never forget being in that hospital room and hearing the doctor say, "There is nothing we can do. And you must take this note to your family doctor immediately and get a shot for yourself and anybody else who's been in your home during the last few days to protect yourselves from the virus that's infected your husband."

Just before Donald fell ill, my brother, Clifford, had come out for a visit. His wife, Kay, had passed away, and Donald and I had gone to Lethbridge, Alta., to be with him during the last days of her life and after her funeral. Clifford was lonely, so I invited him to stay with us and take up bridge in a more serious way. Clifford was leaving on the last day of February when Donald came downstairs that morning and said, "I don't feel very well; I don't think I want to go golfing today." Clifford said that was fine and went to see his brother-in-law instead.

By noon that day, I thought I'd better take Donald to the doctor, so I called the doctor's office and was told to meet the doctor at the hospital. They admitted Donald right away. That evening, Clifford reassured me and said, "Don't worry. They'll give him some tests to find out why he's not feeling well and let you know tomorrow." So I took my brother to the airport the next morning, and when I returned to the hospital, here was the doctor telling me, "I don't think there's anything we can do. If he were a younger man, we might think of a liver transplant, but I don't advise this given his age."

I went to my own doctor's office later that day even though I shouldn't have been driving a car at the time. I told the receptionist I needed to go right in. I couldn't wait. My doctor told me, "There's a Gulf War on, you know." I didn't know what he meant by that and he explained, "We don't have anything with which to boost your immunity, because all the supplies have been exhausted in Canada due to the war."

I came out of his office and called my daughter, Catherine, and my brother, Clifford. I couldn't get in touch with Catherine because she was away skiing, but my brother said he'd come right back. He owned a drug company in Calgary and said he'd bring the supplies we needed somehow. The day after Donald's funeral service, Clifford and I each received a shot to protect us. After the autopsy, we learned that Donald had developed a virus which had attacked his liver. It may have been dormant for a while.

It's very difficult for me to talk about all this. Donald was a devoted husband who always had a kind word for me every day of his life.

How do I deal with loss? Not easily. I deal with loss privately. I don't expect others to carry me through things that I cannot reasonably carry myself. And I don't think a person's religious faith can spare the person hardship. God can't keep you from the ravages of some forms of ill health, regardless of your faith. This is not to say there isn't a loving God, nor do I think that God puts some people on earth with desperate physical impediments to try their strength. We can't blame God for these happenings, nor call upon God to remove them.

Seeing Donald's composure after he'd been told there was nothing more that could be done was a lesson for me. We'd both shed our tears, and Donald faced his death with grief but without terror.

I wonder sometimes whether the United Church can ever be as great a solace to its members as the Catholic Church seems to be to its adherents. When you enter a United church, there isn't the same sense of being in a place of prayer that there is in a Catholic church. I think this carries over into the inner soul of its members, no matter if they're diligent in worship or not.

For the person left behind, it helps to do something worthwhile for others, rather than withdraw into yourself. I know people who are very committed to wellness and prayer programs, but for me personally, I find this a bit too self-centred. It seems to be all about "help me." I'd like to be described in the Book of Life as "one who loves her fellow men." That's how I'd like to be remembered.

Life after death

By Irene McDonald
as told to Terry Dance-Bennink

You get pretty wormy when you die! You eventually become ashes and your body becomes nothing and if there is any part of you that survives, it would be this intangible thing we call the soul. We're not all going to rise up on a Judgment Day in a bodily form, otherwise it would be pretty crowded!

If there is a purpose for life, however, it would be that a soul will be there to enter into someone else's thought or plan. So many songs and poems have been written through the ages about "lost and found souls." But I don't have words to truly describe this soul that I have.

It's a bit like saying I have a conscience. Everybody has an inner self, a sense of guidance. But you can't prove all this. You can have faith in the Mystery and see a new life unfold be it human, animal or plant. You can see the universe expanding and can learn about it, but you don't have your finger on that moment of creation — or destruction.

How do I feel about dying? I would hope that I wouldn't have a lingering existence — the kind I've seen others face who've lost their physical and mental capacities. I don't want any heroic measures taken to save my life. I don't believe in linking somebody up to a mechanical source of life. When death approaches and a person cannot be restored to normal functioning, he or she should be allowed to die.

I've made it well known that I don't want an artificially sustained life. I told my family doctor that I don't want to be kept as Specimen A in a bed, and he understood me. What worries me is the chance I could be in an accident and rushed to the hospital and put on all this stuff before I have a chance to say no. "Could I have it tattooed on my chest?" I asked my doctor who just laughed at me.

I've seen people die and there is a gentle calm which surpasses understanding when you are there and that's what I think dying is. It's part of the mystery.

As for suffering and violence in the universe — if there are imperfections in creation these have come about through growth, genetically or otherwise. It seems to me that the first little cell was created quite perfectly. I don't know why the elephant steps on the mouse except it does. And I don't know why the very same recipe can produce scones that are hard and flat and another time the scones are quite nice. I don't know why this happens. Some things just happen, and animals kill as their method of survival — it's just built into their function.

I don't think God brings about suffering. God would much prefer there wasn't suffering. The suffering comes because something goes wrong *after* creation — it's part of the freedom that each being or creature has. I can't conceive of a God who is all powerful, sitting up on high with a detailed plan, ignoring our suffering. But again, I lack the words to describe this Mystery.

A short but loving marriage

By Helen Simpson as told to Joan Mason

Jim Tanner and I bought this apartment together in Victoria in 1992 — it was our dream place and that's why it is the size it is. When I moved here, it was hard to leave the garden but it was a new adventure. I thought we would have a very happy time together; we had all these plans about places he was going to show me in the B.C. Interior, but it didn't work out. You accept things as they come along. Sometimes you can mourn forever but I couldn't see that. It was just an episode in the road of life.

Jim had been our neighbour for 30 years. We started to square dance together as two couples. Ken and I had been dancing since

1958, and Jim and his wife Mary started to learn. The four of us square danced together for 10 years. Then Mary was unable to dance because of her arthritis, and Ken couldn't dance because of his sight. Both of them felt isolated with having to stay home. For a time, Jim and I would commiserate with one another, and he would visit with Ken and I would visit with Mary.

Then, one morning, he came downstairs to find Mary had died overnight. After Mary's death, Jim kept hanging around, and finally asked me to go for a drive and a couple of picnics. My husband, Ken, had also died by this time. Jim talked about going on a cruise and I suggested going on the boat from Campbell River for four days. He decided that we should go on a cruise and he came back the next day and said we are going to Alaska. I said, "No, I can't accept that from you." He replied, "Of course you can — you mean that much to me." So, I decided that maybe I could.

Helen Simpson and Jim Tanner on a cruise

We went on a seven-day Alaska cruise and explored every stop. He had been in the full-time Navy and we had a second dinner seating and sat at the back of the ship just enjoying the scenery and the silence. We met the nicest people and had a lovely time.

Jim had enlisted in the Navy on the West Coast in the late '20s, was married in 1932 and had daughters Joan in 1933 and Marie in 1934. Then he was posted to Halifax when his wife was pregnant with their third child, Harvey. His first wife died at 34 years of age of a type of leukemia leaving him with three children aged 14, 13 and 6. After a few years, he married Mary, the sister of his first wife.

Jim and I married on May 31, 1992. We knew that Jim had

bone marrow cancer. In an appointment with the oncologist prior to our marriage, the specialist said it could activate in two, three or five years. Jim collapsed just five days after the wedding and had to be hospitalized for a week. After he came home, the long term care people came in and told me that because I had given so much volunteer time and energy to the community, it was time for me to receive some help and we were provided with home support three hours a day, five days a week.

I nursed Jim for the five months until his death and became acquainted with all the people who came to help us. Shannon, the home support worker who was here four days a week, was a dear. She did everything except window cleaning and scrubbing floors and took Jim for a walk each day.

Before he died, Jim said to me that Joan, his daughter would always be there for me and she has been. Marie, his other daughter, lives in Ucluelet, B.C., and keeps in touch. The day that Jim died, I said to my stepdaughter, Joan, "My life is over." She said, "No, Helen, you are going to bounce back."

Bob Stobie, when he was minister at First United, was the only person with whom I discussed my marriage to Jim Tanner. He often dropped in on a late afternoon after making calls. He understood that our wedding ceremony had been conducted by Bert Forsyth with whom we had square danced and that Jim's funeral service was taken by the Navy chaplain because of Jim's long naval service.

I went to church a year later and Bob spoke that morning about Moses climbing the hill and never getting across the water. I couldn't take it as that day was my birthday and the first anniversary of Jim's death. I waited until everyone had left the vestibule and burst into tears. I think that was my first public breakdown.

Church was a real solace to me during stressful times like this, but I couldn't have managed without doing my "daily thoughts." I felt very ignored by the church, however, after Ken died as I wasn't contacted until a year later. We were simply not doing enough follow-up after bereavement, nor follow-up after christenings either. That's why I got involved with the Pastoral Care Committee after a while.

Pastoral care is now recognized as being a necessary part of the church. To me, pastoral care means working with people because they need you. It's still a challenge getting out to people, though, given the numbers on our roll.

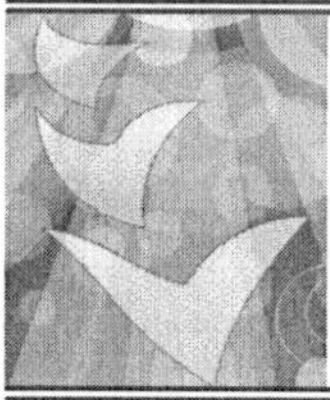

On losing my husband

Excerpt from *Finding Gold In My Memories* by Madge Struthers as shared with Barbara Robertson

After many years of declining health, my husband George had a massive stroke in May 1991. He was hospitalized at the Royal Jubilee in Victoria where the nurses were very supportive of the things I was doing, like taking him for a walk in his wheelchair each day and reading him all the mail. He was transferred to a nursing home in July, and it was downhill after that. We could never quite understand why he was sent there in the first place, for he was unable to swallow and the staff didn't seem to know he was diabetic.

Madge and George Struthers, 53rd wedding anniversary, 1989

My daughter, Elaine, and I tried to celebrate our 55th wedding anniversary with George on July 8. We took him in his wheelchair out to the lovely little retreat behind the lodge and showed him family pictures and took a few photos. He seemed to brighten a little when his picture was taken. Three days later, we thought he'd had another stroke, and the ambulance came and found him in bad shape. He was dehydrated and suffering from pneumonia so he was rushed to the hospital.

Elaine and our son, Jim, were magnificent during this time. Jim took his dad on a chaise longue type of wheelchair for a walk and spent time on the lawn reading the Bible to his dad. Elaine, always full of compassion, talked to her dad, although we never knew if he recognized us or heard anything we said, but we didn't want to take chances. In fact, Elaine was the last person to talk to her dad.

Elaine and I spent all day at the hospital on August 15. Elaine suggested I go home around 6 p.m. and she stayed until about 8 p.m. She had just arrived home when word came from the hospital that George had taken Elaine's advice. Her last words when she left her dad were, "You can go now Dad. We'll take care of Mom."

Our life together for 55 years was an interesting and challenging affair, and George and I never ceased to be thankful for the opportunities we had, and how we had been influenced by our many friends in every charge we were fortunate enough to serve.

Perhaps it would be nice to hear what George himself had to say about our partnership in his speech to the B.C. Conference of the United Church after 50 years of ministry (1935-85).

> *I thank you for this opportunity to express my appreciation to the United Church of Canada for receiving a brash young immigrant into its fellowship, back in the fall of 1929 and making, at least, a conventional cleric out of him. My arrival in the land of promise was marked by the crash on Wall Street and the birth of the Great Depression, but instead of riding the rods or patronizing the soup kitchens and the relief camps of the Dirty Thirties, as countless numbers of my generation of youth were obliged to do — by the grace of God and but for the good offices of the United Church — I was able to spend the next six years furthering my*

education and preparing for the ministry.

I will always be glad that I arrived out west in time to make the acquaintance of the early prairie pioneers. They were a worthy breed of hard-working folk who had the caring heart that made gentle the rugged physique. What an inspiration it was to meet with them on Sundays in the local schoolhouse, where the seats cramped our bodies but a goodly fellowship made glad our spirits.

I celebrated the first anniversary of my ordination by getting married on July 8, 1936, and so began an adventure in partnership that down across the years has been abundantly blessed. Every pastorate we have served has been a thrilling chapter, full of the encouragement of success as well as the disciplines of failure. The ministry has changed greatly since I entered it, of course — the husband and wife partnership and the team ministries of today are undoubtedly more efficient and effective than we were in the horse and buggy days of our youth.

But I am grateful still that my ministry was served in an age when, while my power base may have been in the pulpit, still it derived much of its real relevance from one who was known throughout the parish as the "gracious lady of the manse."

The gift of new life

Excerpt from *Finding Gold In My Memories* by Madge Struthers as shared with Barbara Robertson

At Easter time in 2000, our minister at First Metropolitan in Victoria, Allan Saunders, wrote a letter about the meaning of Easter. Not the sunny chicks, eggs in a basket or chocolate eggs that most of us think of at Easter time. He suggested that when we allow the real meaning to take hold of us, we discover that we also are raised to a fullness of life.

With this message on my mind, I thought of my life as it has unfolded. I discounted what I thought when I was 50 — that I hadn't accomplished anything — and realized that the older I became, I knew I believed in the resurrection as a way of being and living in this world (albeit modestly). Resurrection is about receiving all of life, moment by moment, as a gracious gift.

When we think of Easter as a resurrection — a new life — it gives us the courage to live a life of wonder, grace and gratitude. It enables us to renew our lives after perhaps experiencing mundane or difficult moments. I can honestly say every day seems to bring some special encounter that makes my life both interesting and exciting.

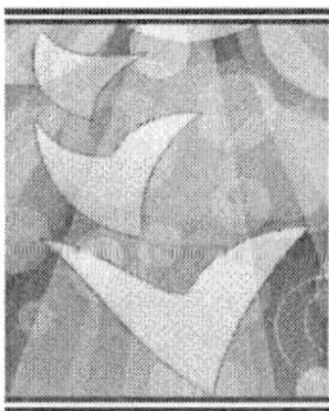

Attack on America: 9/11

Excerpt from *Finding Gold In My Memories* by Madge Struthers as shared with Barbara Robertson

Sept. 11, 2001:

Today, we are all Americans and we go around in a daze after this attack on our way of life, but terrorism forces us to consider some tough questions. President Bush talks of war, but I am hit with another question. What would war solve? Violence begets violence. History has proved this! What did the war between the United States and Iraq accomplish? Only a Hussein more eager than ever to retaliate.

It feels absolutely surreal as we all try to understand what has happened. Personally, I feel that declaring war on a country is not an option, but the terrorists must be held accountable and justice done. This is just the first day — it's only the beginning of the pain and suffering that will be felt as a continent when all the bodies are found and we question our entire way of life.

Sept. 14, 2001:

A day of mourning has been proclaimed for all those who died during this terrible attack. Many other countries have expressed great sympathy and caring. Canada held services in almost every town and city, and it was wonderful to see 100,000 or more people gathered on Parliament Hill in Ottawa. It was a very fine service — the planners kept religion out of it, and I understood their reasoning although I would have liked to have heard a prayer or two.

As I listened to the day of mourning service in Washington, however, the opposite was true. It was almost identical to what you might hear in a church service put on by the Anglicans, the First Baptists, the Presbyterians, or the United Church. I felt the United States was rather arrogant in shutting out all the other religions — the country was not facing the truth of our global living. Here in Victoria, our minister, Allan Saunders, joined in with a number of other faiths, including the Muslims, in a day of mourning service held in Confederation Park.

Speculation has already centred on Osama Bin Laden as the leader of the attack, but it would be a mistake to label the terrorists as "Muslim." We should not stereotype any race or religion because of the terrible acts of a few evil individuals.

Seeking revenge never works — it only causes more hate, rage and heinous crimes. If we used the money that goes into defense, bombs and guns to feed the hungry and clean up our environment and water, the world would be a different place — and not just for us but for everyone. I don't often define my feelings in such a clear way, but in this case, I felt I couldn't leave the issue alone.

A mixed blessing

By Mary Thomas as told to Edeana Malcolm

I lost my husband three years ago and it was a terrible loss, although it was also a blessing. That sounds so contradictory, but Len was developing dementia and getting so exasperated with himself. He couldn't remember all the things that he'd always done so well, like running the electronic things he'd invested in and loved.

He had surgery in Victoria General Hospital, and our daughter Beth came home and was with us for several days after Len came home, but he was extremely difficult. He was on antibiotics intravenously and kept pulling the tubes out and so on. Beth dealt with him much better than I could. He acted as if she were a nurse because she wasn't normally there.

Then Len was taken to Royal Jubilee Hospital for another surgery. I was standing beside his bed giving him supper on a Monday night, I think it was, and our son, Arthur, was sitting in a chair close by. We'd both been talking to Len when the supper came and I served him his supper. I said to Arthur, "Oh, there's an awful draft. That window must be open behind me." So Arthur got up and closed it. Len had been chilled and had complained about being cold earlier, but he kept throwing the covers off. I think he had pneumonia, and it was pneumonia that took him suddenly.

My sister-in-law, Vi, and I were there that last afternoon. He seemed to be sleeping quietly and we talked across him as he lay in the bed. Then she said it was time to go for dinner. She had just brought me back to my condominium and I was getting out of the car when her phone rang. It was our son, Leonard, asking if my sister-in-law would take me back to the hospital because Dad had just died. So she promptly took me back to the hospital.

Quite a few of us were gathered around his bed, but he had gone. It was a very sad time, but at least he didn't have to go through the dementia. His mother had suffered from it, so we knew what it did to you. That was the hardest part. The kids took over and made all the arrangements for the service.

I am certain that I will see my husband again, and my mother and father and a lot of cousins who are dead. Yes, that's one of the great things about our faith.

NOW IT'S YOUR TURN

Some questions to ponder

- **How have you responded to loss and death in your life?**
- **Who or what protects or comforts you in the midst of grief?**
- **Where do you find sanctuary?**
- **What does "resurrection" and "life after death" mean to you?**

BUILDING A FAITH COMMUNITY

In the core of our being, we yearn for intimacy… we want people to share our lives. We want soul friends. — David Benner

Bingo!

Written by May Deller
as shared with Irene Baddeley

May (Turnbull) Deller outside Hamiota United Church, Man., 1949-50

"Who's this?" I say to nobody in particular because I am the only one in the room. It is early on a sweltering Monday afternoon in July. I stand barefooted in the living room of our little bungalow with my arms full of baby diapers and other related items needed when you have two babies to care for.

I thought I'd heard a vehicle approaching when I'd been out collecting the dried wash from the clothesline at the back of the house. Since there are two houses in our farmyard and I was not expecting company, I had paid little attention to the car that now pulls up before our gate rather than across the road at my mother- and father-in-law's yard. I hurriedly toss the wash on to the sofa asking myself as I do so, "Where on earth have I left my shoes?"

Shoes? What shoes? They are nowhere in sight. I glance out the window of the living room trying to gauge the amount of time I have before the unexpected guests knock on the door. Too late! They are already through the gate and approaching the house. I recognize them instantly.

"What brings them here in haying weather?" I wonder. Why, one of them has national recognition for his Black Angus cattle, and the other prides himself on being the best organized farmer in the district. They wouldn't make social calls in haying weather, yet here they are. Such a hot day to be dressed in black suits and ties no less! This is not a social call, of that I am sure. They mean business. I am to be confronted by elders of our local United church in which I have been active since my arrival in the community three years ago. I know in a flash what they have come about.

You know how it is, don't you, when at a time of reckoning, your life can flash before you in an instant? Well, my recent sinful past flashes before me all right.

It is the past Saturday. Two bachelor neighbours and my husband have been loading and stacking hay together on our farm. Thundershowers put a stop to their efforts around five o'clock, which brings all three to the house to escape the rain. I quickly produce an early supper.

As we eat, conversation ranges all over the map until big Jim in an inspirational moment remarks, "Hey, that big blackout bingo's going on in the fairgrounds in town tonight. Let's go."

"Can't," says younger Jim with his mouth full. "Heavy date tonight. Dance."

"Bill?"

"Naw. Guess not. May doesn't believe in gambling. Church says it's wrong," replies my husband, glancing at me.

"Aw, come on May. What's it going to hurt, just this once?" big Jim persists appealing to me with his ever-ready charm and persuasiveness.

A moment of weakness, then decisively, I announce, "I think I will. We know a family that has been hit really hard lately. I'll go and win the thousand dollar blackout for them." (That would certainly justify my straying from the straight and narrow, wouldn't it?)

Before 7 p.m. there we sit with hundreds of cars arranged in rows around the fairgrounds racetrack. Our two-month-old daughter, fed and ready for sleep, snuggles tucked up in her blankets beside me and our two-year-old sleeps like an angel, curled up on the back seat of the car.

Two bingo cards each are all we figure we can handle. We roll the windows down so that we can hear the numbers as they are called through loudspeakers strategically placed around the grounds. We arrange our cards and markers preparing to tackle this serious task. We're ready to try our luck.

The calling starts. Our ears have to be sharp. The rumble of late evening thunderstorms competes with the caller for attention. The air has cooled. We feel a bit chilly but no matter, we hunker down to the business at hand.

"Under the I–15!" We are on our way.

Game after game goes by. Not our lucky day for sure. But the babes sleep on and excitement builds as we start the final game — the BLACKOUT.

"Under the G–clickety-click! Under the B-5!" on the numbers roll.

"No one out there got a bingo yet?" bellows the caller. "It's time for someone to come up with a full card."

I know it will not be me. I have five numbers left. Too many. Maybe another time. No, I don't gamble, remember?

"Under the N-33." That is one of my numbers.

"Under the O-75." Another one of my numbers.

"Under the B-19." A third one, only two to go!

"Come on out there! Someone must have a bingo by now! Under the B-2!"

One more to go. This is unbelievable! "Oh, please let my luck hold," I plead silently.

"Under the G-53!"

'BINGO!" I yell. "Honk the horn, Bill! Honk the horn. Turn on the headlights!"

"Are you sure?"

"Never mind 'are you sure'!" I shout. "Just lean on the darn horn!" I order as I bend across the baby to lean on it myself. "Turn on the lights, turn on the lights!" Startled from sound sleep, the little ones cry out. I frantically try to comfort them.

Over come the officials. "Yes sirree! Here's our big winner folks!" and my name blares over the loudspeaker while car horns all around blow congratulations.

I don't remember any more about that night.

The next morning we head out with my $1,000 cheque. What excitement for the recipient family and for us. Yes, there are strings attached: When they become able, they are to pass the money on to someone else with the same stipulation.

That's the instant flashback, but this is now. These gentlemen are nearing the house. I am tense — not with excitement but apprehension.

A prayer comes from my lips, "God, let us get this over with in a hurry and please keep my babies sleeping for at least another hour!"

"Boy, I'm in for it now!" I mutter as my guilty heart sinks to my boots. "My shoes! Where are my shoes? Forget them; it's too late to find them now," I admonish myself as I wait momentarily for the dreaded knock at the door.

Not forgetting my manners, I greet my visitors warmly, albeit anxiously, and offer them a seat on the sofa. Do I see some corresponding anxiety on their part as they hesitate awkwardly? Of course — the baby laundry! I hastily gather up the offending articles and toss them into the stuffed armchair nearby.

The gentlemen sit stiffly on the sofa, obviously ill at ease. I back into the armchair, sit on top of the laundry, then rise and shuffle it around a little to make room for myself.

Polite conversation ensues (about the weather of course). I excuse myself, retreat to the kitchen, plug in the kettle and prepare tea as rapidly as possible. I do want this visit to be short-lived. "Stay sleeping, my little ones. Stay sleeping," I whisper to myself as I serve my guests tea and cookies. Tea is so useful. Perhaps we will all relax and get the inevitable over with.

Dis-ease stalks the room despite the tea. The men shift their positions often; their teacups rattle in the saucers. I begin to feel more empathy for them. They have their austere Presbyterian principles from their Scottish homeland to uphold. Their job as elders is to oversee the local "flock," one of which has erred grievously and been publicly proclaimed a gambler! (Surely the gateway to perdition to say nothing of the example set for the church's reputation in the community!)

Long embarrassing silences! What to say?

"I might feel more prepared for the forthcoming reprimand," I think to myself, "if I wasn't sitting on the edge of my chair in bare feet and shorts, with baby diapers bunched up behind me and dangling wherever. How can I retain my dignity like this?"

I smile sweetly, swallow another mouthful of tea and take the plunge. "I have the feeling gentlemen that this is not quite a social visit but that you have something more serious to discuss and you're not quite sure how to get started," I offer in the most dignified manner I can muster given the circumstances.

"It wouldn't happen to be about Saturday night's bingo game would it?" I ask them.

Relieved looks pass between the two. (I'll bet they are sweating profusely under all that Sunday-go-to-church apparel, I conjecture to myself. Poor dears.)

One starts to speak, then stops. The other stutters and stops. "Well, come on then," I hear myself saying as encouragingly as I can. "Please, say what you need to say."

Finally one of them blurts out, "Well, yes it is about the bingo game. We know you were there and won the thousand dollars. You are aware, aren't you, that... ." There's a long pregnant pause and embarrassed glances once again.

"Here it comes!" I think, preparing myself as stoically as I can for the forthcoming humiliating lecture.

"Our church... " offers the other hesitantly. "Our church..." another pregnant pause.

"Yes?" I say brightly.

Finally he continues, speaking so rapidly I can scarcely keep up with what he's saying, "Our church, you know," shuffle shuffle, shift shift, "our church purchased an electric organ last year and we wondered if you might consider contributing your winnings to make the final payment on that organ. It would cover it nicely."

He draws a much needed breath, just as a small voice calls

from the bedroom, "Mommy? Mommy?"

"Please excuse me a minute," I gulp. I'm off that chair and into the bedroom in a flash. I shut the door, lift my two-year-old from his crib, hastily tidy him up and dress him, all the while shaking with silent mirth and nervous exhaustion. Gaining rather tenuous composure, I lead him out to the living room, where he grabs me round the bare leg and tries to hide behind me when he sees these strangers.

I manage somehow to stammer a brief reply to my guests' query. They thank me in dignified voices for the tea as they rise and almost trip over each other in their crestfallen haste to depart.

I wait until I see their car drive down the road then I burst into uncontrollable laughter until my stomach hurts and tears run down my cheeks. "Mommy laugh?" queries my son, "Mommy laugh? Funny? Funny Mommy!" and he joins in the moment with laughter of his own.

"Yes, my darling." Still laughing, I gather him in my arms. "It is funnier than you will ever know. Just wait until I tell your daddy this one!"

What I value most in life

By The Rev. Colleen Erb
as told to Terry Dance-Bennink

I value friendship and being connected to people the most. It has a lot to do with the value I place on loving God, your neighbour and yourself. This leads me into ministry wherever I am, including the church, which is why I can't leave the church like some of my friends have done.

Sometimes I'm disgruntled with the church, but this can be a catalyst for change. When I feel out of sorts with the church, I remind myself that I believe in death, life and rebirth. The church follows the same cycle of dying, rising and rebirth — it's all about transformation. I know some people are unhappy with institutional religion. A couple of my friends have left the church completely and haven't found another alternative. But the church is so valuable to me that I can't leave.

The Rev. Colleen Erb delivering a sermon at Sardis United Church, B.C.

There's more than the "temple" here at this church, more than the sermon or the word. Jesus Christ is the founder of our church and he still communicates with us through the body that first gathered so long ago. It's through this body that we connect and link with one another. To cut myself off from the church would be like cutting off the limb of a branch.

A member of the B.C. Conference asked me recently why I was still so involved in the church after having retired in 1993. "I still long to know what's happening in the church and where it's going — how the body is growing, developing and changing," I replied. When I find myself complaining, I tell myself to be more encouraging. It's a hard job ministering to this church.

The church has been my life and the church is still my life and I want to be part of it. I've felt called throughout my life to belong to this church, to be here with my gifts whatever they may be.

If you have a beautiful fireplace with a roaring fire inside it and you take away one of the burning coals and set it apart, it dies. Without the church, no matter how many errors or mistakes it makes, what have you got? The flame goes out. It's like Jesus said. "I am the vine and you are the branches. Abide in me as I abide in you and you will bear fruit." (John 15:5)

I love the way John portrays the church — the body of Christ — as a tree with branches. That's why I've included this passage in my memorial service! The tree is a powerful image of the cycle of life. The branches get knotted, the leaves grow old and fall off, but new life always springs up from the deep roots of the tree.

As I reflect on my whole life, I would hope that I'd be honoured for my faithfulness to God, to the church, to humanity and to life. I cherish life, and especially my life with God, the church, family and friends. I've been honoured for other things in my life like my gifts as a pianist and singer, but the focus of my life has been to answer the call to be faithful to God, my neighbours and myself.

A Christian upbringing

By Ruth Howell as told to Edeana Malcolm

I certainly am grateful for the influence on me of very Christian parents. I was brought up in a Christian home and attended Sunday school and other Christian groups which influenced me for the rest of my life.

My mother sang in the choir. She had a very good voice. So did my sister; for years, even up to the time she passed away, she sang in the choir at church. I didn't have the same musical ability that she had, but I'm also fond of music. In my teens I sang in the church choir at Knox Presbyterian Church, which was on Stanley Avenue then, a couple of blocks from my home. I was 17 when we moved to First United Church. That was when the United Church began in 1925.

Looking back on my life I realize my Christian upbringing meant an awful lot to me. I still think of my Sunday school teachers with affection and am very glad I had them in my life. They were wonderful women. I know I'm repeating myself, but I feel that the Christian influence has a lot to do with the bringing up of children. It's all too easy in today's world for children to get involved in things like gangs.

Practise what you believe with joy!

Written by Helen Mau as shared with Cyndi Frame

The church has meant many things to me. It's a place for worship and a place to learn more about my spiritual life. It's a community of people with a faith who have the opportunity to develop and use their talents together be they gifts in conversation, leadership, character, badminton or friendship.

I think the key to building a true community of faith depends on how much leaders and members practise quite consistently what they believe and in a joyful manner!

I've been connected to many different faith communities over the years. When I lived in Guelph as a child in 1926, I felt deeply connected to St. Andrew's Presbyterian Church. I especially enjoyed the John McCrae Bible Class and CGIT. John McCrae was a member of St. Andrew's Church before World War I and during the war he wrote the famous wartime poem, "In Flanders Fields," which we all had to memorize in English classes in high school.

As a teenager in Sunday school with 100 students and my father as leader, I suggested to a popular male teacher, Mr. Frank Braucht, that we should have a coeducational class for those of us who were in high school and that we should meet in the gallery of

Helen Mau with First Met friends

the church. He agreed to this, and we decided that our class should have a name. We had raised money for a brass plaque to be put on John McCrae's pew so that the church would always remember him. So we decided to call our Bible class, the John McCrae Bible Class.

Frank Braucht taught trades in the Guelph Collegiate Vocational Institute. He was a Boy Scout leader in Guelph and a leader of a popular boys' camp in Algonquin Park. Frank was once named Man of the Year in Guelph. He was brown as a berry in white shorts with a balding head encircled with white curly hair and had a great sense of humour.

When I was working at Bigwin Inn, he came to visit me and asked me to come down to the dock after work for a chat, which I did. I was wearing my white uniform and he asked me to sit down with him and his friend. He knew I would sit in a puddle of water in the dark! I last saw Frank in a nursing home in Guelph and he gave me a bear hug at age 98.

When I lived in Toronto, I was deeply connected to the Eglinton United Church community where I taught Sunday school. We offered an excellent program on the life of Paul with a short movie and specific questions for study before each class meeting. I was also a regular member of our church badminton club.

I lived and taught in Ridgetown, Ont., for one year and Geraldine Boone and I were leaders of a CGIT group of about 30 teen women. We were responsible for the church service one evening, so I ended up leading the worship service from the pulpit. This gave me an appreciation for the work of a minister who must be prepared, knowledgeable and natural when delivering a sermon from the pulpit.

Once I retired to Victoria, I became active in First United Church when the Rev. Bob Stobie was the minister. When First and Metropolitan amalgamated, I was involved in the choice of a new minister — the Rev. Dr. Allan Saunders — along with Sheila MacDougall and Doreen Loosmore. I also served on the executive of the UCW. I wrote and illustrated a history of the

UCW at First United since 1925, which is now in the church archives and an unbound photocopy is in the church library.

Fred Martens and I wanted to improve the use of the lower levels of First United and were involved in helping the Intercultural Association move into the basement of our church. I enjoyed arranging an annual UCW tea for as many as 40 members of the Intercultural Association as our guests. We wanted our UCW members to learn about the differences in family life in other parts of the world.

The joys and challenges of amalgamation

By Sheila MacDougall
as told to Terry Dance-Bennink

Once I decided to join Metropolitan United Church, I soon became an active volunteer. Joan Dowse phoned me one day and asked if I'd like to be the chairman of the Ministry and Personnel Committee. I said, "Yes, I think so." "You would?!" she cried. She wasn't used to someone agreeing so quickly to head up a committee! So I started attending board meetings, and amalgamation soon topped our agenda.

Prior to amalgamation, we held many focus groups to talk about what we wanted in our new church. We decided that we wanted to "attract" people and then "integrate" them into the church. Our next goal was to "transform" people in order to "send" them out into the world. We made lists of what was required under each category.

After much discussion, Metropolitan and First United both agreed to sell their respective churches. We had a bidder — the Conservatory of Music — who wanted one of the two churches, and we agreed to let them decide. A lot of tears were shed on the day we learned that Metropolitan had been sold.

Metropolitan, in my opinion, is a beautiful church with

excellent acoustics. We never dreamed it would be the one chosen, but the Conservatory needed a facility in which to teach music, and Metropolitan had already been zoned as a school.

Both churches had agreed to abide by whatever decision the Conservatory made. But for those who'd been born into Metropolitan and married and raised their children in this church, it was a very hard decision to accept.

"Yes, we sold our church, but we invaded the other one!" I told one woman. "Nobody ever admitted that before!" she replied.

We came to our new church ready to work. There weren't huge cultural differences between the two churches, although First United had Presbyterian roots and Metropolitan had Methodist roots prior to the creation of the United Church. It was ridiculous, however, to have two big United churches two blocks apart, both with a dwindling membership, so we agreed to come together.

Early challenges

We experienced a number of challenges during the early days. Trying to merge two different ministerial teams and office systems was one of the biggest challenges. We had a minister at Metropolitan during our first year as an amalgamated church who was convicted on a sexual abuse charge. He was a great teacher and counsellor and many people loved and trusted him. But some of our members felt deeply betrayed and traumatized by his behaviour. Despite all this upheaval, we continued to integrate the ministry teams at both churches.

Our next challenge was to undertake the physical renovations of our new church and this, too, caused some controversy. Not everyone agreed with the proposed redesign, but we seem to be relatively happy today with the changes that were made.

The organ was also an issue. We had to decide whether to renovate the existing organ or buy a new one. We decided to save money and, under the leadership of our choir director, to buy an electronic organ. Everyone had access to all the information which made it a very democratic process.

What to do with the space in the basement was the next hot issue. After much debate we opted to house the Intercultural Association which has been very good for the church.

Despite all these challenges, I'm proud of our church. We've done well, even though we're not perfect. I find it interesting that after all our various upheavals, we're back to the governance model we started with. We originally intended to create separate teams such as property and finance with representatives coming together in a management team. But we decided at a certain point not to have these teams, leaving individuals in charge of areas like property and finance. These individuals began to orchestrate what Council should be doing which was not our original intent.

Today, we have separate teams and a representative from each team sits on Council with management reporting to Council, which is a much better model. We also had a congregation chairman in the early days who'd chair various forums. We haven't gone back to this role yet, but I hope we do as it allows people to air their questions and get answers.

What I'm most proud of is the fact we managed to work together without any serious breakdown of communication and social ties. Most teams worked extremely well together. Irene McDonald, for example, stepped up to the plate and said she thought the merged UCW units could handle all the funeral receptions for a while, relieving the Pastoral Care Committee of this responsibility. The UCW handled this for four years which was wonderful.

Sheila MacDougall and Irene McDonald, friends for life

We don't hear much any more of, "Well, at Metropolitan

or First, we used to… ." We have a lot of new members now, as quite a few people have joined since amalgamation.

Listening comes first

My advice to other congregations contemplating a merger is to listen to one another first and foremost. An amalgamation team is also very important. The orchestration of the sale of the buildings was handled very well and in a way that could be accepted by everybody. Property and money can be touchy subjects.

We also had to resolve the issue of choir masters, because we had two choir directors at the beginning. They got along well together, but some of the choir members had more difficulty. The young male director decided to move on, and Frances Pollet remained our choir director.

First Met has moved along with the times. In 1988, there were terrible eruptions in many United churches over the issue of sexual orientation, but we resolved it. We were also ahead of ourselves in how we handled the leadership of our Sunday school. Some members felt all we needed was a volunteer, but despite repeated efforts on my part, I couldn't entice any volunteers to step forward to lead the Sunday school. Many churches had begun to pay their Sunday school superintendents, and it was time for us to explore this option.

When Megumi Matsuo Saunders expressed a desire to take it on, it was a great solution. We've never looked back. The Sunday school is like a mini church — the children come and go. Megumi doesn't have the same kids three Sundays in a row, because they've got all kinds of other commitments. That's just the way it is.

I'm proud of how we've moved into today's world. We've been a bit slow in fundraising, but the stewardship campaign last year was a big success. The move to paying for roles that were formerly filled by volunteers horrifies a few people, but times have changed. Take hospitality for example. Our women used to clean the kitchens and prepare the food, but today, many women are either working or they've retired. Just because we did it a certain way 50 years ago doesn't mean we have to do it the same way today.

I've always been interested in new ideas. Our core values, however, haven't changed. We remain loyal to our Christian roots and the Bible stories.

An exemplary amalgamation

By Irene McDonald
as told to Terry Dance-Bennink

During my retirement years, I became more involved with the United Church and especially the UCW. I'd joined First United in 1969, but when we amalgamated with Metropolitan United in the mid '90s, I found it a trying time. I felt discouraged sometimes, because I'd been chair of the Ministry and Personnel Committee and wondered how we were going to meld the two ministry teams.

One of our ministers also became involved in a court case during this period. I thought he was an exceptional minister in the pulpit, so I felt very disheartened and let down by this development, not just by the person involved, but by the national office of the United Church. All of these matters are well documented, so I won't go into them here. It was a time of forgiveness and reconciliation. Without forgiveness, there can be no reconciliation.

The merging of UCW units was exemplary. My unit amalgamated with a Metropolitan unit and we chose the name Harmony for the new unit which reflected our feelings. We did everything we could to bring harmony within the congregation. I was sure that when we amalgamated, the new church would be located at Metropolitan.

I was quite overwhelmed when I learned the location was First Church. I felt that the people from Metropolitan would be

First Met UCW friends, 2003

terribly sad to leave such a gorgeous sanctuary, and my heart went out to them. I would have felt much more comfortable going into their sanctuary than they, perhaps, felt entering ours.

I was president of the UCW at our church for six years, and I'm very proud of the fact the UCW provided the hospitality for all the funerals and memorial services held at the church. Whenever there was an occasion to provide refreshments for 40 up to 400 people, I was in charge of organizing the hospitality which was quite a challenge. At first, we used to do our own baking, but after amalgamation, we bought the food and tried to set it up in whatever manner the family wished, using a silver tea service or simply coffee mugs. We attempted to be of comfort to the family.

On the 125th anniversary of Canadian confederation in 1993, I received an unexpected honour when I was presented with the Commemorative Medal for Volunteerism by the Right Honourable Raymond Hnatyshyn. Being a volunteer has its joys and sorrows, and I will continue to help where needed, even though I'm 91 years old.

Still room for change

I sometimes wonder why I've remained in the United Church. I really do. The church has evolved in the last 60 years and it has grown into what is commonly referred to as a "faith community."

I believe the emphasis should be placed on the *Christian* aspect, for faith can be so broadly based. The United Church is a Christian faith community, so when the church takes on the role of political action, it should do so from a Christian perspective.

The United Church, I think, is still in a conventional faith mode in its Sunday school curriculum. I wonder if much has changed in the teaching of the birth, death and resurrection story since I was in Sunday school?

When I sit in the pews on Sunday morning with my fellow members, I feel I'm not the only one who questions the bodily resurrection of Christ. People bring their intellect and knowledge with them to a Sunday service. The idea of someone coming back to life is questionable — unless, in fact, they weren't dead to begin with.

So what does the Resurrection mean to me? Life resurrects itself. Anyone who grew up on a farm sees this all the time. The grain grows, the seed appears, it falls into the ground, another crop sprouts up and you do everything you can to select the best seeds for re-planting to ensure the cycle continues. But do I think my life is going to be resurrected in this way? I don't think so.

After I die, my cells aren't going to be resurrected in the form they once were. But each person leaves an imprint, a ripple on the surface of life which continues on.

I think all churches need to take a look at their commitment for good and assess whether some of their activities should be done by the world's people, not just the church. World governments and international courts should exercise a greater influence over every nation.

Our Mission and Service work and local housing projects like Our Place are laudable, but we are simply keeping a finger in the dike. We're not solving the root of the problem, which requires the whole community to act, not just a small group of Christians.

If you look at the demographics of Canada, it seems unlikely that the United Church of Canada will survive due to the number of people entering the country from other cultures, religions and faith communities. The number of people who are Christian-oriented is shrinking in proportion.

The Christian faith will never die — there will always be a Christian faith — but we have to recognize that across Canada we have many churches closing for lack of funds at a time when the Canadian economy is strong. We have to ask ourselves why. I think it's because the Church is not fulfilling its purpose to its individual members, namely, care of the soul. We have become too busy with "busy things."

I'm not a theological scholar, but I'd like to see a greater message delivered from the pulpit and quieter harmonies in our hymns: more care of the soul. Our choirs do a good job of capturing the soul of music but lately, our hymns often resemble campfire songs.

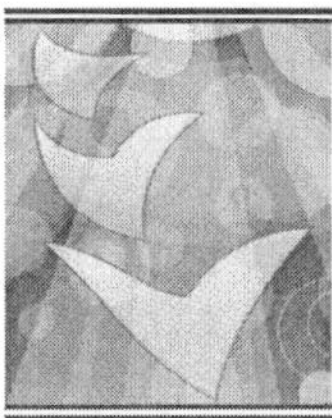

From babies to girls to elders

By Helen Simpson as told to Joan Mason

No longer was the mystery of communion hidden, when my sister, Dorothy, and I became part of Dr. Wilson's communicants class of 1928 at First United. I never had a chance to be involved in a girls' group such as CGIT because we lived out in Saanich and my father didn't have a car until 1925.

When I was 17, my parents sent me to the Young People's Society at First United. For a whole year, I sat and looked on and made no attempt to belong to the larger group of 175–200 people ranging in age from their late teens up to their 40s. Finally, I made some friends.

I assumed responsibility for the Nursery Department at our church from 1938 to 1944 and had a wonderful pool of young women, including my sister, Muriel, who acted as helpers with the two- to four-year-olds while their parents attended church. The ladies' Cradle Roll group worked with us and prepared the annual Christmas Party.

From babies, I went on to Intermediate Girls. In the late '60s, we tried an experiment with team teaching. Aldyth Swainson and I had the 12-year-olds, Jean Fields and Alice Waddell the 13-year-olds, and Donna Denike and Jean Goulson the 14-year-olds. We met together to prepare the lessons every two weeks. It was a wonderful experience.

Although I was never a member of the Women's Association, from time to time I took on a number of special projects. In the Rev. Hugh Hunter's time, Aldyth Swainson, Daisy King and I pledged to assume responsibility for organizing the catering of congregational events for a period of three years. To keep expenses down, we used volunteers to make the sandwiches and asked church members to bring squares for dessert.

Looking back now after having stepped down from five years' responsibility on the Pastoral Care team, I feel I graduated from babies to girls to the congregation as a whole and finally to the elderly in my church involvement.

Camp Pringle is born

About the time Ken and I were married, I was asked if I were interested in becoming a CGIT leader. I decided that since the young people were looking for activities and church was our lifeblood, I would get involved. Leona Aitken was a member of a group when I was a leader during the Rev. Moir Waters' ministry. I met some wonderful people through CGIT, especially at church camps. That for me was *the* thing to do. Most United church camps at that time were held at Camp Thunderbird or Ocean Park or Cultus Lake.

I was on the Conference and Presbytery camp committees as well as being connected with CGIT. In 1950, we were looking for property suitable for a campsite. The first time we visited the property that is now Pringle, it was rather boggy, having rained heavily for a week. We had a very strong camp committee in

Victoria and started to build the camp from 1952 on. We had a work party in there every Saturday morning from Good Friday to July 1st to get the camp ready.

Bob McKinnon, who had also been a secretary in the YMCA War Service, and I would start with a list on Monday night and phone every single church in the area to get volunteers for the weekly Saturday work party. In 1952, Mother looked after my daughter, Pat, who was a year old, and I was up there the whole summer with my four-year-old daughter, Elizabeth. My husband, Ken, used to come up twice a week and bring the orders of day-old bread and other supplies in the car. It was a horrible gravel road in those days.

I lived there as camp manager in 1957 when the Rev. Laura Butler came for the first time as director of the intermediate girls. I also met Aldyth Swainson when she came to Camp Pringle in 1952 as a leader in the Girls' Camp, and we've done things together ever since.

The Sewing Club (1937–1992)

The Sewing Club, 1977

A group of us from Young People's found we had much in common and when two of us were expecting in 1937, we decided to invite some of our friends to do our embroidering and knitting together — and the Sewing Club was born! For most of us, it was a link that provided support and many years of friendship.

The Sewing Club met every two weeks in one of the members' homes. We developed our own baked specialties (none too elaborate) and together learned new crafts and sampled new recipes. We bore our babies, married them off and welcomed the grandchildren. We lost two members in the earlier years, one due to an aneurysm and the other due to breast cancer.

I was always involved with babies. Olive and Ed Smith had three boys. When Olive delivered twins and their son, Murray, was just 15 months old, she needed help. Ed was working as the head pharmacist at the Jubilee Hospital and worked Saturdays.

So I would bike over to the Smiths on Lincoln Road on Saturdays and help Olive bathe the three younger children. That done, we would roll the washer out into the middle of the kitchen floor, put through the laundry and then attach the hose and drain the water down the back steps to the vegetable garden. The next year, I helped Reita and Gordon Robson when they had their first baby.

The Sewing Club stayed together as a group from 1937 to 1992 and we never had an argument. The group got down to seven women. In later years, three of the group had dementia and it was hard visiting them. Olive Smith and Elsie Simmonds died in 1989 and 1990 and four more died during the 1990s. It was the strength of the friendships in that group that meant so much to me and made me what I am today. I have been gifted all my life with wonderful people who helped me in so many different ways.

Life in a manse in the '30s

Excerpt from *Finding Gold In My Memories* by Madge Struthers as shared with Barbara Robertson

I've always been thankful that our first charge (ministerial assignment) after we got married was Sovereign, Sask., in 1936. We spent six happy years in this community which had about 100 residents when we arrived.

Our first manse in Sovereign, Sask., 1936

We got our drinking water by the pail from a well three blocks away from the manse. The school was just across from us on the next street, and a grocery store, post office, hardware and butcher shop were on the main street. We could buy meat for 10 to 15 cents a day. Our salary when we started was $1,100 a year.

We were truly welcomed as bride and groom and had to get used to being addressed as "Mr." and "Mrs." Struthers and having a beautiful manse to live in with everybody coming and going. The large glassed and screened veranda was used for many things.

Before the war, the kids came over from school at noon and played ping pong on that veranda. On a rainy day, a local woman would go out on the road and pick a tub full of mushrooms and bring them to our veranda for people "to come and get it" and they did.

After the war, we set up two quilt frames and another frame in the dining room for quilters who came whenever they could spare a few hours. Many came in the morning around 10 a.m. with a sandwich and I'd make tea at noon. We didn't have a washing machine for a year or two, so we used tubs and a plunger and hung our clothes outside to dry. In wintertime, our clothes became like stiff boards, and at least once, George was phoned and told his underwear was hanging upside down.

We really had quite a lot of company: people passing through the town or speakers at the school or community hall were frequent house guests at the manse. When Dr. Schnell made his rounds for the Bible Society, he came in limping one day.

"Madge, my feet are killing me, can I soak them?" he asked me. Out came the Epsom salts and a basin of nice warm rain water and his groans of pleasure were something else.

The Sovereign people were very active in the church and our Young People's Society, in fact, became quite famous. Sixty-five of them came regularly for Sunday evening meetings — some from as far away as 10 miles arriving by horse and sleigh. The big event remembered to this day by those who were there was the New Year's Eve Dance put on by the young people — quite a dress-up affair. Honorary patronesses welcomed the dancers as they entered the hall. We heard that the bootleggers from Rosetown were dismayed when they were not allowed in to sell their wares.

At 11:30 p.m., everyone marched up the street to the church where my husband, George, conducted a "watch night service." The church was packed to the gills. At midnight, I played the chimes to bring in the New Year, and then all of us — Catholics, Lutherans and United church members — returned happily to the hall for refreshments.

In the Dirty Thirties we had to make our own fun and we did. A young music teacher and I put together a minstrel show in Sovereign and toured other towns as well. We also put on three-act plays, the most famous of which was "The Ghost of Spooky Tavern." Just before my son, Grant, was born, I was asked to sing at a concert in the hall, so I sang "Mighty like a Rose," which some people still remember.

On my parents' anniversary, I travelled to Saskatoon for the celebration with my two-year-old son along with other relatives. On the return trip home, a heavy snowstorm came up and we were stranded for 12 hours covered in snow. Divine providence must have been with us for around 9 a.m., we heard shovels scraping the road and digging us out.

Our first car

We had stopped in front of the only building on that stretch of road 40 miles from Biggar on the way to Rosetown. The building was a store owned by a couple who invited us all in (we must have been 30 in total) and they were terrific. They offered us all coffee, toast, a boiled egg, cheese and jam, and I shared some of the goodies my mom had packed for me before we left. I then understood the parable of the loaves and fishes.

We always had to keep an eye out for the weather in Saskatchewan, especially in the winter. During our term at the town of Sceptre, six of our United church women drove to Gull Lake one day to attend a presbytery banquet. We set out in a car driven by Mrs. Mahaffy, but the road was not gravelled in those days. As we crossed a narrow road over a large slough, we all held our breath as Mrs. Mahaffy kept us on the straight and narrow, but as we climbed the rather steep hill on the other side, we discovered the mud had congealed around the wheels and we were stuck.

Never mind, we had five ladies who took off their shoes and stockings and we pushed the car up the hill! All this activity made us a little late for the banquet, and we caused a stir when we entered with our shoes and stockings in our hands and walked through to the back where we washed our feet. In some ways, it smacked a little of biblical times.

The train's arrival brings relief

During the '30s, most people needed a leg up and even at Sovereign, we had relief cars coming, dropping off apples from the Annapolis Valley in Nova Scotia and dried cod from Newfoundland. The town had its share of hoboes as we called them, but they could be, after all, your brother or mine. A hobo's life was a rough existence unless he struck a town at harvest time and found a job, usually hard labour and for shockingly low pay. At the manse we had quite a few of these men come to the door for food.

I played many roles as the minister's wife. One night around 1 a.m., a neighbour knocked sharply on our door in quite a state. Her husband needed an enema and she wanted me to come over and give him one! I had worked at the hospital before marrying George so some people pinned the title "nurse" on me. I had all the paraphernalia at home, however, so I followed her up the lane and it went off without a hitch.

On another night, we heard a rather timid knock on our door around 2 a.m. and a little child's cry. On opening the door, we found a little girl from many blocks away on the outskirts of town. I think she was about five years of age and had woken up to find her parents missing. She was very cold and had put her galoshes on and a coat over her nightie.

We brought her upstairs and she cuddled with me in our bed. George went up town and checked the house but no one was home. It was the next day before the parents came back and were contacted. Nowadays, they would have been reported to social services, but they were very young and, perhaps, they didn't realize what they'd done.

Many years later, I gave a talk to an open forum of newly graduating ministers who wanted to know about life in a manse. Quite a few of the students were married long before they went into the ministry; they'd been longshoremen or fishermen, so the lads and their wives were not acquainted with manses.

They'd been sent on a student mission field trip and were shocked to find everybody in town staring out of their windows at them when they arrived, and when they went into the manse, to find, horror upon horror, apple sauce, bacon, eggs, milk and bread in the fridge. They seemed to find it quite embarrassing to say the least.

I told them they had to wake up and recognize they were in a wonderful occupation. "In what other occupation do you find you are loved before you even get there? The local people feel they know you already and are ready to accept you fully. The goodies in the fridge are to welcome you, so you won't have to scramble for groceries on your first night."

When I handed these students their awards later at the University of British Columbia, they were all very chummy. I felt honoured to be asked to share my experience with them.

Friends for life in the UCW

By Mary Thomas as told to Edeana Malcolm

I'm passionate about my church, first and foremost, and the United Church in particular. I find my sanctuary in church, and I find it with some of my friends. I don't have friends now in quite the way that I had when I was younger. Seeing friends is part of going to church and I really enjoy this. I ran into one dear old friend recently when we were going in and saw others to just speak to briefly.

I remember when we were youngsters how my mom always enjoyed meeting friends at church, and we, of course, enjoyed seeing the other children with whom we went to school — it was good to see them at church too.

I feel deeply connected to my UCW group. Several members are close friends and have been for a long time. We were originally called the Doreene McLeod unit, but we got so big we had to split up and became three groups.

What we got from each other was love, as well as assistance in dealing with our children. It was such a relief to find that everybody else had many of the same problems with their children as I did; it helped to talk about how to deal with these issues. That was one of the most important benefits, I think, when I first joined the group.

Mrs. McLeod was the person who urged me to join; she was the one who originally organized the groups. It was wartime and a lot of young women had husbands who were in one or another of the services, either waiting to be called or had been called somewhere away from home. I was in a different situation because I had my husband with me.

Faith: a gift from my parents

By Esther Younie as told to Sheila MacDougall

I was brought up in a Protestant Christian home and faith has always been a part of my life — no blinding revelation — it's just there and will be forever when needed. I've always been a church attendee just as my parents were. They've been the main influence on my life.

My mother was a teacher and received her BA in 1912, and my father grew up on a farm and obtained a degree in agriculture from the University of Guelph. Dad was also a superintendent of the Sunday school and we used to travel with our horse and buggy to Sunday school every week at 10 a.m., followed by the church service at 11 a.m. Sometimes we visited other families after church; many informal friendships developed among those church families.

As a result of my upbringing, I've made church a central part of my life. I'm not a fundamentalist, but I enjoy a formal kind of service. My husband,Watson, and I tried a number of United churches in St. Catharines, Ont. We moved on until we found a welcome and a group we could join. We especially appreciated the couples' clubs. At St. Paul Street United Church, the group drew names and we entertained one another and really got to know people that way.

In Victoria, we tried various churches but finally moved to a downtown church, Metropolitan United. On our first Sunday, we were putting money in the parking meter outside the church when we were intercepted by Jean and Walter Gibson. "You don't need to put money in the meter on Sunday," they told us. "Now let us show you the way into the church."

We were given a warm welcome and soon joined the Actimets. We loved our new friends, some of whom had been in the service like us during the war, and we enjoyed the social events including the bridge club.

Life hereafter is a puzzle. I believe we live in people's memories and pass our genes on to the next generation as those before us have done. As one who is nearly 90 now, I've endured many things, but I feel that life is good and I've had a wonderful life. I've been blessed with good parents, a loving husband and marriage, children of whom I am very proud, and so many great friends.

NOW IT'S YOUR TURN

Some questions to ponder

- **What community of people have you felt deeply connected to?**
- **What does "church" mean to you?**
- **Do you have any stories about your church you wish to share?**
- **What is the key to building a true community of faith?**

THE MANY FACES OF GOD

Every creature is a book about God.
— Meister Eckhart

In the heart of God

Written by May Deller as shared with Irene Baddeley

I've become increasingly aware of the hand of God in all that surrounds me which gives me great joy. It is God or Mystery that has encouraged me to seek the truth wherever it might lead. One of the most significant truths I've learned is that not only do I and all of creation have "God" in our innermost being, but all of creation is in the heart of God. That is a tremendously joyful and satisfying centre with which to "greet the unseen with a cheer" as the poet, Robert Browning, put it.

What nourishes my spirit the most is my relationship with the natural world as well as with human beings. I'm grateful for all the goodness, beauty and truth that breaks in on me every day. For me this has always included the written word and the arts, which I see as a dialogue and relationship with the author, performer and creator.

Faith is a gift that arises from this nourishment. You can read and pray forever and still not "have" or "keep" faith. I do not seek faith; it is a gift.

God is in our midst

By The Rev. Colleen Erb as told to Terry Dance-Bennink

The image of God that speaks to me the most is of a loving, all-embracing presence. God is close, intimate and personal — not something way off in the distance. God is within me, in my heart, a holy place that needs loving attention.

God is also in other people. This morning, for example, during my meditation time, a friend who was quite upset called me. She wanted to retaliate against someone who'd hurt her but knew this was not the best way to react. Our talk together became part of my prayer time this morning. God was in our midst.

I had a close brush with death last year after my stroke and it took me a while to recognize God's face in this scary experience. When I was lying in the emergency room at the Langley Hospital, I never mentioned my role as a retired minister. But when I left the emergency room on Christmas Eve, the nurses came over and hugged me. When I went up to the ward, it was the same thing. When I was finally discharged and went down to say goodbye to the nurses, one of them said to me, "Your work isn't finished yet," as she gave me a big hug.

God kept surprising me during that hospital stay. The nurses were like bright shining lights. I couldn't really see this at the time because I was too busy trying to understand what was happening to my body. I knew in my head that God was there, but in my heart, it was like a dark night. My energy was zapped.

But I do remember awakening to a deep sense of my dad's presence. When I was lying there on the stretcher, he came to me and said, "If you have to come now, don't be afraid, I'm here."

In discussing my stroke later with a trusted friend, she asked me, "Was God in that experience for you?"

"I don't know," I replied. "I prayed for healing but I didn't have a deep sense of God as I'd expected."

When you're dying, you hope to really feel God, but sometimes your physical and mental state may not allow you to experience this. My friend then asked me about the nurses. All of a sudden, I realized that God was there in those caring people: the nurse who helped me to the bathroom, the nurse who reminded me my work isn't finished, even the staff with little bedside manner.

When I went down for a CAT scan on Christmas Day, I told the attendant that I was scared, and she said, "Oh, don't worry, it will be all right." This exchange helped me. It's through these kinds of interactions that God speaks.

God is in the muck with us: that's what I discovered. God didn't cause my illness or the loss of a friendship, but afterwards, I sensed a fuller picture of God's friendship. Everything became more precious and intensely beautiful after this brush with death. All became gift. My friends and family suddenly became much more important to me.

I've always tried to encourage people, but after my stroke, I began to tell my friends and family how wonderful they are — even the people who work in banks and restaurants. I went into a Tim Horton's recently for a coffee and asked the server if anyone had told her what a great job she's doing. She said "No" and started to cry.

So part of my ministry now is with the bank tellers and restaurant servers — to establish a rapport with them and call them by their names. Now that I've retired from most of my committee responsibilities, I'm out in the "marketplace," trying to bring some light into the darkness. Small acts of kindness can lift people to a different plane.

Many routes to God

In my prayer time now, I just sit down and ask God what direction is best. I don't stick with one mode of prayer. I'm flexible and let the Spirit guide me each morning. Sometimes I practice *lectio divina*, a way of meditating deeply on a piece of scripture. I've also explored John Main's approach to Christian meditation using the mantra, *maranatha*, as well as centering prayer. I've read a lot about the mystics like Julian of Norwich, Hildegaard von Bingen and Teresa of Avila.

I've been attracted to many different forms of prayer, but a while ago, none of them seemed to serve my purpose. I needed to change the way I was praying and understand things differently. It's not the experience of prayer that counts but the outcome.

After this insight, I modified my prayer life and relied on various approaches, depending on my need at the time. I like lectio divina because I'm able to focus on what stands out in a scripture passage, chew on it and then write about it. The words become ingrained in my heart and often return to me later on which helps me become more sensitive to God's presence throughout the day.

But sometimes I just ponder the passage and listen to what God is saying to me, and then I write. Sometimes it's just a prayer of quiet. Sometimes I simply pray for direction in the prayer time itself.

When I was having a bad time in my life, I just sat with the music that Joyce Rupp sent me. Sometimes I get the hymnbook out and sing one or two hymns or read the words. Sometimes I cry all the way through my prayer time, like I did after I hurt my back in an accident. God seemed to cry along with me. It was part of my healing and it was powerful.

I'm not bothered by the lack of a fixed routine. It's more creative this way. On Saturdays, I deliberately change my schedule. I may take a Joyce Rupp book or another inspiring book and go to a local restaurant for a coffee and bagel. Or I might go for a walk with my coffee. Sometimes I write my prayers in my journal.

I feel I'm led to do what is needed which is a form of grace. It could be singing, crying, painting or writing. Journal writing, however, is my foundation. I have miles of material in my journals! I fill two or three each year as I reflect on my prayer time and what comes to me during my time alone with God.

Jesus in my life

By The Rev. Colleen Erb
as told to Terry Dance-Bennink

We don't often talk about Jesus these days, but he's a vital presence in my life. Jesus was both human and divine, and his mission was to usher in the kingdom of love on earth, but no one got it! His followers wanted him to be an earthly king — a king on a throne to rule, to battle injustice, to bring peace and to give them food. They didn't understand his mission, but he went ahead anyway.

Is there a difference between Jesus and us? Well, we're human and divine too, and we have the same spark of God inside us. We can choose between good and evil. Jesus had this same freedom, but according to scripture, he didn't succumb to evil, and that's the difference between Jesus and us. He refused to jump off the temple or bow down to Satan or turn stones into bread, because he didn't want people following him for the wrong reasons. He wanted them to follow out of love.

Jesus faced the same temptations we do, but he didn't succumb to evil because his life was steeped in God. He overcame the human desire for power and fame, because he believed so deeply that he and the Father were one. We are one with God, as well, but we are more prone to temptation than Jesus was and to making wrong choices.

Jesus is important in my life because he is the bringer of life. He's a saviour. We don't use this word often nowadays, but Jesus saves us from death and brings us new life. Through his death, his sacrifice, he brings us into union with God. This is old theology and people don't even talk about it today, but I remember sharing this conviction with a class years ago, and they just about left in tears. They'd never heard this before, how Jesus became our sacrifice.

We talk about Jesus reconciling us with God, but what does this mean? Through his death, he interceded for us and brought us into relationship with God. Our sins are forgiven.

I can't accept Tom Harpur's suggestion in *The Pagan Christ* that Jesus didn't exist as an historical figure. I look at the 66 books in the Bible and the four Gospels and ask myself why would anyone bother to compile all this, if there wasn't something real going on? I choose to believe that Jesus lived and walked on this earth as a real human being. He's our hope, for if he can do what he did, so can we. In fact, he predicted we'd do even greater deeds than his.

Jesus was a revolutionary because he stood out against the legal codes of the day. He was revolutionary in his approach to life, in his thinking and acting, and in his stance for good over evil. But he was also a fun-loving man. I think Jesus had a sense of humour! He liked to drink wine and hang out with his friends.

Some people think Jesus was being rude, even catty, when he responded to the woman who asked for bread by saying, "You shouldn't give food to the dogs." She replied, "Even the dogs eat crumbs beneath the table." I think they were simply enjoying a joke together, but not many people see it this way.

I wouldn't be surprised, either, to learn that Jesus was married. It wouldn't bother me a bit. He may have been in love with Mary Magdalene, and she was certainly in love with him. As a human being, Jesus incarnated all forms of love — *filia*, *eros*, and *agape* — not just *agape*.

Jesus was a friend: a friend to children, Zacheus, the tax collectors, his disciples and to his followers today. When he lived on this earth, he cared deeply about his friends and was truly disappointed when they left him high and dry.

The Beatitudes reflect the core values of Jesus. They're not a set of Ten Commandments but speak to the spirit with which we should live our lives. And the parables reveal an image of God (and Jesus) as a companion, a friend and a shepherd to us all.

God seeks and saves the lost. No one is going to be lost or destroyed. Why would we come to the end of our lives only to discover that Jesus is no longer a shepherd? Nothing in life is lost; it's all gathered up into love.

Jesus is light for me. He is also hope, joy, peace and healing. And he's still with us. I'm speaking in the present tense because Jesus *is*!

An answer to our prayers

By Mona Hundleby as told to Terry Dance-Bennink

My son, Glenn, had a close brush with death when he was eight years old, and I certainly felt God's presence then. Glenn was outside playing with a friend in the lane at the back of our house. He went to his friend's home in order to play with his friend's golf equipment. Somehow, Glenn was in the way when his friend swung and missed the ball and then let go of the club. The club hit Glenn's head just above his eyebrow.

A neighbour of mine saw it happen and dashed over to my house and told me to call an ambulance quickly. I went with Glenn to the hospital in the ambulance. They took him up for X-rays and told me to go home as it would be some time before they'd know the results. It was what they would refer to today as a life-threatening injury.

I took a taxi home and discovered my husband, Roy, and daughter, Pat, waiting anxiously for me on the front porch. I told them what had happened, so Roy phoned the hospital for an update. They said a brain specialist from Vancouver just happened to be in Victoria that day attending a meeting and he was operating on Glenn at the time. The hospital staff said they weren't sure Glenn would live.

A neighbour came and sat with us as we waited at home for news. It was after midnight when the hospital finally called. The surgeon had removed six pieces of bone from his brain. That's when I knew our prayers had been answered. I don't remember praying that much before this awful accident, but we sure prayed hard that night. I had a real sense that God had answered our prayers.

When I pray at night these days, sometimes I just say to God, "I think it would be better if you handled this!" Sometimes, when I have good days, I can tell God's looking after me. I'm religious, but I don't preach it. I just try to live it. I also talk things over with Jesus. I talk to both of them — God and Jesus! The message I'm getting these days is that I can't give up. I can still help people in small ways. When I can't do any more for people down here on earth, they'll have me up in heaven.

A sense of Presence

By Sheila MacDougall
as told to Terry Dance-Bennink

Your faith is just a given until something happens in your life which really makes you question it. After my husband, Jack, died, I thought "How can you do this to me, God?" At first, I wondered why that Presence had allowed Jack to die, but I soon realized there was a purpose behind his death, even though it was awful to lose him.

When my son, Ken, died six months later in the same year, my grief was all one. It was too soon after Jack's death for me to process Ken's death. I was numb and Ken's death almost passed by. But in the midst of my grieving, I became aware of that Presence.

I didn't like what was happening to me, but as I waited, I began to see the purpose or the meaning. Having suffered these two terrible deaths in my own life, I became a much better nursing instructor. I was far more compassionate towards my students.

Shortly after their deaths, I started reading about the power of positive thinking and imaging. And I remember a friend of mine who visited me in Regina shortly after Jack's death. She drove up in a truck and said, "I don't know what to say to you, but I'm here." She and I had always talked about everything. I started telling her about the power of positive thinking and my sense that there's something beyond yourself.

I call it God, I've always called it God. You have to have something beyond yourself to believe in: a Presence. I don't believe in the old man in the sky stuff. But a sense of Presence has stayed with me all these years and it's stabilized me. I don't have to say that I believe in this or that, but I do believe there is a Presence, there *IS* a Presence, which orchestrates a lot of what you're up to and helps you.

Sometimes I ask God, "What's that about?" I don't always get a direct answer, but eventually, the answers come. They always have. You can make a mistake, but there's always a reason why you were allowed to make the mistake. So don't worry about mistakes.

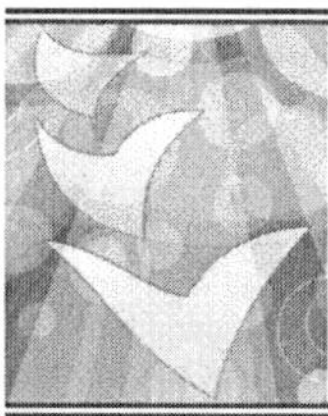

Scripture as story

By Sheila MacDougall
as told to Terry Dance-Bennink

As a child, I understood that some things were just a given: There was a God with a son named Jesus who performed all kinds of miracles. This God was a white man who lived up in heaven — there was never any question in those days that God was male.

As I grew older, my image of God changed. I attended various churches and it was quite a while before I realized that what I thought and felt about God was not necessarily shared by those who sat beside me in the pew.

The Bible, in my view, is a book of beautiful stories, some factual and some enhanced, because the writers want you to get the point, the big picture. It doesn't matter how factual the stories are. I enjoy meeting Hindus and Muslims who have their own sense of that Power beyond them. I don't think it matters what you call this Presence.

Our church has changed its policies on a number of controversial issues over the years, but very few debates have caused me angst. I had no problem, for example, with the gay question. It was never a stumbling block for me.

My sense of God as Presence sets me apart a bit from others in the church, but I just keep on listening. I knew quite early on that biblical stories about the great flood, Moses in the bulrushes, and the virgin birth weren't historical events but simply stories or metaphors. I think of them all as wonderful stories with a teaching or message.

The Christmas story and the Easter story are easy to understand. These stories date way back to Egyptian times, long before Christianity was founded, which increases my respect for their message. There's something to learn in such stories. I believe Jesus was a real person, just as Mohammed was a real person and so was the Buddha. They were all real people and great teachers in their day. I don't have any problem with this at all, although I don't know whether my parents would have agreed with me. My mom loved to argue, and I never wanted to upset her. My father, on the other hand, was more open and flexible.

With my own family, I don't feel the need to proselytize. They don't attend church but at Christmas time, my daughter-in-law likes to read the Christmas story. I refer to it as a *midrash*, a type of biblical interpretation, passed down over the ages. I don't preach.

But I really enjoy some of the Old Testament stories, like the one about Moses in the bulrushes. I've used it in my work as an example of caring, caring for the baby hidden in the bulrushes. That story is also found in the Koran. The story reveals how the queen wanted to care for this child, even though he wasn't an Egyptian baby. And the wet nurse happened to be the actual mother of the child. This story cuts across many ethnic and faith traditions.

The story of Job interests me too. What I admire the most about Job is his patience. You have to be patient in life, even though some things can seem unbearable at the time. The Old Testament is filled with stories like this. I like to ponder the Old Testament stories more than the New Testament, although the stories of Jesus healing also attract me. Healing is a much broader thing than simply mending the flesh.

I don't pray to God every day, but my healing touch ministry is a spiritual practice which is very important to me. The other night, we had a great meeting of all our healers, and I had a strong sense of God's presence or energy. I pray spontaneously; whenever and wherever I feel like it, and during healing touch, I invite that presence and power to flow through me. The image of an old man in the sky is a rather child-like way of imagining God, in my view.

The image of Jesus teaching and healing floats back to me sometimes. The other night, I told the healing touch group that we're not talking about a cure, we're talking about healing. I wanted to make sure they didn't expect our clients to get up and walk. If I can give a person some peace, that's what healing is all about.

One woman disagreed with me and replied, "But Jesus taught that you can get up and walk, so why can't we expect this?" I hear where she's coming from, but I think our ministry is more about healing than a physical cure. The people who come to our sessions regularly often remark on the sense of peace they feel when they leave us.

Did Jesus cure as well as heal? No, I don't think so, but perhaps over time, a person can recover his or her health. Physical healing comes with relaxation. The body has to rest. My nursing background makes me a bit sceptical, but I firmly believe that healing occurs. God also helps those who help themselves, and we need to use the medical treatments that are available.

Every hour you have in this life is precious. It's a chance to give and share with others. By taking a treatment that is successful or perhaps unsuccessful, your behaviour influences and teaches others. It's an individual's choice, but we have all these new medical discoveries, so why not use them?

A personal relationship

By Ross MacKinnon as told to David Bray

My mom and dad were both quite involved in the church. Dad had been what they called an Elder. I grew up in a family that said grace before meals, and you went to church on Sunday and you believed there was a God in existence who knew everything that was going on.

Dad taught Sunday school for a while, and I went to Sunday school the whole time. In those days you said the Lord's Prayer in the morning at school every day. A lot of kids don't know this prayer any more.

When the going gets tough, it's really neat to have some relationship with the Lord. It does something for you that material things don't do. It's not just because you go to church every Sunday — it's having that *personal* relationship with the Lord that is there every minute of your life.

And yet because we live in a material world, we tend to forget this and get messed up in things; all we see around us are the material things.

If you bring this up with a lot of people, they feel uncomfortable, perhaps because it's something you can't see. In this day and age, people don't even believe there's a spiritual dimension to life at all.

I kind of feel that my relationship with the Lord has just gradually deepened over the years. There are little things that happen — you could call them coincidences. You can always explain things as, "Well, it was a coincidence." But when you look back, you can see how the Lord guides you. People can write it off as being a coincidence, but I don't think it is.

The Bible says Jesus is the Lord and there's only one way and it's His way. Because we were given free will, however, we get kind of stubborn and think, "Well, maybe I know better." But over the years you find it's better to let the Lord direct you; you may not always know where you're going, but it's better to trust and keep things open.

I don't think I've experienced an epiphany or a defining moment in my life. It's just been a deepening awareness that the Lord is very real.

I don't speak up enough about things, and I guess we're admonished by the Bible to acknowledge the Lord in everything that we do and not be ashamed of this.

I don't particularly like some of the things the United Church does nowadays. We seem to worry so much about offending someone and we're so politically correct. I don't think the church is scripturally correct sometimes, but I attend church because it's where I was baptized and I can worship the Lord there.

Travelling opened my eyes

Written by Helen Mau as shared with Cyndi Frame

I've travelled all over the world and have learned a great deal from most religions including the faith traditions of India, China, Malaysia, England, Scotland, the Vatican, Judaism, the United States and Canada.

My faith has certainly helped me to live with a positive and hopeful attitude. I've tried to follow the examples of Jesus and Paul and to practise compassion, tolerance, humility, kindness, friendship, generosity and forgiveness.

I've had to struggle to forgive sometimes when faced with deception by friends and my husband, and when my father's religious prejudice and intolerance led to the break-up with my first love who was a Roman Catholic.

Two books, in particular, have strengthened my faith. Abram Maslow's book *Religion and Peak Experiences* helped me see what people at different levels of personal growth can experience spiritually, based on their need for security, belonging, self-esteem and self-actualization. I feel I'm at the fifth level of needs but I've reached this level because of the good fortune in my life.

I've also been greatly influenced by Dr. Benjamin Bloom's book *Cognitive Objectives*. He stresses the need to know; understand what you know; apply what you know; synthesize new ideas from what you know; and then to evaluate circumstances based on what you know. In my doctoral work at Columbia University in New York, I tried to get teachers in my field to teach beyond the level of memorizing facts and theories and to encourage their students to move towards action related to each of these objectives.

My image of God and Jesus has definitely changed over the years. I see Jesus today as an ordinary man of his time who was chosen by God to show the world how to live an exemplary life of compassion, goodwill, love, sincerity, simplicity, inspiration, brotherhood, humility and how to be a risk-taker.

In my earlier years, I didn't see the significance of all these qualities nor that Jesus really exemplified them all within his short life on earth.

If I got to ask God one question now, it would be to continue to show me the way to exemplify the same qualities practised by Jesus.

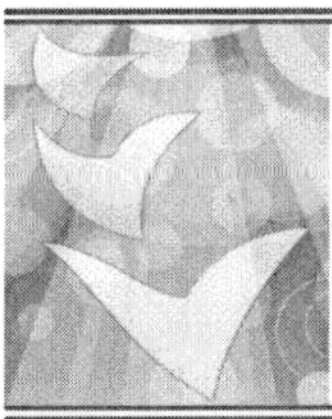

How I've experienced the Mystery

By Irene McDonald
as told to Terry Dance-Bennink

I've already mentioned that conceiving and giving birth is certainly one of the great mysteries of life. I don't have language to describe what God probably is. To describe God as a person would not reflect my feelings about God at all. When I hear people say, "Our Father/Mother God…," I say get me away from that. You're putting breasts and testicles on God. That isn't who God is.

God is an infinite mystery to me. I think there is a supreme hand in the universe but much that is written in the Bible should not be taken literally. I can't relate to people who still have a conventional faith, who believe the Bible is the Word of God, and that Adam and Eve, for example, really existed.

I have three or four good books at home about the myths people have believed in through the ages. A Christian mythology emerged many centuries after other ancient mythologies. I simply can't subscribe to the claim that there was an actual virgin who gave birth to a person who was not human.

I think a person named Jesus was born who led an exemplary life. Whether Jesus had the power to change water into wine, I do not know, but he certainly examined his social world. His teachings encapsulated the wisdom of God and the principles of ethical living. Some people like him are being born today. Perhaps Jean Vanier is an example. He's spent his life helping people to better themselves, with great compassion.

I'm sure that every era has produced at least one noble person who has done wonderful things. Jesus was one such person in his time. He groomed his disciples to help people better their lives. But brutal things happened in his era and, of course, he soon became a threat to the rulers of the day. The same thing happens on a regular basis today when somebody becomes a threat.

How do we handle people who threaten us? I wish some of them would shake us out of our lethargy. We should be more cognizant of their needs and tackle them with greater zeal. Why do we tolerate homelessness in Victoria?

Has my image of God and Jesus changed over my lifetime? My family talked a lot around the table when I was growing up, but I can't remember ever getting into a conversation with my parents or sisters and brothers about whether Jesus was God. It just never entered into our conversation. I don't know what my sister would say today if she read what I've just said.

Anyone who believes in an all-powerful man in the sky who commands wars or brings about peace is living a dream. We are the people who command wars and bring about peace. That power is invested in people. I also don't think God intentionally creates people with disabilities just in order to test their strength and faith. I don't believe that at all. Imperfections in people are simply inevitable.

Do I pray to God? Not in the sense of, "Please God, this is a dreadful day, could you do something about it?" No, no, not that kind of prayer at all. When I attempt to communicate with God —and I'll use the word "prayer" although it may not be a good word — I pray to keep my soul. I don't have words to describe what my soul is, but when I lose my life, I would pray that my soul would be kept.

My sanctuary

I'm the kind of person who relies on my own resources. I've not been one to go to somebody else with my aches and pains or troubles. I've been fortunate to have some strength of reason and have been able to make some decisions by myself. I cannot imagine going to a clergyman and saying, "Come and help me." Nor do I remember going to a teacher when I was young and saying, "Help me."

I do remember, though, being confronted with difficult things in my education which required the help of professors or teachers. I would seek an appointment and ask them how I should tackle the problem, but I never felt that they should solve it for me.

I find sanctuary by sitting quietly in a room with someone I know who is feeling the same woes as me. Just to have a quiet communication with that person, not necessarily spoken, gives me solace. I find it comforting to know there's somebody there who would pick me up if I did fall down.

A church sanctuary also gives me solace, but today, the only church sanctuary that I feel is a true place of prayer is St. Andrew's Cathedral. My own church no longer feels like a place of prayer; it feels much more like a social institution. That's not bad, because there are a lot of social problems that the church is responding to and I admire the people who work diligently on social issues. But it is not a church that nourishes my soul.

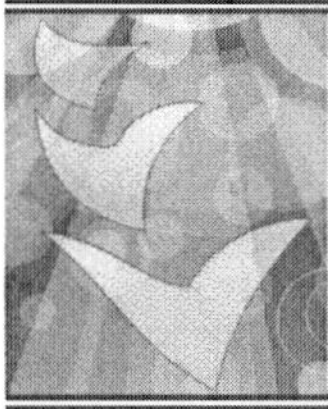

God is always with me

By Mary Thomas as told to Edeana Malcolm

God is always with me. This feeling has been my saving grace all my life. When I ran into problems with the children I was teaching or with my own children, I prayed.

At one time, my husband, Len, wasn't able to work for a while, and I certainly sent up a lot of prayers to God to help me look after Len and the children so he'd get well and return to work again. He was off work for three or four weeks, and we had no other income so it was difficult.

There have been hard times, too, with our children. Our youngest, Arthur, had pneumonia four times during his first year, so we sent up a lot of frantic prayers because he was so prone to pneumonia. We often had to take him to the hospital where he'd be given antibiotics and so on. He got so that he dreaded seeing our doctor because of the needles.

I've always thought God was a presence with me all the time. I don't have a specific image of him that is like a human being. I think of him as a spirit that is around me, in me, a part of me. I think I've always felt that way — that God isn't something specific, not something that I can touch or anything like that.

Jesus has become less of a personal kind of person over the years and become more of a spirit too. While he's always the son of God, the two have merged a lot in my worship. When I was young, I thought of Jesus as more of a person, somebody I would have loved to have known. I felt that I was fortunate to know God because he was so much a part of my life.

One of the last things I always ask God before I go to sleep is to take care of all my family, and they're getting to be quite a few. I ask God to bless them with continued good health and to draw them closer to him as he has drawn me.

One small difference that my faith has made is that when we get together as a family, they always ask me to say grace. And they always know that I would like to go to church if I have the opportunity. Whenever I visited a new city with them, they knew that I would probably want to go to church on Sunday and they'd try and arrange it.

Sometimes I feel as if maybe I haven't done enough. But my mother and father set the example. They didn't push me or my sister or my brother, and my brother ended up with faith the same as my own and much the same attitude to many things. He's five years younger than I. So I hope my faith helps my four children to cope whenever they need strength to solve a problem or get through something.

NOW IT'S YOUR TURN

Some questions to ponder

- **How and when have you experienced God or the sacred in your life?**
- **Has your image of God and Jesus changed over the years? If so, how?**
- **Has your faith made a difference in your life? If so, how?**
- **Do you believe in the power of prayer (to heal, to intervene)?**
- **If you got to ask God one single question, what would it be?**

MORE WORDS OF WISDOM

There are years that ask the questions and years that answer.
— Zora Neale Hurston

Stay focused on the light — *The Rev. Colleen Erb*

Treasure your friends — *Sheila MacDougall*

Live every moment to the best of your ability
— *Irene McDonald*

Pursue your passions and stay healthy
— *Helen Mau*

Stay focused on the light

By The Rev. Colleen Erb
as told to Terry Dance-Bennink

I'll never forget a sermon I heard given by the Very Rev. Bruce McLeod a long time ago when I was in Pincher Creek, Alta. I remember only one line: "Out there in the midst of the encircling gloom, there is a light."

No matter what, no matter how dark your life may seem, keep your focus on the light. There's always hope no matter what. Anytime we experience death or a loss in our life, we discover hope, sooner or later, even in the darkness. God is with us in the muck. So my message to the next generation is d*on't give up*.

There's so much darkness in our world today — war, violence, economic crisis, environmental degradation. As a church, we need to preach hope. I remember the days of the invasion of Pearl Harbor when we had to cover our windows at night to keep our light from shining outside, but we still used to sing songs of hope at school — "the light will come again." And we wore bright clothes in those days to cheer ourselves up. But I don't hear this today on the radio or TV, and everyone seems to wear dark clothing.

Our church should encourage people to have hope and show them how to live amidst the muck and the pain, to keep on going. We have to stay focused on the light and connected to one another.

Treasure your friends

By Sheila MacDougall
as told to Terry Dance-Bennink

I value my friends, and my family, of course, the most. But it's the network of friends that is really important to me. I'm not sure

Sheila MacDougall with B.C. Cancer Society friends

why. Perhaps it goes back to my upbringing in a rural part of Saskatchewan, where I developed a strong sense of community. I still remember all the families I grew up with, and when I encounter anyone from "back home," it's wonderful to compare notes.

Ottawa wasn't quite the same which is probably why I didn't stay. And when Jack and I got married, we moved often and were expected to be instantly involved in every new community. Jack was very good at remembering people and quite social, and I stepped right in beside him.

I had to struggle a bit after Jack died, because all of a sudden I was alone. But I returned to nursing and made all kinds of new friends among my school mates, and we still keep in touch. When I married Mac and moved to Victoria, it was much more difficult, because Mac wasn't social at all. But I quickly decided to get involved in First Met and the Cancer Society, and began playing competitive bridge. My parents also lived in Victoria, so there was a nucleus of friendship ready to grow.

It takes work to maintain a friendship. I don't see or talk to some of my friends that often, but I try to maintain contact. What I value most in life are relationships — I enjoy being with people. This Christmas, instead of sending out Christmas cards, I'm going to phone all my friends! And I may go to New York to play bridge with a woman who's 60. She's a lot younger than I am, but it doesn't seem to matter. Life wouldn't be stimulating if I wasn't learning and exploring.

My sustenance comes from continuing to learn and to do. I'm not ready to sit back and I don't think I ever will be. Perhaps some day I'll have to accept the reality of less energy, but not yet! I'll keep on doing whatever I can. There will always be people like the woman I'm companioning now who need help and friendship. We've become good friends. I had to work at our relationship at the beginning, but now we're friends for life until one of us is gone.

When I die, I hope to be remembered as a friend, a good friend. I'd like a church funeral, and you can celebrate my friendship that day!

If I had to give a title to my life story, the word "fulfillment" comes to mind, but it's not quite the right word as it sounds too blah. I've led a rewarding and stimulating life and I feel blessed. My life has not been all pretty and easy, but I believe my purpose is to do useful and stimulating things and to learn about new ideas, people and places.

In addition to friendship, I also value tolerance and the ability to listen. Tolerance has been a thread throughout my life. I had to tolerate my mother's intolerance to a certain degree — that's just the way she was. I had to make some adjustments in my second marriage as well. I just backed off if an argument got heated. And in the church, I've found that tolerance is essential.

Sheila MacDougall at her computer

My nursing career probably taught me a lot about tolerance and accepting the people I cared for, regardless of their warts. And listening is the key to tolerance. I learn so much by listening because it helps me understand where the other person is coming from.

My advice to the next generation is: Never give up! Seek your place in life and enjoy the moment, too. It's important not to spend all your time working or cleaning your house. Take the time to enjoy other people. Pursue your dreams and don't say, "I can't do that." If you want something badly enough, you can get it. You don't need to stay in one track, like law or nursing. I've followed different paths at certain points in my life. It's never too late to try something new.

I also think it's important to give back to society and to those who have less — to share your time, money and talents. It can be quite an education, although you have to strike a balance between meeting your own needs and caring for others.

Live every moment to the best of your ability

By Irene McDonald as told to Terry Dance-Bennink

My advice to the next generation is to live every moment to the best of your ability. I hope that I'll be remembered as someone who made an earnest attempt to fulfill my various missions in life to the best of my ability.

Don't go through life half-heartedly. Give it your best, so when you're finished, you can say, "I gave it my best shot." I guess I'm a perfectionist in that regard. I don't like to iron my linen half-heartedly.

I have one other piece of advice: don't stop learning. I'm still growing and learning at age 90! I like to take courses and keep up with current affairs. I scan more than one newspaper a day and have just finished reading all about the CIA in the United States — a fascinating book. If I hadn't caught this nasty cold, I would have started another computer course at Camosun College. It's important to be conversant with the new technology regardless of your age.

If you stop challenging your mind, you've in effect died. Keep your mind active and stop whining about the weather or the state of your body!

I hope I'll continue to keep growing and learning.

Pursue your passions and stay healthy

Written by Helen Mau as shared with Cyndi Frame

I have many words of wisdom for the next generation! Here are 30 of my favourite strategies for enjoying life and staying healthy.

1. Discover and pursue your passions and keen interests.
2. Cherish your health, practise good nutrition and get enough sleep and exercise.
3. Get to know and enjoy a variety of people.
4. Know your values: rank them in order of importance when making a choice between two or three best options.
5. Be fearless and live dangerously.
6. Simplify your life; have a file system and shred regularly.
7. Monitor your income and expenses; look at patterns over the year.
8. Update your will every two years.
9. Express your wishes at death in writing to make it easy for caregivers after you've passed on or if you become incapacitated.

10. Try to get a second opinion from a doctor you trust when hospitalized or having a special health exam.
11. Be reasonable about your expectations of caregivers.
12. Love your neighbour as yourself. Don't expect others to do what you wouldn't expect of yourself.
13. Make young friends throughout life, especially in your 50s; this will help you stay young at heart.
14. Be realistic but compassionate with those who suffer from mental health problems.
15. Enjoy work and leisure.
16. Find joy in small things.
17. Read the Bible daily. Ask yourself, what did this passage teach me?
18. Don't sweat the small stuff; remember, it's only small stuff.
19. Recognize that failures and mistakes lead to wisdom if you take the time to reflect.
20. Take the initiative and be proactive.
21. Learn about different cultures. Think about the qualities in your own culture and how they influence what you do, think and say.
22. Obey the rules of your own culture for the sake of good relationships.
23. Keep an open mind and keep learning.
24. Take a 10-minute break every 50 minutes because we all do our best work for about 50 minutes.
25. Smile and the world smiles with you.
26. Be grateful — gratitude creates an attitude that gives you latitude.
27. Listen for the "ahas" or "wows" in life and enjoy them fully over and over.
28. Expect change to be good and it often is!
29. Recognize that self-control can give you time to think.
30. Enjoy creative thinking. It's challenging and pleasurable!

NOW IT'S YOUR TURN

Some questions to ponder

- **What do you value the most in your life?**
- **What is the single most valuable thing you've ever learned?**
- **What is one of the hardest things you've ever done?**
- **What are some "unforgettable moments" in your life?**
- **What words of wisdom would you share with the next generation?**

THE ELDERS' GALLERY

Biographies and Wisdom Learned

MAY DELLER

At age 17, May Deller became a teacher responsible for seven children spanning seven grades. Since then, May has volunteered in both church and community organizations throughout her life. She's an independent thinker, a thought-provoking writer and a talented poet as the excerpts in this book reveal.

Born in 1933, she grew up in the village of Hamiota, Man., and graduated from Grade 12 at age 16. May was the third of six children of Grace (Atkinson) and Norman Turnbull and spent her summers on the family farm at Binscarth, Man.

After high school, May accepted a position as a permit teacher at Randale, a rural school north of Shoal Lake, Man., and met her future husband, Bill Deller, during this time. After a year in Shoal Lake, May attended normal school as the teacher training college was called in those days, and then taught Grades 5 through 8 in Beulah, Man.

She married Bill in 1953 and joined him on his farm in the Municipality of Shoal Lake, actively working alongside him in the fields as well as the house. They raised three children together, which May describes as one of the most satisfying experiences in her life.

The family moved from the farm in 1976 to the town of Neepawa, Man., where they lived for 11 years. In 1986, May and Bill moved to Brandon, Man., before retiring to Victoria in 2000.

To read May's stories, see the following chapters: Early Memories; Love and Friendship; Accepting Loss and Death; and Building a Faith Community.

○ ○ ○ ○ WISDOM LEARNED ○ ○ ○ ○

From May Deller by Irene Baddeley

Do you believe that sharing stories can be life-changing? I do. May Deller's stories and wisdom have touched my soul, warmed my heart and truly inspired me.

I first encountered May in a workshop about "Writing our Stories" a few years ago. We were paired together and had to verbally tell each other a story in three minutes or less. While I fumbled around trying to tell my brief story, May immediately knew what her story would be and told it with such clarity and pathos that I was spellbound.

When our church launched the Spiritual Companions program last year, I asked for May Deller as my elder and what a privilege it has turned out to be. We've met many times, and May has shared both her struggles and her high moments. I admire the way she moves forward with hope and simply does what has to be done. I stand in awe of her ability to capture the essence of a happening in her life and make it into a story of insight, love and compassion.

Here are just a few of the "simple" truths I've learned from May:

- Save time for yourself, no matter how demanding your life is, otherwise you risk becoming disenchanted and powerless.
- Laugh at yourself — be human.
- Listen beyond the spoken words and don't worry about silent moments. Much can be understood even when left unspoken.
- Forgive when you think it's quite impossible.
- Come to terms with the things that can't be changed in your life.
- Nourish your spirit by relating to the natural world as well as the human.
- Be grateful for the goodness, beauty and truth which come through the written word and the arts.
- Love unconditionally as Jesus did.
- Remember that not only does God live in us, but we live in the heart of God.

○ ○ ○ ○ ○ ○ ○ ○ ○ ○

THE REV. COLLEEN ERB

The Rev. Colleen Erb fell in love with music and God at an early age.

Colleen was born in Calgary, Alta., on Jan. 19, 1928, and moved to Victoria with her parents and brother when she was 12 years old. She attended South Park School and Victoria High, and at age 15, went to work at the Empress Hotel. Colleen continued to study music, graduated with her piano teaching and performance diplomas and taught piano to students in Colwood and Victoria for seven years.

She was an active member of Metropolitan United Church, and through the Rev. Laura Butler, in her late 20s Colleen sensed a call to ministry. Colleen left home and her parents — one of the hardest moves of her life — to study at the United Church Training School in Toronto.

Despite a gruelling course of study, she graduated and was sent to Pincher Creek, Alta., where she had a five-point charge covering 1,000 sq. miles in the foothills of the Rockies. After four years, she was called to Chilliwack, B.C., in 1966 as a Director of Christian Education, where she also added singing to her musical repertoire and teaching credentials.

Her call to ordination surfaced in the 1970s, once again at the prompting of the Rev. Laura Butler, and after another hard slog of studies, Colleen was ordained at St. Andrew's Wesley Church in Vancouver in 1980, which she describes as one of the happiest days of her life.

Gordon United in Victoria called Colleen shortly afterwards which, she says, was "a perfect match," and she ministered to 250 families until she retired in 1993 after 31 years in ministry.

Since retirement, Colleen has become a vital member of First Metropolitan United Church in Victoria: singing in the choir, leading a women's spirituality group, offering spiritual direction and enjoying time spent with her many friends. Her latest call, she says, is to "feast on her life" and share her reflections with others through the Spiritual Companions program. The church has been her life and she hopes she's been faithful to God, her neighbours and herself.

To read Colleen's stories, see the following chapters: Love and Friendship; A Life's Call; Accepting Loss and Death; The Joys and Challenges of Growing Older; Building a Faith Community; The Many Faces of God; and More Words of Wisdom.

○ ○ ○ ○ WISDOM LEARNED ○ ○ ○ ○

From the Rev. Colleen Erb by Terry Dance-Bennink

I've been deeply moved by Colleen's *relationship* with her God. God is not an abstract source of energy nor an unknowable mystery for Colleen, but an active, personal, infinite source of love and compassion, and so is His son, Jesus.

From Colleen, I've learned to let go of endless mantras and simply dialogue with this Being who has loved and protected me from the word go and always will. I've learned there are many ways to converse with God — no one way is right for all people at all times.

Colleen's brush with death after her stroke last year took us into many deep conversations about dying and life after death. I've been struck by her willingness to be vulnerable, to acknowledge her fears about death, despite her "Rev." title. We both share a conviction that life on this earth is not the end. The soul does not die. We will be reunited with loved ones and our God in some form or another in a dimension beyond time.

As a newcomer to Victoria two years ago, friendship and community mean a lot to me as they do to Colleen. We've acknowledged that friends can't always fill the void of loneliness, but they sure help. I'm grateful for Colleen's friendship; we seem to be two kindred souls.

Lastly, she's taught me not to give up on church. No one and no thing is perfect in this world, and if you cut the branch off the tree, life stops flowing. We all need friends, we all need community and the church, for all its warts, *is* Christ's body today.

○ ○ ○ ○ ○ ○ ○ ○ ○ ○

BARBARA HENDERSON

Barbara Henderson is one of those rare breeds — a native Victorian.

She was born in her parents' bedroom in Vic West in 1915, one of five girls. Family life revolved around the church. Barbara's father, who immigrated to Canada from England as a shipwright, was superintendent of the Sunday school at Victoria West United Church, and her mother was known as the "Mother of CGIT in Victoria." The family joined Metropolitan United Church in 1928, and Barbara remains an active member of the amalgamated First Metropolitan United Church to this day.

Barbara became a teacher of commercial subjects in Prince Rupert, B.C., and Port Coquitlam, B.C., and then an inside instructor in the High School Correspondence Dept. of the provincial government. In 1939, she met her husband, Kenneth Whitworth, a marine engineer, who joined the Navy when World War II escalated. Tragedy struck the family after the war ended, when Ken drowned along with the entire crew of a tug and barge caught in a very bad storm on the way to Alaska.

Barbara was left with two young girls and very little money, so she went back to work and found solace in the books of Catherine Marshall. She met her second husband, Keith Henderson, in a fairy-tale romance. He was a bachelor and a baritone in the same church choir and the rest is history. After 36 very happy years of marriage and five grandchildren, Keith died in 1993.

Barbara lives on her own in a condo today, still reaching out and caring for her many UCW and neighbourhood friends. Her daughters keep a close eye on her. She starts and ends each day with a prayer and is convinced God hears and answers her prayers. At 92, she says she's ready to go, but she hopes it won't be before September 2008 when her first great-grandchild is due.

To read Barbara's story, see the following chapter: Love and Friendship

○ ○ ○ ○ WISDOM LEARNED ○ ○ ○ ○

From Barbara Henderson by Gloria Stott

Many words come to mind when I think of what I've learned from Barbara Henderson. Here are just a few.

Modesty: Barbara never takes credit for all her accomplishments in life and always thanks others for what they do.

A Christian: She's been an active member of our church since 1928 and is always thinking of ways to help the church. She's gathered many religious articles and spiritual quotations.

Spontaneity: She can quote the Bible or say a prayer at a moment's notice.

Strength and perseverance: She's managed to get through all the ups and downs in life, including the loss of two husbands.

Thoughtfulness and kindness: No matter what happens, Barbara has a kind word of understanding and forgiveness.

Leadership: She has the ability and confidence to take charge and make things happen.

Calmness: Barbara never seems to get upset. She keeps a cool head.

Gracious hostess: She always welcomes friends and neighbours to her home in a friendly, gracious manner.

Absolute trust: Barbara's faith in the Lord is firm. She's ready to meet the Lord whenever He wants to take her.

Gratitude: The title of her life story, she says, could be "Blessings of Life."

Barbara has been a blessing in my life.

○ ○ ○ ○ ○ ○ ○ ○ ○ ○

RUTH ISABEL WILSON HOWELL

Victoria-born Ruth Isabel Wilson Howell is our centenarian! She was born in Victoria on Aug. 25, 1908, the oldest of three children, and grew up in the Fernwood area of Victoria. She attended the Knox Presbyterian church when it was located on Stanley Avenue but after church union in 1925, the family moved to First United Church. Ruth was 17 at the time.

She attended Girls Central School and Victoria High School, before going to Victoria College in Craigdarroch Castle and then on to normal school. Ruth taught elementary school in Smithers, B.C., Nanaimo, B.C. and Victoria before she married Jack Howell in 1941 in Vancouver. Ruth and her husband had two children and enjoyed a happy marriage until his death at age 78.

When Ruth lived in Smithers, she was active in the Sunday school, choir and CGIT. At First United, she was involved in the Doreene McLeod Central women's group, which later became Harmony UCW. They were a close group of friends who supported each other as they raised young families during the war years and afterward. Ruth was especially close to her sister, Jean, who was also an active participant in First Metropolitan church life until her recent death at age 90.

Ruth Howell was very happy to be chosen as Queen for a Day on Oct. 31, 2007, at Oak Bay Lodge where she lives. She is looking forward to her first great-grandchild in June and her 100th birthday in August 2008.

To read Ruth's stories, see the following chapters: Early Memories; Love and Friendship; The Joys and Challenges of Growing Older; and Building a Faith Community.

○ ○ ○ ○ WISDOM LEARNED ○ ○ ○ ○

From Ruth Howell by Edeana Malcolm

Mrs. Howell sits in her wheelchair waiting for me. She's wearing her best clothes and her hair is neatly combed. She has prepared for my visit; the church newsletter and the Lenten booklet are beside her. Her eyes light up when she sees me. I feel like an honoured guest.

This woman, if you took the time to notice her among those who look too much like heaps of cast-off clothing as they doze in the early afternoon sun at the seniors' lodge, is a woman filled with dignity. The hardest thing about being 100 years old and physically limited is the humiliation to which she is exposed. But she does not complain. In fact, she accepts her fate with graciousness. Just as she appreciates my visits, she appreciates the staff at this seniors' home who assist her with her daily ablutions.

How uplifting is this dignity in the face of difficulty. Over and over, she says to me, "My attitude has to be gratitude."

Well, no, it doesn't. She could be bitter and angry like the dozens of others I see around me. But because she isn't, because she smiles, because she appreciates, everyone else around her is blessed by her presence.

Thank you, Mrs. Howell, for the wisdom you show me by your presence.

○ ○ ○ ○ ○ ○ ○ ○ ○ ○

MONA GRACE HUNDLEBY

July 11, 1918–Nov. 2, 2007

Mona Hundleby dedicated her life to helping others. Together with her husband, Roy, she founded Victoria's first counselling centre during the 1960s, which is thriving still some 40 years later and offers a testament to the solid foundation laid by both of them.

Mona and Roy studied with such world-renowned psychologists as Dr. Carl Rogers, Dr. Herbert Otto and Virginia Satir, and developed more than 85 workshops and community programs for lay and professional counsellors in Victoria and the Lower Mainland areas, in conjunction with the University of Victoria, the clergy and many professionals.

Mona began her training as a CGIT leader, a Sunday school teacher and Young People's leader in the United Church. Mona's earliest church memories are of Metropolitan Methodist Church and its beautiful stained glass windows. She later became an active member of Belmont United Church and helped establish the United Church's George Pringle Memorial Camp at Shawnigan Lake, B.C. She and Roy also spent several summer vacations helping to build the United Church Training School at Naramata, B.C.

After she "retired," Mona volunteered and led groups at the Fairfield Seniors Centre, and she and Roy logged more than two and a half years of sailing time on various cruise lines.

Mona was heart-broken to lose her husband in 2005, after 65 years of such a unique and happy partnership. It was the hardest moment of her life, but she continued to care deeply for her many friends, new and old — as well as her beloved son, Glenn, and daughter, Pat McClung, three grandchildren and five great-grandchildren.

Shortly before she died, she told her spiritual companion: "I've talked to God and told him he can put me to work as soon as I get there. I'm sure there are people in heaven who need help."

To read Mona's stories, see the following chapters: Love and Friendship; A Life's Call, Accepting Loss and Death; and The Many Faces of God.

○ ○ ○ ○ WISDOM LEARNED ○ ○ ○ ○

From Mona Hundleby by Terry Dance-Bennink

I became one of Mona's new friends a few months before she died on Nov. 2, 2007 and was honoured to record her reflections on her life. Her most moving story is entitled "On Heaven and Dying."

Mona had lost her beloved husband, Roy, after more than 60 years of marriage a few years earlier, and she was having many "close encounters" with Roy and a beautiful angel. Some might say they were just dreams, but she and I shared the conviction that life and love continue beyond the grave. "All things are possible in this world," she told me as we talked about heaven and dying.

Mona wanted to rejoin those she loved, but she also wanted to share her life story with others. Sixty-one pages later, we celebrated its conclusion and distributed her "book" to all those who attended her memorial service, courtesy of her two children, Glenn and Pat.

One of the most valuable things Mona learned in life was how to relax, and she counted swimming in warm water as her preferred way to unwind. Mona died very early in the morning of Nov. 2, 2007, and I woke up suddenly from an unusually peaceful and beautiful dream at the very same time. In my dream, I was walking on a wide, smooth golden beach and as I entered the calm, warm water, I exclaimed, "I can swim here after all, even though it's Victoria — how wonderful!" I like to think it was Mona's way of reaching out to reassure me, because she'd promised to let me know she was OK.

Mona had a lively relationship with her God and used to have daily chats with God and Jesus. Her faith and trust continue to inspire me, along with her zest for life. "Travel now, not later," she urged me. And so I am. Mona enjoyed growing older and looked for love even in the face of death. She and I remain spiritual companions.

> *I want to thank Terry for the huge difference she made in the last six months of my mother's life. Mom was happy during that time because she had purpose and a sense of completion to her life on earth by having her story written down.*
> — Pat McClung, Mona Hundleby's daughter

SHEILA MACDOUGALL

Loving parents and a strong sense of community shaped Sheila Josephine (Plewman) MacDougall, the woman who became a dedicated nurse and later a nurse educator, then a church and community leader. Sheila was born on Aug. 10, 1922, and grew up on a farm in Lashburn, Sask., during the Depression. Sheila married a bank manager, John (Jack) Rennie Rice and together they reared three children. Church was a spiritual and social anchor for the family in the midst of many moves.

Jack died suddenly of a heart attack in 1970, and Sheila's teenaged son died in a tragic car accident a few months later. Sheila returned to work and service as an antidote to despair and grief. She became a nurse educator at Wascana Institute in Regina, Sask. She married her second husband, Dr. Walter MacDougall, a few years later.

They eventually retired to Victoria, where Sheila became the chair of council of the newly amalgamated First Metropolitan United Church, and steered the congregation through a turbulent period. Fundraising, hospitality and the healing touch ministry at First Met have all been blessed with Sheila's energy.

Church is not her only world. As a former provincial president of the B.C. Cancer Society, Sheila and her team helped to raise more than $13 million for the province. In her downtime, Sheila likes to explore the planet and has travelled to nearly every continent. She also plays competitive bridge in between her service commitments and travelling adventures.

As both an elder and a spiritual companion herself, Sheila will go down in history as one of First Met's most dedicated and faithful pioneers.

To read Sheila's stories, see the following chapters: Early Memories; Love and Friendship; A Life's Call; Accepting Loss and Death; Building a Faith Community; The Many Faces of God; and More Words of Wisdom.

○ ○ ○ ○ WISDOM LEARNED ○ ○ ○ ○

From Sheila MacDougall by Terry Dance-Bennink

Energy comes first to mind when you meet Sheila MacDougall, but there's far more to this elder. At the top of my list of wisdom learned from Sheila is the power of positive thinking. After losing her first husband, the love of her life, followed shortly by the death of her teenaged son, Sheila recovered by turning her back on negative thoughts.

Her positive thinking has been matched with service to others. As a nurse, an educator, a fundraiser and president of the B.C. Cancer Society, and a council chair of a newly amalgamated church, Sheila has shown a passion for listening and caring. She values friendship, more than any worldly accomplishments — a timely reminder for me to treasure relationships more than goal achievement. And never hold a grudge, she adds.

"Seek your place in life and enjoy the moment," is another piece of Sheila wisdom, coming from the lady who's travelled all over the world, often on her own, and is still going strong at age 85. Growing old has its challenges, but Sheila looks for the joy.

Sheila's God is a sacred Presence. If she asks for guidance at a fork in life's road, she receives it. "If you wait, the answer will come, sooner or later," she insists. Sheila hopes she's been a "fairly faithful servant."

In my eyes, she's an exemplary servant and an inspiration to senior boomers like me who hope to age with her grace. I will never forget this woman who simply wants to be remembered "as a friend, a good friend."

○ ○ ○ ○ ○ ○ ○ ○ ○ ○

ROSS MACKINNON

Robert Ross MacKinnon served in Kenya as a pilot with the Royal Air Force during World War II. He was born in Victoria, B.C., on May 20, 1923, the oldest of three sons of Donald and Jean MacKinnon from Glasgow, Scotland.

He grew up in the Victoria neighbourhood of Fairfield, about half a mile from his present home, playing road hockey, basketball and other sports, making rafts, getting his pants dirty and doing what most boys do.

Ross attended Sir James Douglas Elementary School and Victoria High School and after spending one year at Victoria College in Craigdarroch Castle, he joined the Royal Canadian Air Force.

After graduating as a pilot, a posting overseas led to service in 209 Squadron of the Royal Air Force stationed in Mombasa, Kenya. The end of hostilities in 1945 brought his return to Victoria College and then the University of British Columbia, followed by his graduation with a B. Comm. degree.

Ross married Patricia Scrivener, also a native Victorian, in 1950 and their family consists of two adopted daughters. During most of the 1950s he also flew in the RCAF reserve.

Ross spent 40 years with Revenue Canada–Taxation in the Victoria District office as an auditor and supervisor and earned his Certified General Accountants degree over a four-year period.

Throughout his working career, and during retirement, Ross has always had a prime interest in church work in various capacities, including teaching Sunday school. Since retirement, he volunteers annually to assist low-income taxpayers file tax returns.

To read Ross' stories, see the following chapters: Early Memories; The Joys and Challenges of Growing Older; and The Many Faces of God.

WISDOM LEARNED

From Ross MacKinnon by David Bray

I was intrigued when I first heard of the Spiritual Companions program. Here was a chance to learn from people with more life experience, listen to their lives and reflect on my own and to hear some darned good stories.

There would be no problem interviewing people, I told myself. As a journalist, I've been questioning people for as long as I can remember. But those are different interviews — get the story, get the quote, get out. You don't have to connect with those people or get involved with them or build a personal relationship. You get what they can give you and you go home.

This was different. Here were people who, though they were not making news, also lived through important times and made important contributions. They lived through war and difficult circumstances I know nothing about. They have been places in life where I may be going and, perhaps, they can pass on a tip or two I can use on my way through.

I have been inspired by Ross for the warmth he showed someone who walked into his house as a complete stranger asking nosy questions. I am inspired by the way he keeps active — perhaps the true secret of life — physically and mentally.

I am struck by the fact that while we are separated by a generation we are not too far apart. I am encouraged by his openness and willingness to share personal and sometimes private things so that one day, when someone might be asking questions of me, I will not hesitate to answer.

KIT MACMILLAN

"Be your own person" is Kit MacMillan's advice to anyone married to a minister. She should know as she was married to the Rev. Ian MacMillan for 47 years until he died in 2000. Kit consciously chose not to get overly involved in church activities as she felt one minister in the family was enough.

Kit was born in Winnipeg on Dec. 31, 1926, and raised as an Anglican for the first 20 years of her life. After recovering from a bout of T.B., she became a registered nurse at Winnipeg General Hospital in 1950. She toyed with the idea of becoming a deaconess before she married Ian in 1953, who she says "challenged every theological idea I ever had and made me think." She soon realized she didn't need a PhD to have a meaningful faith.

After her three sons grew up, Kit returned to nursing in Edmonton. She specialized in geriatric and rehabilitation nursing because she found seniors so interesting and loved listening to their stories. When the family moved to Richmond, B.C., she volunteered with a weekly seniors' luncheon program encouraging elders to connect with others.

Kit and her husband arrived in Victoria the same day as the Rev. Dr. Allan Saunders, and they chose First Met because they didn't want a "wee little church." She guards her time carefully and prefers one-on-one relationships with people and her phone ministry, rather than cooking in the church kitchen.

Despite some health challenges, Kit continues to be a vital, active member of our church at age 80. Her sons and six grandchildren are her delight.

To read Kit's story, see the following chapter: The Joys and Challenges of Growing Older.

○ ○ ○ ○ WISDOM LEARNED ○ ○ ○ ○

From Kit MacMillan by Terry Dance-Bennink

Kit MacMillan was one of our first speakers at our New Vistas Program, a lunch-and-learn series for seniors, in March 2007. She made three points which stuck in my mind — the sign of a good preacher: acknowledge your creator, take care of your body and help someone in need every day. It sounds simple, but Kit practises what she preaches.

I sit beside her sometimes at our 9 a.m. communion service on Sundays, and she always has a smile and a friendly word for me. She's not a bubbly extrovert type, but you can tell she cares.

I admire her spunk and independent spirit. She's carved out her own life, separate from her minister husband, and avoids the trap of "church busyness." This gives her time for one-on-one relationships — a good reminder for me whenever the challenge of editing this book feels overwhelming. Stay focused on the friendship between elder and companion, not "the book!"

Losing her husband eight years ago was a hard blow, but despite her tears, Kit reached out and found support within our church community. "Ask and you shall receive" is one of her favourite scripture passages (Matthew 7:7). I hope I will be as brave and faithful if my 72-year-old husband dies before me.

I lost my mom to Alzheimer's a few years ago, so I found Kit's humorous take on memory loss reassuring. "By the time you're old enough to be called a wise elder, there's more than one encyclopedia tucked away in your brain, and frequently, the search machine is a little slower. Why worry about it?"

Kit treasures her many friends, including "bright people in their 50s and 60s." Perhaps I'm one of them. I'd certainly like to be.

○ ○ ○ ○ ○ ○ ○ ○ ○ ○

HELEN ELIZABETH (DICKIN) MAU

As a young child, Helen's close bonds with her many uncles and aunts affected her in positive and enduring ways. Helen Elizabeth (Dickin) Mau was born on Apr. 26, 1921, in Guelph, Ont. Her mother's five siblings placed a high value on education and encouraged Helen to strive for perfection in her professional life.

Helen's father, from a farming family of five, loved experimenting with foods throughout the years, and this would later encourage Helen in her choice to study nutrition and home economics.

Earning her bachelors of health sciences and pedagogy, as well as a masters in pedagogy at the University of Toronto, Helen then went on to complete her doctorate in education at Columbia University in New York City with a focus on creativity.

She taught at San Francisco State University from 1954-87 and, mentored by Frank Sperling, she developed a graduate interdisciplinary program on family budget and credit counselling. Helen helped shift the focus of the San Francisco Board of Consumer Credit from debt management to budget counselling which enabled many families to get out of debt.

In both her professional life and volunteer community service, Helen's leadership and teaching skills have been appreciated. Always active in every church she attended, Helen was an early leader in CGIT in Ontario. Helen came to First United Church in Victoria in 1987. She became very active on many committees and was secretary of the UCW, assembling a Memory Book which is in the church archives. Helen was also instrumental in welcoming the Intercultural Association to the First Met building on Balmoral Road.

Helen married Charlie Mau in New York in 1952. Though they had no children of their own, joining this larger close-knit Chinese family afforded her many opportunities for learning about Chinese culture. Through their travels to the far corners of the globe, Helen broadened her intellectual and spiritual horizons.

Helen's philosophy of life is striking and unforgettable: "Enjoy work and leisure. Listen for the 'Ahas' in life. Be fearless. Live dangerously!"

To read Helen's stories, see the following chapters: Early Memories; Love and Friendship; A Life's Call; Accepting Loss and Death; the Joys and Challenges of Growing Older; Building a Faith Community; The Many Faces of God; and More Words of Wisdom.

○ ○ ○ ○ WISDOM LEARNED ○ ○ ○ ○

From Helen Mau by Cyndi Frame

Of the many attributes I admire in my new friend, Helen Mau, what I love most is her warmth, her inherent trust in others, her openness to new learning and striving to be her best. Yes, that is a long string of top qualities to lump into one sentence — but this is Helen.

When I am with her, I am inspired to continue giving to others, no matter one's age or limitations, for she shows me by example that others may benefit from our gifts. I admire her consistent respectfulness for other cultures and faiths, broadened perhaps by her rich experiences of travel throughout the world.

Over the last few months, Helen's stories of her time at First Metropolitan United Church and her involvement in its life, the UCW, and the Intercultural Association have made First Met come alive to me in a new way. I see a deeper and richer history of caring people through her stories, a gift I hadn't yet received when I chose First Met as my church family three years ago.

My friendship with Helen developed slowly. If she didn't feel well, she listened to her body's needs and respected herself. I'm learning to listen to my limitations as well as I carefully and respectfully pursue time together with her. Change is constant — our bodies/other people/jobs/church buildings — but Helen teaches me that nothing needs to stop us from growing and learning. When we stop growing, then we age.

Thank you, Helen, for your friendship and your inspiration to me to keep growing and giving.

○ ○ ○ ○ ○ ○ ○ ○ ○ ○

IRENE (KING) McDONALD

Irene (King) McDonald is a multi-faceted woman. A teacher of gifted children, an RCAF veteran involved in highly secret code-breaking operations during World War II, a sex education pioneer in Victoria, a former national fundraising chairman of the Canadian Cancer Society, a UCW leader for decades, a devoted wife and mother — these are only some of the challenging roles Irene has played throughout her 91 years.

Born on a farm in Ghost Pine Creek, Alta., on June 15, 1917, Irene grew up in a loving family of seven children during the Depression. At age 18, she became a teacher in a one-room prairie school house, responsible for 10 grades. In 1943, she joined the RCAF Women's Division and operated the Enigma machine used by the Allies to crack the German "unbreakable" code.

She met her husband, Donald McDonald, while they were both stationed at the Western Air Command in Vancouver and they were married on Mar. 1, 1945. A daughter, Catherine, was born on June 15, 1946. The family moved to England upon Donald's military transfer where they observed the indomitable spirit of the British first hand.

Upon their return to Ottawa in 1954, Irene began teaching gifted children and served as an executive member of many professional teaching bodies. After Donald retired from the military, the couple moved to Victoria in 1968 and Irene's next challenge was to help implement Victoria's first sex education program in the schools.

Upon her retirement from teaching in 1975, she soon became an active fundraiser for the B.C. Cancer Society and along with her close friend, Sheila MacDougall, helped raise $13 million in one year. After a brief period as national fundraising chairman of the Canadian Cancer Society, Irene transferred her incredible energy to The Canadian Club in Victoria as well as the newly amalgamated First Metropolitan United Church. A member of the UCW since 1969, Irene played a crucial leadership role during this demanding time.

The loss of her husband, Donald, in 1991 was the saddest period of her life, but Irene continues to be active within First Met, plays competitive bridge, and keeps in close touch with numerous friends. At age 91, she declares she's still "growing and learning."

To read Irene's stories, see the following chapters: Early Memories; Love and Friendship; A Life's Call; Accepting Loss and Death; Building a Faith Community; The Many Faces of God; and More Words of Wisdom.

○ ○ ○ ○ WISDOM LEARNED ○ ○ ○ ○

From Irene McDonald by Terry Dance-Bennink

As a fellow educator, Irene's life speaks to me. I've been touched by her deep respect for the thousands of young people she's encountered throughout her teaching career. But she's no "milquetoast," as she puts it, and she sets high standards. If she'd been my teacher when I was young, I would have been challenged! A passing grade is not good enough — live every moment to the best of your ability, she insists. She's the kind of teacher everyone needs.

Irene is a very private person and I had to coax her to engage in this life review process, but by sharing her life wisdom, she's found yet another way to educate the next generation. Whenever I think of Irene, I try to pull up my socks and refrain from moaning and groaning! A wimp she is not.

I've thoroughly enjoyed our far-reaching conversations and the breadth of Irene's thinking. She's no biblical literalist, that's for sure, and she's not afraid to challenge her church. She searched for words to describe her God and the term "Mystery" kept cropping up. She'd be speechless, like Job, she said, if she got to ask God one question. She values a quiet, contemplative approach to worship rather than "campfire singing." Irene's face of God enriches mine.

Irene has taught me to treasure the days I have left with my husband and to keep in closer touch with my friends. She's also shown me that turning 60 this year is no big deal — like her, I may have 30 more years to keep on growing and learning and giving life "my best shot."

○ ○ ○ ○ ○ ○ ○ ○ ○ ○

HELEN LUCILE SIMPSON

Helen Lucile Simpson helped found Victoria's Family Caregivers Network after decades of caring for family members and others.

Helen was born in Courtenay, B.C., on Oct. 24, 1914, the eldest of four children of Robert Prendergast and Lucile Halliday. The family moved to Victoria in 1919 after her father returned home from World War I.

Her father bought a general store and post office at the corner of Carey and Tillicum Roads where Helen assisted him from age eight. Helen attended McKenzie Avenue Public School, Victoria High School and Victoria College at Craigdarroch Castle. She attended First United Church on Quadra Street during the 1920s and became a CGIT leader, Sunday school teacher and member of the Young People's Society.

Helen married Kenneth Simpson on June 10, 1936. After the death of twins in 1938, she was at loose ends. In 1940, she joined the YMCA as the first female committee member in the history of the YMCA. She supervised Camp Thunderbird at Glinz Lake, B.C., for three years and became the YMCA's Director of the Social Education Program in 1943.

In 1944 she joined the YMCA War Service, which assisted returning servicemen, including a party of British prisoners of war from Hong Kong, and later became a staff member of the Citizen's Rehabilitation Council.

Her two daughters, Elizabeth and Patricia, were born in 1948 and 1951. Helen continued to volunteer with numerous community groups while also caring for her mother, aunt, uncle, foster sister, two sisters-in-law and her husband during the last 12 years of his life.

Putting her caregiving experience to work, she helped found the Family Caregivers Network in 1989, chairing the board for two years and serving in other capacities for many years, including as chair of the pastoral care committee at First Metropolitan United Church.

After 52 years of marriage, her husband, Ken, died in 1988. In 1992, she married John James Tanner, a friend of 20 years. He passed away just five months later. Helen is an avid gardener and genealogist, though in recent years her gardening is limited to deadheading the plants in her apartment building gardens and tending to the plants on her balcony.

To read Helen's stories, see the following chapters: Early Memories; Love and Friendship; A Life's Call; Accepting Loss and Death; The Joys and Challenges of Growing Older; and Building a Faith Community.

○ ○ ○ ○ WISDOM LEARNED ○ ○ ○ ○

From Helen Simpson by Joan Mason

I first met Helen Simpson through the Victoria Genealogical Society but really got to know this "feisty little lady from British Columbia" when we were matched in the Spiritual Companions program.

We share a love of family history and gardening. We are both eldest children who learned early the importance of hard work. Helen is a woman ahead of her time who made history as the first female program secretary in the history of the YMCA and who worked outside the home when most of her friends were homemakers. She combined her career with volunteer work and caregiving.

From Helen I have learned the value of not simply belonging to a group, but of getting involved for the long haul. Whether it was the church, the Lions Auxiliary, or the Family Caregivers Network, Helen saw a need and pitched in. It has earned her a deep satisfaction and the enduring love and respect of her friends and colleagues.

At the same time, she understands the importance of not making herself indispensable, encouraging others to lead and continue the work of the group. She leads by encouraging others, something that has been an inspiration to my own leadership of the Epiphany Explorations planning team at the church.

Helen's life has had its challenges and losses, but her faith in God and her acceptance that some things are not meant to be helped her carry on. She surrounded herself with friendship, helping her sewing circle friends with their children after her own twins died and sharing her home with servicemen and their families during the war, and Hungarian refugees later on.

When she shouldered a heavy burden of family caregiving, she sought out others in similar situations and was a founding member of the caregivers support group. From her I have learned that I do not have to face problems alone; the support that friends and family can give is invaluable. Thanks be to God for Helen!

MARGARET (MUIR) STRUTHERS

Margaret (Madge) Struthers has friends all over Canada due to her outgoing nature, generosity and compassion. She was born in Elfros, Sask., in 1913 to Scottish parents and spent the first five years of her life on a farm until her family moved to Saskatoon. She grew up on the prairies and has many vivid memories of the Great Depression.

Her voice and piano lessons revealed genuine talent and she played on one of Canada's first nation-wide radio shows when she was only 13. Music continues to inspire Madge to this day.

The Rev. George Struthers was a friend of the family for several years before Madge decided he was the man for her, despite her initial impressions of him as being "too old and too wise!" Madge spent the next 55 years as the "gracious lady of the manse" as her husband once described her.

She and her husband ministered to seven United church congregations in western Canada, including the Saskatchewan communities of Sovereign, Sceptre, Eston and Regina, and B.C. communities of Burnaby, Dunbar and Victoria. As a minister's wife, she has fed, watered and cared for literally thousands of people.

Madge has also been active in many United church organizations, choirs and fundraising campaigns. In her later years, she devoted herself to visiting nursing homes and entertained residents with her humorous "nursing home ditties."

She gave birth with great difficulty and lost a much-loved five-year-old son, but is delighted to have a daughter, Elaine, and son, Jim; four grandsons; and four great-grandchildren. She has amazing stories to tell of "making friends out of strangers" and wrote a 230-page memoir entitled *Finding Gold in My Memories* in 1999, excerpts of which are printed in this book.

To read Madge's stories, see the following chapters: Early Memories; Love and Friendship; Accepting Loss and Death; The Joys and Challenges of Growing Older; and Building a Faith Community.

○ ○ ○ ○ WISDOM LEARNED ○ ○ ○ ○

From Madge Struthers by Barbara Robertson

Madge is a perfect spiritual companion and we both come from Saskatoon, which is a bonus. Madge is an optimist and although she's 95, she's not lost her enthusiasm for the people and events she's experienced throughout her life as a minister's wife. She even managed to go to the Symphony Splash in Victoria last summer with help from her family. She wouldn't have missed it for anything.

Madge is truly gifted in living life to the fullest. She had a happy childhood despite the hard times of the Depression and always had a large circle of friends who enjoyed music and dancing. She had several boyfriends before she met and married the Rev. George Struthers, the love of her life.

Music, choirs, drama, leadership and hospitality all came naturally to Madge. Despite only a few years of music lessons, she turned them into concert level performances.

I admire Madge's sincerity, her trust in God and her interest in this project. She wants her stories to be remembered! Before we even thought of *Stories United*, Madge had compiled 230 pages of her memoirs in a large book. Several copies have been given to family members and relatives in Scotland.

Madge has a talent for relating her joys (and only a few sorrows). She has a keen sense of humour and feels that life has blessed her. What an inspiration she is!

○ ○ ○ ○ ○ ○ ○ ○ ○ ○

MARY ELIZABETH (PASK) THOMAS

Mary considers growing up on a farm in Saskatchewan during the Depression to be her good fortune. Her birth certificate lists her birthplace as Section 28, Township 20, Range 1, west of the second meridian. Her father and uncle had come from England in 1899 to homestead two quarter-sections six and a half miles north of Esterhazy, Sask., at Zeneta, a station on the Canadian National Railway. They built a house there in which Mary Elizabeth Pask was born on Feb. 20, 1917.

Mary attended Zeneta Public School and Regina Normal School and taught in rural Saskatchewan for three years. In 1942, she came with a friend to Victoria to take a summer course toward her teaching certification. Here she met her future husband, Leonard Cookson Thomas. They married a year later in Saskatchewan and came back to Victoria, where they had four children — Elizabeth, Sheila, Leonard and Arthur. Mary Thomas now has 12 grandchildren and 13 great-grandchildren. Her husband, Len, died in 2005.

Mary Thomas still attends First Metropolitan United Church where she has been an active member for many years. She was involved in the Harmony UCW group and is good friends with my other spiritual companion, Ruth Howell.

To read Mary's stories, see the following chapters: Early Memories; Love and Friendship; Accepting Loss and Death; Building a Faith Community; and The Many Faces of God.

○ ○ ○ ○ WISDOM LEARNED ○ ○ ○ ○

From Mary Thomas by Edeana Malcolm

When I visit Mary Thomas, I know that I am speaking to a pioneer. Her life growing up in Saskatchewan during the Depression seems so far removed from today, and yet it is not. It is here now in her memory and I have been so privileged to catch a glimpse of it through her eyes.

I can see young Mary and her sister Anne singing harmony as they milked the cows or held squirming piglets in a gunnysack as they drove across the dry prairie. They hauled water twice a week, fattened their own calves and did their lessons in a one-room schoolhouse. These are some of the memories she cherishes today, when we can flip a switch or turn a tap and instantly have all the light, heat and water we want.

Mary Thomas has taught me how blessed I am, and the lessons have been sweet indeed. Her soft-spoken words tell the truth about the tough survivor that she is. Her twinkling eyes reveal the spark of a vivacious personality beneath the deceptively meek exterior of a 91-year-old woman. Thank you, Mary, for the lessons you have shared with me so far. I look forward to many more.

○ ○ ○ ○ ○ ○ ○ ○ ○ ○

EILEEN THORN

Despite losing her vision when she grew older, Eileen Thorn is an indomitable woman.

An only child, Eileen was born in 1919 in Edmonton, Alta., to Mary Jane and Mansel Jenkins. She lost her mother to cancer when she was only four years old and was brought up by her father and aunt and uncle in Moose Jaw, Sask. As a child, she loved singing in the choir at St. Andrew's United Church.

She worked as a stenographer for Prairie Airways until she fell in love with her husband, Kenneth Thorn, who declared,"That's the girl I'm going to marry," after only one date. Kenneth's job with Imperial Oil took them to Hamilton, Ont., where a daughter, Sheryl Anne, and a son, John Edward, were born. They moved many times but eventually settled in Victoria and joined Metropolitan United Church in 1971.

A series of losses came Eileen's way in the 1990s, starting with the death of her cousin, Glenys, who was like a sister to her. Kenneth, Eileen's husband, died of Alzheimer's disease in 1995 and another close friend, her bridesmaid, died around the same time. Eileen says it was the love and support from her church Actimet friends which helped her through these major losses.

Eileen's daughter died of a heart attack at age 55 in 1996, and then Eileen's own health deteriorated. She's lost much of her vision due to macular degeneration and glaucoma and also suffers from osteoporosis. She thought she'd never walk again, but with the help of a walker and a white cane, Eileen continues to live an independent life and enjoys her friends and seven grandchildren and seven great-grandchildren.

A fire gutted the bathroom in her apartment suite in October 2007 due to careless use of a blowtorch by a neighbour, but Eileen's faith in God remains unshaken.

To read Eileen's story, see the following chapter: The Joys and Challenges of Growing Older.

○ ○ ○ ○ WISDOM LEARNED ○ ○ ○ ○

From Eileen Thorn by Gloria Stott

I enjoy my friendship with Eileen very much. Before I pick her up to go to church on Sundays, we watch the Hour of Power on TV. Afterwards, we enjoy talking in the car about the hymns we liked on the show and, especially, the guest speakers each week. Eileen is such a devoted Christian lady and her faith and goodness are inspirational.

In spite of all the losses and hardships in her life, she remains a happy person and counts her blessings instead of thinking negative thoughts. Nothing seems to get her down for too long. Her optimism and faith in God help her a lot. She also has a loving family and many friends for whom she's thankful.

When I meet her in the Fellowship Hall after church for coffee, her Actimet friends surround her. When I arrive, she always smiles and graciously asks me to have a seat nearby and join them.

Eileen has made me realize that whatever happens in life, God will see us through it. We just have to trust in Him and although God has a timetable of His own, He will always be there for us. It's a very comforting feeling, and I'm grateful that she reminds me of this.

She told me one day that she doesn't have much patience. But I think she has lots of patience which she's learned through the years.

○ ○ ○ ○ ○ ○ ○ ○ ○ ○

ESTHER (MARTIN) YOUNIE

Going on 90, Esther Younie still counts her blessings.

Born on June 4, 1918, Esther grew up on a farm in Guelph, Ont., the child of parents who brought up their children to be strong Christians. Her mother was a teacher and her father had a degree in agriculture.

Esther graduated from high school and became a home economist. During the war, she joined the Aircraft Detection Corps of the RCAF. By the war's end, she was an officer responsible for the Women's Division in Winnipeg.

Upon her discharge, she returned to southwestern Ontario and found work as a home economist with the Ontario Agriculture Dept., training local leaders to offer courses in cooking and sewing for girls. She met her husband, Watson Younie, at this time and they were married at her parents' home.

They raised a son, Norman, and a daughter, Lys, on a farm near St. Catharines, Ont. Once the children started school, Esther held several jobs as a dietitian with the Hotel Dieu in St. Catharines, the Niagara-on-the-Lake Hospital and the T.B. Sanatorium. Esther also loves to sew and enjoys teaching people how to achieve better results.

Esther has been an active member of the United Church ever since childhood. When she and Watson retired to Victoria in 1987, they joined Metropolitan United Church and subsequently, First Metropolitan. They've enjoyed the Actimets Club and numerous social events put on by the church.

Watson Younie died in 2007, and this is Esther's first year of bereavement. She misses her husband a great deal and is also coping with serious health issues of her own. But as she approaches the age of 90, she still believes life is good: "I've been blessed with wonderful parents, a loving husband and marriage, children of whom I'm very proud, and so many great friends."

To read Esther's stories, see the following chapters: Love and Friendship; A Life's Call; and Building a Faith Community.

○ ○ ○ ○ WISDOM LEARNED ○ ○ ○ ○

From Esther Younie by Sheila MacDougall

Loyalty is a characteristic that has impressed me as I've listened to Esther's story and gained her friendship. She is so loyal to her family, past and present, and proud of their accomplishments.

The loyalty and pride in family is reflected in her reluctance to record any behaviour which could be viewed as unseemly — perhaps in society's view or what Esther is afraid society might think. She accepts the events of her life as "just the way it is," but doesn't feel the need to put them all on paper. I've come to appreciate the fact that she trusts me, that it is OK for me to know, but she doesn't want the details of what she entrusted to me to go into the written story.

We have parallel lives in many ways — growing up on a farm and a simple church background. She was in the Women's Division of the RCAF. I worked for the Navy in Ottawa. We were both teachers. Her insight into the dyslexia of her husband and son is amazing. She is a beautiful seamstress, and still bakes her own bread! She taught these subjects and expresses the joy of helping others learn.

Her faith is a simple one. We have talked easily of the amalgamation of Metropolitan and First — not always totally agreeing — but understanding one another. Here again is a loyalty to the former Metropolitan and its minister.

○ ○ ○ ○ ○ ○ ○ ○ ○ ○

THE STORY BEHIND THE STORIES

The Spiritual Companions Program

by

Terry Dance-Bennink
Program coordinator and editor

SPIRITUAL COMPANIONS

A lay visiting program to honour our stories

The spirituality of the aged is a spirituality of story-telling…
the aged among us are rare parchments,
waiting to be read by those of us who will take the time to listen.

— Margaret Guenther

INTRODUCTION

"**Hearts with ears and a pen.**" That's how elders describe 12 lay volunteers at First Metropolitan United Church in Victoria who've been trained as spiritual companions to help elders reflect on their life experience and harvest the wisdom in this newly published book *Stories United.*

We've included a final "story" in our book that describes the origin and design of the Spiritual Companions program for those who wish to harvest their elders' wisdom as we've done. You can learn from our experience in:

- **Assessing needs**
- **Getting trained**
- **Making the match**
- **Offering support and supervision**
- **Gathering the stories**
- **Evaluating the program**

ASSESSING NEEDS

Our goals

The elder survey

Story-telling resources

Learning from others

Like many other churches, First Met has a growing proportion of members who are over the age of 60, but we're not dismayed by this greying of the church. We see it as an opportunity to help older adults and seniors continue the life-long process of learning and growing.

First Met has grown rapidly in the last few years with many young people and families joining the church, but more than 50% of our membership is over the age of 60 (35% over the age of 70 and 20% over the age of 80).

Close to 300 First Met members are "elderly"; two-thirds of them are women and more than 80 of them need regular pastoral visiting

Our demographics reflect provincial trends. The number of B.C. residents aged 65 or over is expected to double in the next 25 years because of the baby boomer bulge and the fact we are living longer, according to the B.C. Premier's Council on Aging and Seniors' Issues.

The City of Victoria, in particular, is a magnet for retirees from across Canada seeking a warmer climate. First Met is located in the heart of the city and wants to reach out and serve this growing segment of the city's population.

The church identified outreach to older adults as one of its top five priorities in 2007. A successful local fundraising campaign together with a modest grant from the Watkins Fund for Senior Adults at the national office of the United Church of Canada gave birth to the **Spiritual Companions** program early in 2007. We identified five goals:

Our goals

1. **Build a sense of community among elderly, frail members of First Met who may feel disconnected from the church;**
2. **Establish a bridge between long-standing and newer members of First Met to ensure the wisdom of our elders is passed on through an Honour Our Stories project;**
3. **Tap into the goodwill of members of the congregation willing to volunteer their time and be trained as "spiritual companions";**
4. **Reduce the growing pressure on the church's pastoral staff to meet the individual needs of a diverse membership; and**
5. **Help First Met grow as a community in which elders are valued and involved regardless of their age or physical circumstances.**

We've also been inspired by our own national church. The Spiritual Companions program embodies the spirit of the Ethical and Theological Statement on Aging approved by the 37th General Council of The United Church of Canada in August 2000:

> *We believe the church is called to celebrate the milestones of older persons…and challenge the exclusion of older persons by our own culture and our religious institutions… We are called to recognize, encourage, and support initiatives by older adults to explore meaningful and satisfying options, and to offer their experience and wisdom to the church and the community.*

The elder survey

After setting our goals, we consulted with church elders and surveyed possible program models. A new member of the congregation took on this challenge (a senior boomer) with support from First Met's Minister of Pastoral Visitation. As program coordinator, she prepared an interim report along with a detailed training program by March 2007 in consultation with others. We accomplished the following:

- assessed the needs of First Met elders through individual interviews with elders and staff, meetings with UCW units and the Pastoral Care Committee, and a review of church statistics;
- identified elders' priorities for spiritual learning and nourishment through the New Vistas program survey;
- researched 26 different models of lay visiting/spiritual companionship in North America;
- designed a pilot training program for volunteer spiritual companions; and
- submitted recommendations for a comprehensive ministry to older adults at First Met.

The elders spoke out loud and clear. Here's a sample of what they told us:

- *We don't want to be shelved or forgotten as youth take over! We still want to play a role.*
- *Many of us have given decades of our life to this church and now we need pastoral care ourselves.*
- *Isolation is a big thing; elders miss their families and need emotional support. We want to talk about our spiritual journeys and needs. Telling our stories is a great way to connect.*
- *One-on-one visits are key. Group activities are more difficult for the elderly. A visit tells an elder 'you are still important to this congregation.'*
- *There are only four functioning UCW groups left. Who will take care of the UCW women as they grow frailer?*
- *While we work on the Emerging Spirit program to attract younger families, we must remember the faithful of many years.*
- *Some of us feel dry and spent. How do we nourish and renew ourselves?*
- *I'm still eager to learn things but I want time to reflect.*
- *Many older volunteers are exhausted. Some older people feel overwhelmed by the pace of growth in our church.*
- *Music, rituals, social celebrations and story-telling are great ways to nourish older adults.*
- *Let's get back to loving one another instead of organizing more lectures for our heads.*

We also reviewed past initiatives to minister to elders in our church including an elder visiting program, the UCW model of Christian caring, various health and wellness initiatives, communion and teas for shut-ins, and one-on-one pastoral visits by staff.

We concluded that one pastoral care minister can't possibly meet the demand, which is why the church has recently added a quarter-time Minister of Pastoral Visitation to our staff. He's much appreciated. But lay visitors are also clearly needed given our demographics. "We are all ministers," one elder reminded us. In the early days of Christianity, lay ministry was the foundation of the church.

Story-telling resources

After 70 plus years of "doing," many elders told us that it's time for them to harvest their lives, to reflect on lessons learned and pass that legacy on to others. They loved the idea of sharing their life stories with a companion, so we decided to make this a unique focus of our lay visiting program.

> *Old age is the time when the meaning of the play becomes clear to us… to become an elder, we must stop rushing madly about, learn to get quiet, mix all the ingredients together meditatively, bake the cake and allow it to rise in its own time.*
>
> — *Rabbi Zalman Schachter-Shalomi*

Story-telling is a wonderful way for elders to:

- honour and bless their past
- give meaning to their lives
- share their wisdom with others
- prepare for death through a spiritual life review
- decide if they wish to change their "story" in any way
- experience healing from isolation as another person listens compassionately to their story

In our interviews with elders, we suggested they might want to ponder such questions as:

Who or what has nourished me in my life?

What were some of my early dreams and goals?

What are my dreams now?

Where do I find sanctuary?

What were three of the most life-fulfilling moments in my life?

Three of the most stressful?

What are some of my regrets, "if only's" or "I wish I had's"?

How have I experienced God, the holy or the sacred?

Has my image of God changed during my life?

Has my faith made a difference in my life?

What do I value the most in my life?

What's the underlying thread of my life story?

What words of wisdom would I share with others?

We identified many local resources to help us honour elders' wisdom including members of the congregation with writing expertise, local personal historians, self-publishing firms and countless books and CDs.

Learning from others

How should our spiritual companions be trained? That was our next question, so we researched 26 different models in North America before deciding to "design our own." Those training models included:

- Hospice Victoria's palliative care training program;
- A local pastoral care program for visitors to extended care facilities;
- Counsellor training offered by Victoria's Citizens' Counselling Service;

- The Seniors Serving Seniors training program;
- Pastoral care initiatives at several local churches;
- Aboriginal practices involving elders and storytelling;
- The lay visiting program at Richards Memorial United Church in London, Ont.;
- The Caring for Seniors program offered by York-Simcoe Ministries in Ontario;
- The Elderspirit initiative at Penticton United Church;
- Telecare in Edmonton;
- Spiritual direction programs sponsored by the Pacific Jubilee program and Regis College in Toronto; and
- Many United States models including programs offered by the Stephen Ministry, the United Methodist Church, the Sacred Art of Living & Dying Centre in Oregon and the Spiritual Eldering Program.

We learned a great deal from this research but concluded that **no single program met our needs**. We had to weigh factors like our focus on the elderly, story-telling and gathering, our timeframes, the cost and our location. The Honour our Stories project, in particular, required a unique approach. We also chose to focus on **spiritual companionship**, rather than simply friendly visiting, and drew distinctions among spiritual companionship, spiritual direction, and psychological counselling.

GETTING TRAINED

Roles of elders and companions

Skills/competencies of spiritual companions

Volunteer/elder recruitment

The training program

Defining spiritual companionship

Evaluation of the training

We hope to nurture a mutual spiritual friendship between elders and companions — rooted in love, honesty, intimacy, mutuality and accompaniment. This dream seems to be coming true in most cases. A dozen lay volunteers have been trained and matched with 15 elders, and the pairs visit together every two or three weeks for at least an hour.

Every program model we surveyed stressed the importance of good training. The depth and quality of the training shapes the outcome. Our volunteers can be described as "hearts with ears and a pen" and offer the following:

- a listening presence and emotional support and empathy with lifestyle changes, loneliness, decision-making and problem-solving;
- a witnessing presence to encourage elders to reflect on their life experiences and faith journeys and record the lessons in writing; and
- referral to other church or community resources as needed.

Roles of elders and companions

We invite participating **elders** to:

- reflect on their life and faith stories;
- share their wisdom with their spiritual companion;
- leave a legacy for the next generation (orally and/or in writing);
- receive emotional and spiritual support with lifestyle changes, loneliness, decision-making and problem-solving if needed and requested; and
- show an active interest in their companion to ensure mutual dialogue.

We invite **companions** to:

- listen with empathy to their elders' life and faith stories and reflect on their own;
- help their elders recall and record their memories and conduct a life-review;
- offer emotional and spiritual support with lifestyle changes, loneliness, decision-making and problem-solving if requested;
- refer/connect their elders to church or community resources as needed;
- attend monthly volunteer training/support sessions; and
- keep a confidential half page written record of visits including the date, time, issues discussed, and what is going well or not well in the relationship.

Skills/competencies of spiritual companions

We promote the following skills/competencies in our companions.

Attitudes

- a compassionate listener *(a heart with ears)*
- warm and friendly
- non-judgmental and broad-minded
- interested in elderly people and their stories
- flexible
- honest
- committed to this vital Christian ministry as a personal call

Skills

- good communication skills
- interviewing skills to evoke and record life stories

- problem-solving skills *(not a "let me fix it for you" approach)*
- able to share some of their own life stories while maintaining the focus on the elders' needs
- able to respond appropriately to grief, depression and loss
- able to recognize and respond to early forms of dementia
- able to assess basic spiritual needs (hope, forgiveness, meaning and relationship issues)

Knowledge

- aware of church and community resources to refer or connect the elder when needed
- understands the joys and sorrows of aging, myths about aging and ministering to the elderly
- understands the need for confidentiality and the ethics of pastoral care
- committed to their own self-care and spiritual growth and learning
- comfortable with the use of simple spiritual resources such as praying with another person, journal writing, taking care of the body, etc.

Volunteer/elder recruitment

We generated interest in the program among potential volunteers through:

- articles in church Sunday bulletins
- brief talks from the pulpit explaining the purpose of the program
- an information meeting for those interested in the program
- personal follow-up with individuals suggested by church leaders
- completion of a volunteer profile and self-assessment form

We hoped to recruit up to 12 volunteers as spiritual companions in the pilot program last spring. A total of 17 volunteers completed the initial training program and a fast-track version in the fall. We currently have 11 active volunteers playing various roles. Several initial volunteers withdrew due to their own health concerns and time constraints.

Our volunteers range in age from 50 to 85 (two-thirds are in their 50s and early 60s). We have one male companion and the rest are women. Most are retired or semi-retired, and half of the volunteers are relatively new members of the church.

Elders were recruited through similar means, although we relied mainly on names submitted by the Pastoral Care Committee. These individuals were phoned or visited to see if they'd be interested, and most were. We had more interested elders than volunteers.

An elder profile form was completed for each elder that identified their contact information, current living situation, family/church background, health concerns, and the best time and place to visit.

We hoped to recruit up to 24 elders, and 23 elders initially agreed to participate, although several had to withdraw later due to health problems. Fifteen elders are currently involved in the program and several others remain on our list to be matched when more volunteers are recruited in the future. The elders are primarily women (14 out of 15) and range in age from 75 to 100. The majority are "shut-in" although several are still active leaders in the church who want to share their life-stories.

The training program

Two people designed the training program: the program coordinator (a former college vice-president academic and trained spiritual director); and an experienced Victoria counsellor/trainer. We studied other training programs carefully and designed a seven-week, 18-hour training program with the following outcomes:

Learning outcomes

- understand the joys and sorrows of aging;
- practise a variety of self-care strategies;
- experience listening and communicating like a "heart with ears";
- identify ways to ensure mutual sharing while keeping the primary focus on the elder's needs;
- understand the importance of boundary-setting to avoid burnout;
- clarify possible ethical challenges that could arise in an elder/visitor relationship;
- identify what is helpful and not helpful in responding to grief, loss and death;
- experience the power of biblical figures as role models for spiritual friendship;
- clarify the difference between friendly visiting, counselling, spiritual direction and spiritual companionship;
- practise the use of simple spiritual resources such as praying with another person, journal writing, etc.;
- understand how life stories can be means of healing;
- practise various interview techniques through case-studies and fieldwork;
- identify spiritual and community resources for networking/referral;
- commit to ongoing volunteer support and supervision; and
- clarify and affirm personal gifts for this vital ministry.

We felt that an 18-hour training program over seven sessions was the bare minimum. A custom-designed, 145-page training manual was prepared for each participant. The sessions unfolded based on the following themes and local resources.

Session 1 Orientation: introductions and self-reflection

The purpose of the spiritual companions program

The joys and sorrows of aging *(led by a retired minister)*

The volunteer's spiritual growth, self-care and support/supervision

Session 2 Visiting/companioning an elder: the joys and challenges *(led by an experienced pastoral minister)*

Mutuality, boundary-setting, confidentiality and ethics *(led by a counsellor and the Parish Nurse)*

Session 3 Being present to grief, loss and death (led by a Victoria Hospice counsellor)

The spiritual challenge of death (led by First Met's Minister of Pastoral Visitation)

Session 4 Biblical models of spiritual friendship (led by Tim Scorer)

Christian spiritual companionship (led by the program coordinator)

Session 5 Life stories as healing: content and techniques to evoke/record stories *(led by Dan Curtis, a documentary filmmaker and personal historian)*

Session 6 Life stories as healing: fieldwork experience (practice interviews)

Session 7 Spiritual and community resources for networking/referral *(led by a local expert on seniors' resources and the Parish Nurse)*

Matches with elders: review of proposed matches

Ongoing support and supervision

Evaluation of the training program

Defining spiritual companionship

You don't have to be a professional to be a spiritual companion. The potential for spiritual friendship lies undetected all around us in friends, spouses and family members.

So what do we mean by a "spiritual companion?" How does a spiritual companion differ from a friendly visitor, a counsellor and a spiritual director? Our companions offer their elders more than just a friendly, sympathetic ear, but steer clear of counselling or spiritual direction.

There's no firm dividing line between friendly visiting, counselling, spiritual direction and spiritual companionship. It's a continuum and one is not better than another. We've defined the roles in this way:

A friendly visitor offers emotional and/or physical support to a person who may feel isolated, lonely and have difficulty accessing community resources. A friendly visitor is a good listener, empathetic, warm-hearted, knowledgeable about community resources and willing to share a bit about his/her own life. A spiritual dimension may or may not enter into a friendly visit.

A counsellor offers crisis or problem-oriented, short-term counsellor-led therapy in which the counsellor relies on various psychological tools and models to help the client determine his/her path forward. A spiritual dimension may or may not be evoked.

A spiritual director accompanies another with a clear focus on the directee's spiritual journey and experience of God. A good spiritual director is characterized by personal holiness and trust in God, a life of prayer, experience on the spiritual path, genuine love and compassion for the directee, and a willingness to face her/his wounds and be vulnerable.

A spiritual companion builds a *mutual* spiritual friendship rather than a relationship where one person is the guide/director; it is characterized by love, mutuality, honesty, intimacy and accompaniment. All aspects of life may be discussed, but special attention is paid to the spiritual dimension.

Evaluation of the training

Two-thirds of the participants rated the effectiveness of the training program as "excellent" and one-third rated it as "very good" in June 2007. Participants praised the

- openness, vulnerability and caring spirit of the facilitators and presenters
- wonderful variety of topics
- enthusiasm of the participants
- opportunity to practise skills
- great leadership, well-organized sessions
- practical, life-affirming applications

Participants appreciated, in particular, learning the difference between counselling, spiritual companionship, and spiritual direction; how to conduct a good interview; how to approach the subject of loss and death; and the importance of self-care as a volunteer.

Suggested changes included: make it a longer program; spend more time on practice interviews/listening; integrate more relaxation exercises; give more time for group discussion; and address the issue of accompanying elders suffering memory loss.

A three-session, fast-track training program was offered in the fall of 2007 due to interest among three new volunteers. The seven-week program was condensed due to the experience and skills of the new volunteers, but the longer training is preferable.

MAKING THE MATCH

We commissioned our volunteers in a ceremony at the June 17, 2007, Sunday service, and elder/companion visits began during the summer. Pastoral Care Committee members drew up a list of proposed matches, based on their knowledge of individual elders and companions and completed elder profile forms.

Some changes were made due to illness/poor health on the part of elders, but most matches have proved life-affirming for both the elder and the companion. For elders' feedback on the program, see *Evaluating the Program.*

A staff member introduced companions to their elders in person, and an introductory letter explained the purpose of the program and the roles of elder and companion. Most elder/companion duos meet every two or three weeks, but some duos meet more often.

OFFERING SUPPORT AND SUPERVISION

We hold monthly meetings with our spiritual companions to offer support and supervision. The purpose is to:

- deepen the spiritual friendship between elders/companions through individual reflection and peer feedback;
- resolve an impasse or "sticking point" in a relationship;
- refer an elder to church or community resources if needed;
- promote self-care practices to avoid burnout;
- strengthen skills in such areas as listening, boundary-setting and spiritual discernment through experiential exercises;
- share the results of story-gathering and develop story-catching skills among volunteer "scribes";
- reflect on the meaning of elders' stories; and
- share companions' life stories in response to those of our elders.

A typical agenda consists of:

- an opening prayer
- sharing of self-care practices by volunteers
- update on visits: the joys and the challenges
- wisdom learned from our elders
- sample of an elder's story and reflection
- *Stories United* Editorial Committee report
- closing prayer

The volunteers take turns preparing the opening and closing prayers, and we pay special attention to self-care practices at the start of each meeting since most of us are involved in other church activities as well. First Met is a busy church! Several companions also face health problems of their own. We offer each other mutual support and encouragement whenever possible.

The sharing of "wisdom learned" from our elders is a highlight of each meeting and quite moving. An elder's story of losing her beloved husband and son within a six-month period, for example, made us reflect deeply on the meaning of death and how to accompany someone who has suffered in this way. We've also discovered that our elders hold very different beliefs about life after death. Each person's experience of the holy or sacred is unique — God has many faces.

If problems arise in an elder/companion relationship, the program coordinator and/or First Met's Minister of Pastoral Visitation offer individual coaching and support.

GATHERING THE STORIES

Why saving our stories matters

Themes and favourite questions

The joys and challenges of gathering stories

Producing a book

Why saving our stories matters

We were fortunate to have Dan Curtis as our story-gathering coach. Dan is a personal historian with over 20 years experience as an independent documentary filmmaker for such broadcasters as TVOntario, the National Film Board, CBC and Citytv. He conducted two of our training sessions and gave us wonderful handouts on why preserving our life stories matters, types of life narrative, life story resources, the benefits of life narratives to patients, interviewing techniques and some reflective questions.

"Our lives are as unique as our DNA," Dan told us. "Unless we chronicle our personal histories, they will in time be forgotten. Think back to a favourite grandparent, parent or friend who is no longer alive. As each year passes, it becomes harder and harder to remember their stories. And with that a priceless legacy is lost."

We all have stories to tell, Dan stressed, and listening to the stories of others is an act of love. He shared with us the work of Dr. Sherry Ruth Anderson, a psychologist in a Toronto chronic-care hospital, who discovered that elderly patients are eager for listeners. "I was really touched by what seemed to be these gold mines of experience in people's lives that had never been honoured as wisdom," Anderson said. "When somebody is listened to with openness, it seems to unlock a treasure chest."

The Pulitzer Prize-winning writer, Studs Terkel, puts it even more bluntly. "I think we're suffering from a national Alzheimer's disease —

there's no memory of yesterday." Perhaps this is why the StoryCorps project in the USA has struck such a chord with the American people. It certainly has inspired us.

"Drawing from more than ten thousand interviews, StoryCorps — the largest oral history project in the nation's history — presents a tapestry of American stories, told by the people who lived them to the people they love." (*Listening Is an Act of Love,* edited by Dave Isay.) This book has been a template for *Stories United.*

Life stories are also healing. Dying people simply want to tell their stories and talk with someone about living with dying, according to Dr. David Kuhl who conducted a 10-year study of what dying people want. In the same vein, Dan Curtis identifies five benefits of life narratives to patients including:

- **Affirmation**: I'm more than my disease. Those caring for me have acknowledged my personhood.
- **Legacy**: Something lasting will transcend my death. I hope that I will be remembered and that my story will provide some comfort to my family in their bereavement.
- **Purpose**: By doing this work, there is still meaning to my life. I am contributing to others.
- **Pattern**: I see more clearly a purpose and meaning to experiences that often seem random and discontinuous.
- **Support**: Having a care provider, friend, family member or personal historian actively listen and encourage my life stories is bearing witness to who I am and the significance of my journey.

Old age is a time for harvesting the meaning of one's life which is why we've chosen "Harvesting Elders' Wisdom" as the sub-title for our book *Stories United.* Many of our elders were raised on prairie farms during the Depression and know the realities of harvesting intimately. To "thresh" means to pound cereal grain to remove the husks and separate out the seeds. As we grow older, we are called in the same way to sift through our lives, to remove what is no longer meaningful in order to celebrate the life-giving seeds.

"I've been feasting on my life as I tell my story to my companion!" one of our elders declared recently in surprise. She was delighted to discover it's OK to step back from the busyness of church life and reflect on her journey in the company of a new friend.

Themes and favourite questions

We used the reflective questions developed by Dan Curtis as a starting point in our journey with elders, and added questions as we went along. We encouraged companions to get to know their elders first without any pressure to record their conversations initially. We suggested they review the highlights of an elder's life before focusing on the reflective questions below. We recommended no more than six to 10 one-hour interviews for this purpose in order to avoid producing a full scale "biography."

Once a sense of mutual trust was established, the companions invited their elders to contribute stories to our book and to have their memories formally recorded through audio-tape or hand-written notes. Four elders chose to write their life stories themselves.

Elders were asked to sign two different release forms, approved by a lawyer, which confirmed their willingness to have excerpts of their story edited and published in a book produced by First Met, with non-exclusive copyright owned by the church. Companions signed a similar release form confirming their volunteer status and copyright ownership.

We agreed to let the themes emerge after a trial period of story-gathering. To select excerpts for our book, we knew we needed some universal themes or categories, but we wanted to let the process shape the outcome.

After six months, we had gathered more than 700 pages of stories! We analyzed the content and selected the following eight universal themes with *sample* questions listed under each theme. We've included these questions at the end of each chapter in our book to encourage readers to reflect on their *own* life journey.

Early memories

What is one of your favourite childhood memories? Use your five senses to describe it *(sight, sound, touch, taste, and smell).*

What is your earliest memory?

Where and when were you were born? What did your home look like?

Can you describe your relationship with your parents and siblings?

What was it like to grow up during the Depression and war time?

What were some of your early dreams and goals?

Love and friendship

Who was the most important person in your life?

What was the happiest moment of your life? The saddest?

Who or what has nourished you in your life?

Who or what have you nurtured and cared for?

Who or what has challenged you to grow in your life?

Whom do you wish to thank in your life and for what?

Whom do you wish to forgive and for what?

A life's call

When you reflect on your life of service, what are you most proud of?

What is your greatest accomplishment in life so far?

What are three of the most life-fulfilling or satisfying moments in your life? Three of the most stressful moments?

Can you describe a sacrifice you've made? How did it change you.

Would you make the same sacrifice now, knowing what you know?

If you were to be honoured for something in your life, what would it be?

How do you want to be remembered?

If your life were a movie or a book, what title would you give it?

The joys and challenges of growing older

How have you faced the joys and challenges of growing older?

What are your dreams now?

What would you still like to do or be before you die?

What do you wish to let go of? What is dying in your life now?

What are some of your regrets, "if only's" or "I wish I had's"?

Accepting loss and death

How have you responded to loss and death in your life?

Who or what protects or comforts you in the midst of grief?

Where do you find sanctuary?

What does "resurrection" and "life after death" mean to you?

Building a faith community

What community of people have you felt deeply connected to?

What does "church" mean to you?

Do you have any stories about your church you wish to share?

What is the key to building a Christian faith community?

The many faces of God

How and when have you experienced God or the sacred in your life?

Has your image of God and Jesus changed over the years? If so, how?

Has your faith made a difference in your life? If so, how?

Do you believe in the power of prayer (to heal or to intervene)?

If you got to ask God one single question, what would it be?

More words of wisdom

What do you value the most in your life?

What is the single most valuable thing you've ever learned?

What is one of the hardest things you've ever done?

What are some unforgettable moments in your life?

What words of wisdom would you share with the next generation?

The joys and challenges of gathering stories

Gathering stories has been a new experience for most of our volunteers. We've had a learning curve! Five of the 11 companions have formal training or experience as writers, but the remaining volunteers have varying skills. Nonetheless, they've done a wonderful job of capturing the essence of their elders' lives, sometimes with help from a more experienced writer.

We keep reminding ourselves that it's the relationship which matters most — the mutual spiritual friendship between elder and companion. Publication of well-written stories is secondary.

Some elders took to pondering the reflective questions with enthusiasm; others were a bit intimidated at first. We stressed the importance of elders telling their stories in their own way. Personality and background play a role in how a story is told. Some elders preferred to recount historical and personal anecdotes with the meaning implied. Those with a more philosophical bent articulated their opinions and life experience in some depth. The stories in our book are as diverse as our elders.

The stories have been prepared in the first person based on informal conversation with a companion. We've tried to retain the elder's original voice as much as possible. As transcribed and edited oral histories, the tone is informal.

To make sure our elders were comfortable with the process, we interviewed them in January 2008, and 100% said they've found the program worthwhile; see *Evaluating the Program.*

Producing a book

The idea of a book crystallized in the fall of 2007 because we wanted to share our elders' wisdom with others and leave a legacy within the United Church of Canada. We struck an editorial committee in January 2008 to assist the editor with the challenging task of preparing a 300-page manuscript by the fall of 2008 in order to launch the book at First Met's Epiphany Explorations Conference in January 2009.

Choosing the excerpts from so many beautiful stories was hard, but we agreed the published stories should:

- relate to one or more of the universal themes
- reflect the diversity of our elders (gender, age, origins, occupation)
- be lively, interesting stories

We've avoided overly detailed personal or family information, story duplication, and sensitive material, i.e. criticism of an individual by name, reference to court cases, etc.

All submitted stories, regardless of whether they're published or not, will be housed in First Met's archives and elders will receive a copy of everything they've shared with their companion.

In addition to the stories, the book contains an **Elders' Gallery** with each elder's photo and biography, along with a photo of the companion and the **Wisdom Learned** from their elder. We've also included this **Story behind the Stories** — a case study of the program — at the end of the book for those who may wish to learn from our experience.

We hope the **book reviews** on the back cover from such well-known people as Lois Wilson, Marion Best, Tim Scorer, and Herb O'Driscoll testify to the book's value and integrity.

We set the end of April as our deadline for story submission which put some pressure on a few companions, but they rose to the occasion. Interviewing/transcribing elders' stories, however, is more time-consuming than we expected and requires special skills.

In hindsight, if we were to repeat the process, we might distinguish the "writing" task from "companioning." Those without writing experience could establish a relationship with their elders and then invite a "writer/ interviewer" to join them for a limited time in order to record key stories. This might encourage more volunteers without writing skills to participate in the program.

Another challenge was our lack of sufficient technical equipment. The five "writers" used personal tape-recorders for their interviews, but we lacked the funds to buy additional equipment to support other elder/ companion duos.

One weakness of the program is that it's labour-intensive given the emphasis on building a long-term, mutual spiritual friendship. If the emphasis on writing is lessened in the future, however, we may attract more volunteers while preserving the focus on an *oral* sharing of life/ faith stories.

We hope the book itself, *Stories United*, will encourage other elders to follow the same process next year. Small study groups may spring up with participants willing to read the book and ponder the same questions, and perhaps write or share their stories in pairs or in a group setting. A shut-in elder could also use the book for individual reflection and, perhaps, invite a family member or friend to help record their stories.

Some practical tips

A book is not the only option for celebrating elders' wisdom. A First Met UCW unit prepares a booklet each Lent based on various themes and invites many short, but moving, contributions from members of the congregation. If cost is an issue, very simple means can be found to compile and share elders' stories.

We chose a book format because we had such great material. A small local self-publishing firm printed 1,200 copies of the book within four weeks of delivery of the manuscript. First Metropolitan United Church is the publisher of the book and holds copyright. We've secured an ISBN number and the book is catalogued with Library and Archives Canada.

A local graphic designer laid out the text and photos, and a graphic artist designed the cover. The six-person Editorial Committee handled the editing, copy editing and proofreading. A great deal of volunteer time, however, was required. The editor's role was almost a full-time job for at least six to eight months. A job description for the editor and terms of reference for the Editorial Committee are on file. Realistic timelines were mapped out and the project was completed within a year and a half. We priced the book to recover our costs, not to make a profit.

Our primary market for the book is the United Church of Canada. We hope to sell the book to elders/companions and their families, First Met members at large, registrants at the 2009 Epiphany Explorations Conference, our local presbytery, B.C. Conference, Christian bookstores, libraries, other denominations, and local seniors' and community organizations. The United Church Resource Distribution in Toronto will promote and distribute the book across Canada.

Our marketing tools consist of a promotional flyer, an order form, a poster, a bookmark, our website, Church bulletins and newsletters, book reviews, local media coverage, outreach to seniors' and community organizations, but most importantly, direct one-to-one contact with interested individuals.

A celebration of the Spiritual Companions program and an official book launch were scheduled to take place at a First Met Sunday service in November 2008. The program was also slated for a plenary session of the Epiphany Explorations Conference in January 2009.

EVALUATING THE PROGRAM

An overall assessment

Ongoing evaluation is key to a healthy program and essential if you wish to secure church support.

In our application for seed money to the Watkins Fund at the national office of the United Church of Canada, we promised to conduct a final evaluation of the program by early 2008. We requested feedback from participating elders, the volunteer companions and our sponsor committee, the Pastoral Care Committee. Through group discussion and individual interviews we answered the following questions.

Did we reach our target audience: those most in need?

Yes, we did as the majority of participating elders (66%) are shut-in and/or facing serious health issues and definitely appreciate having a spiritual companion. The remaining elders are still active but quite elderly and want to share their life stories before their health declines.

Some companions noted that most of our participating elders are white, middle class, and female, but this reflects the composition of elders in our congregation. As the face of our congregation changes in the future, we will pay attention to diversifying participation.

The volunteers also noted that each elder/companion relationship is unique and they appreciate the program's flexibility. We've been careful not to insist on a "one size fits all" approach. More elders wish to participate in the program in the future. We hope to launch a third volunteer recruitment drive next winter once the book has gone to press.

Are the participating elders satisfied with the program?

First Met's Minister of Pastoral Visitation interviewed all the elders in person or over the phone during January 2008. A few elders had only just been "matched" so their feedback was preliminary. *All the elders without exception said their experience with the program had been worthwhile.* Two-thirds of the elders felt we'd achieved our goals "very well" and one third felt "somewhat." Here are few sample comments:

- *Everyone should have the opportunity to complete a life story review!*
- *It was suggested recently that we should feast on our lives, and that's exactly what I've been doing in telling my companion my story!*
- *I wasn't very excited about the program at first, but now I highly recommend the experience.*

- *My companion and I have so much in common and so much to share.*
- *My companion has become a wonderful friend and recorded my story with sensitivity and good humour. The sessions are always special times.*

When asked to describe their companion in two or three words, elders said:

- *My companion has a special way of saying, 'and then…?' which sends you deeper than you expected to go.*
- *I could not ask for a better friend.*
- *He's a good communicator and listener.*
- *My companion is wonderful and the right type of person to do this because she has a church relationship and we share a genealogical interest.*
- *I believe we have learned a lot from each other.*
- *She's delightful and has so much energy.*

How well are we meeting the program's five goals?

The elders seem quite satisfied with the program and the companions feel the same way. In discussion at a monthly meeting, the companions recommended we include another specific goal: record the life history of participating elders before they die. That's how importantly they view the life-review process.

The volunteers feel the intergenerational program is a rich learning experience. The peer support at monthly meetings has given volunteers more than they expected to receive and they recommended we highlight this benefit when recruiting new volunteers.

The Minister of Pastoral Visitation and the Parish Nurse believe the program has definitely lessened the pressure on the church's pastoral staff.

Finally, the volunteers noted that many programs focus on helping the elderly as a form of charity, but this program feels more balanced in terms of mutual sharing and growth between elder and companion. "It's a labour of love, of mutual listening and learning," one 85-year-old elder/companion observed.

Have the volunteers received adequate training and support?

The volunteers rated their training during the spring of 2007 very highly. Six months later, with some experience under their belts, they commented that the depth of training had surprised them at the time, but they now see why it was needed. They flagged interviewing/transcribing elders' stories as an issue, however, because it's more time-consuming than originally expected and requires special skills.

The volunteers value the monthly support meetings highly, especially the regular reminder to take care of *themselves*. The frequency of meetings (once a month) seems just right. "By focusing on listening and learning," said one companion, "we are better visitors as a result. Our visits are not like institutional church visits."

Have older adults/seniors been fully involved in the program's design and implementation?

The Pastoral Care Committee which sponsors the program consists of members who all are over the age of 60. Elders were fully involved during the program design stage through 20 individual interviews with the program's coordinator. Participating elders have recently been interviewed to make sure they are satisfied with the program. And four of the 11 companions are over the age of 65.

Are the human and physical resources sufficient?

Our resources are sufficient, assuming continued modest support from First Met's Stewardship fund. The year 2008 has seen added expenses due to production of the book but we intend to cover production expenses through sale of the book.

The volunteer commitment, however, is significant. The coordinator currently puts in a 35-hour work week (with a modest honorarium for 8 hours/week) and the volunteer companions are investing considerable time as well, not to mention the commitment of the Editorial Committee members. This pressure should ease after the book is published.

Is the program sustainable on an ongoing basis?

Yes, it is and *Stories United* should be an effective way to expand the program. Next winter, we hope to start a new group for interested church and community members using the book as a resource. Participants could take each theme in the book and respond to the reflective questions in a group setting. Oral sharing could be complemented with written stories if participants wish.

Elders who are shut-in could also use the book to ponder their own life stories in the company of trusted friends or relatives. The book should have a ripple effect well beyond the current companions and elders.

What changes, if any, should be made to the program's design?

Our volunteers suggested the following:

- recruit and train new volunteers next fall/winter but remain flexible based on their individual gifts/experience;
- secure more specialized resources for story-gathering and recording;
- organize a wonderful celebration when the book is launched;
- encourage companions to answer the same questions posed to elders as a way to foster their own spiritual growth;
- ask elders to evaluate the life-story review process once it's completed;
- revisit the nature of spiritual companionship, as distinct from friendly visiting, counselling and spiritual direction, now that we have some experience; and
- deepen our own spiritual formation as companions: reflect on how we are accompanying another soul on a sacred journey.

Securing church support

Right from the start, we've had the enthusiastic support of our Lead Minister, which is critical. His "can do" attitude has encouraged us to aim high. Our Parish Nurse provided valuable support to the pilot project during the research and design stage. And the Minister of Pastoral Visitation continues to play a critical role, bringing decades of pastoral care experience to our meetings, along with a generous dose of Down East humour!

The Pastoral Care Committee has also been extremely supportive from the get-go. The current chair made sure we did our homework this year in drawing up our budget and our final evaluation report which was recently approved by First Met's Executive Committee. The Executive Committee appreciated "the quality and diligence represented in the final evaluation report" and noted it was one of the best they'd seen.

Please see the *Acknowledgments* section of the book for the names of all those individuals who have helped birth *Stories United.*

The entire congregation is kept informed of our progress through monthly articles in the church newsletter, and elders spread the word through informal networks. Our local presbytery and B.C. Conference supported our initial grant application to the Watkins Fund and continue to support our work.

We want to share this bountiful harvest of elders' wisdom and hope others can learn from our experience.

A closing prayer

Many and marvellous are your gifts to us, O God.
We thank you for but one of them —
the gift of story.
For in this gift we see the essence of what it is to be human —
the adventure and hope of the beginning,
the difficult and amusing struggles of the middle,
the joys and sorrows of the resolutions,
and not the least,
the fellowship and communion
of sharing the stories with each other.
For this blessing,
we give you our heartfelt thanks. Amen.

— Edeana Malcolm, companion and poet,
shared at a Spiritual Companions meeting

BIBLIOGRAPHY

Anderson, Suzanne. *Self-Publishing in Canada*. Duncan, British Columbia: Half Acre Publishing, 2004.

Arrien, Angeles. *The Second Half of Life*. Boulder, CO: Sounds True, 2005.

Association of Personal Historians (APH). *APH Member Toolkit*. www.personalhistorians.org, 2007.

Baines, Barry K. *Ethical Wills*. Cambridge, MA: Perseus Publishing, 2002.

Baldwin, Christina. *Storycatcher, Making Sense of our Lives through the Power and Practice of Story*. New World Library, 2005.

Benner, David. *Sacred Companions: The Gift of Spiritual Friendship & Direction*. Illinois: Intervarsity Press, 2002.

Bibby, Reginald. *The Boomer Factor*. Toronto: Bastian Books, 2006.

Birren, James E. & Cochran, Kathryn N. *Telling the Stories of Life through Guided Autobiography Groups*. Baltimore & London: The Johns Hopkins University Press, 2001.

Cameron, Julia. *The Right to Write*. New York: Tarcher/Putnam, 1999.

Chittister, Joan. *The Gift of Years: Growing Older Gracefully*. Ottawa: Novalis Press, 2008.

Ellis, Neenah. *If I Lived to be 100: Lessons from the Centenarians*. New York: Three Rivers Press, 2002.

Gentzler, Richard H. *The Graying of the Church: A Leader's Guide for Older Adult Ministry in the United Methodist Church*. Nashville, TN: Discipleship Resources, 2004.

Gerard, Philip. *Creative Non-fiction: Researching and Crafting Stories of Real Life*. Cincinnati, Ohio: Story Press, 1996.

Goldberg, Natalie. *Writing Down the Bones: Freeing the Writer Within*. Boston & London: Shambhala, 2005.

Groves, Richard. *The American Book of Dying: Lessons in Healing Spiritual Pain*. Berkeley, California: Celestial Arts, 2005.

Guenther, Margaret. *Toward Holy Ground: Spiritual Directions for the Second half of Life*. Cambridge, Mass: Cowley Publications, 1995.

Haugk, Kenneth C. *Christian Caregiving: A Way of Life*. Minneapolis: Augsburg Publishing, 1984.

Hutchison, Joyce & Rupp, Joyce. *May I Walk You Home: Courage & Comfort for Caregivers of the Very Ill.* Notre Dame, Indiana: Ave Maria Press, 1999.

Isay, Dave. *Listening is an Act of Love: A Celebration of American Life from the StoryCorps Project*. New York: The Penguin Press, 2007.

LeDoux, Denis. *Turning Memories into Memoirs*. Maine: Soleil Press, 2006.

Morgan, Richard L. *Remembering Your Story: Creating Your Own Spiritual Autobiography*. Nashville, TN: Upper Room Books, 2002.

Peace, Richard. *Spiritual Autobiography: Discovering and Sharing Your Spiritual Story*. Colorado Springs: Navpress, 1998.

Pelaez, Martha & Rothman, Paul. *A Guide for Recalling & Telling Your Life Story*. Florida: Southeast Florida Center on Aging, Florida International University, 1994.

Reimer, Derek. *Voices: A Guide to Oral History*. British Columbia: Government of British Columbia, 1984.

Rosenbluth, Vera. *Keeping Family Stories Alive*. Vancouver: Hartley & Marks, 1997.

Tirabassi, Maren C. & Tirabassi, Maria I., eds. *God in My Life: Faith Stories & How & Why We Share Them.* Cleveland: The Pilgrim Press, 2008.

Schachter-Shalomi, Rabbi Zalman. *From Age-ing to Sage-ing*. New York: Warner Books, 1997.

Silver Threads Service. *The Memory Book*. Victoria, B.C., 2007.

Wakan, Naomi Beth. *Late Bloomer: On Writing Later in Life*. Toronto: Wolsak & Wynn Publishers, 2006.

Wakan, Naomi Beth. *The Memory Bag*. Qualicum Beach, B.C.: Lightsmith Publishing,1999.

Webb, Marie White. *Building a Ministry for Homebound and Nursing-Home Residents*. Nashville, TN: Discipleship Resources, 2003.

Welty, Eudora. *On Writing*. New York: The Modern Library, 2002.

Zinsser, William. *Inventing the Truth: The Art and Craft of Memoir.* Boston: Houghton Mifflin, 1987.

Useful Websites

Association of Personal Historians, www.personalhistorians.org.

Lifebio. Templates for producing autobiographies and biographies. Includes book production, www.lifebio.com.

Turning Memories: The Editor's Manual, www.turningmemories.com.

LifeSketches & Heirloom Memoirs Publishing. Online writing classes and editorial services, www.alifesketch.com.

About the editor and contributor

Editor and contributor, Terry Dance-Bennink is a writer, personal historian, educator and spiritual companion. She created the Spiritual Companions program at First Metropolitan United Church and is a former vice-president academic of an Ontario community college and a retreat centre program director. She has a master's degree in adult education and a diploma in spiritual direction from the University of Toronto. Listening to and preserving elders' life stories is her passion.

How to order the book

To order a copy of *Stories United*:

- Visit First Metropolitan United Church's website: www.firstmetvictoria.com or call (250) 388-5188 or write to: First Metropolitan United Church, 932 Balmoral Rd., Victoria, B.C., V8T 1A8

- Visit the United Church Resource Distribution's website: www.united-church.ca/ucrd or call (416) 253-5456, ext. 1211